365 DEVOTIONAL READINGS FROM

MARTIN LUTHER

DAY*by*DAY

IN GENESIS

Founded in 1869 as the publishing arm of The Lutheran
Church—Missouri Synod, Concordia Publishing House gives
all glory to God for the blessing of 150 years of opportunities
to provide resources that are faithful to the Holy Scriptures
and the Lutheran Confessions.

Copyright © 2019 Concordia Publishing House
3558 S. Jefferson Avenue, St. Louis, MO 63118-3968
1-800-325-3040 · cph.org

Edited by Dawn Mirly Weinstock

Manufactured in China

1 2 3 4 5 6 7 8 9 10   28 27 26 25 24 23 22 21 20 19

365 DEVOTIONAL READINGS FROM

MARTIN LUTHER

DAY
by
DAY

IN GENESIS

CONCORDIA PUBLISHING HOUSE • SAINT LOUIS

INTRODUCTION

Martin Luther viewed himself first and foremost as a professor and teacher of Scripture. It was his calling from God, which he had received through the Church. Because of his certainty of this call and his faith in the truth of God's Word, he confidently challenged the false teachings of the Roman Church; in fact, it was his sworn duty to do so, one part of the formal oaths he took on October 19, 1512, when he received degree and title: "Doctor of Bible."

For the final ten years of his life, Luther expounded the Book of Genesis in the classroom, moving through every chapter and almost every verse and word. He called Genesis "an exceedingly evangelical book" because it is "made up almost entirely of illustrations of faith and unbelief, and of the fruits that faith and unbelief bear" (Luther's Works 35:237). Along with his detailed commentary on Galatians and Romans, Luther's work on Genesis reveals his firm belief that every word of Scripture is to be read, meditated upon, and inwardly digested so that the Holy Spirit can continuously strengthen us in faith in Christ, our Savior.

To that end, these devotional thoughts have been gathered by my colleague Mrs. Dawn Mirly Weinstock in her typical masterful fashion, from the eight volumes of the English translation of Luther's *Lectures on Genesis* (1535–45). The best way to use this book is in concert with reading the Book of Genesis. Before reading Luther's commentary, read the whole chapter of Genesis (or at least the section in which the focus verse is included). While we think we know the accounts of creation, the flood, Abraham's wanderings, or Joseph's dreams, Luther often picks out small details for emphasis—and the broader context will prove helpful. Sometimes reading all the devotional thoughts on a particular chapter at once, then going back to individual devotions in sequence may prove helpful.

Luther's comments on Genesis encompassed a wide variety of themes throughout the ten years of his lectures: vocation, marriage, prayer, the theology of the cross, the Trinity, the two natures in Christ, the work of the Holy Spirit, God's two ways of governing, the Law and the Gospel, to name only a few. But the most consistent message by far is the promise of the Savior, which the patriarchs believed as a future event and thus were saved. Again and again, Luther reminds his hearers (and now us as readers) that we have the inestimable blessing of reading Genesis in the sure knowledge that the promise has been fulfilled, that the Seed, Christ, has come, was crucified for our sins and was raised for our justification, and now lives and reigns to all eternity. And because the Holy Spirit has called us through the Word to faith in Christ Jesus, we have the same sure promises of forgiveness and eternal life given to Adam, Noah, Abraham, Isaac, Jacob, and Joseph, and at our death, we also will be gathered to our people.

Let me use Luther's own words by which he introduced his lectures on Genesis so long ago, now to commend this book to you: "I hope that this work be of some benefit to the godly, and that it will please them" (Luther's Works 2:235).

— Rev. Paul T. McCain

In the beginning, God created
the heavens and the earth.

GENESIS 1:1

Created by God

he first chapter [of Genesis] is written in the simplest language; yet it contains matters of the utmost
importance and very difficult to understand. It
was for this reason, as St. Jerome asserts, that among the
Hebrews it was forbidden for anyone under thirty to read
the chapter or to expound it for others. They wanted one to
have a good knowledge of the entire Scripture before getting
to this chapter. . . . God has reserved His exalted wisdom and
the correct understanding of this chapter for Himself alone,
although He has left with us this general knowledge that the
world had a beginning and that it was created by God out of
nothing. . . . The very simple meaning of what Moses says,
therefore, is this: Everything that is, was created by God.

The Beginning

ith these words] I have the conviction that Moses wanted to indicate the beginning of time. Thus "in the beginning" has the same meaning as if he said: "At that time, when there was no time, or when the world began, it began in this wise, that heaven and earth were first created by God out of nothing in an unformed condition." . . . What will you assume to have been outside time or before time? Or what will you imagine that God was doing before there was any time? Let us, therefore, rid ourselves of such ideas and realize that God was incomprehensible in His essential rest before the creation of the world, but that now, after the creation, He is within, without, and above all creatures; that is, He is still incomprehensible. Nothing else can be said, because our mind cannot grasp what lies outside time. God also does not manifest Himself except through His works and the Word, because the meaning of these is understood in some measure.

The earth was without form and void, and darkness was over the face of the deep. And the Spirit of God was hovering over the face of the waters. And God said . . .

GENESIS 1:2–3

The Mystery of the Trinity

oses teaches that on the first day the heaven and the earth were created, but an unformed heaven, that is, without any separation of the waters, without luminaries, and not yet raised up; likewise an unformed earth, without animals, rivers, and mountains. . . . Water and abyss and heaven are used in this passage for the same thing, namely, for that dark and unformed mass which later on was provided with life and separated by the Word. . . . Indeed, it is the great consensus of the Church that the mystery of the Trinity is set forth here. The Father creates heaven and earth out of nothing through the Son, whom Moses calls the Word. Over these the Holy Spirit broods. As a hen broods her eggs, keeping them warm in order to hatch her chicks, and, as it were, to bring them to life through heat, so Scripture says that the Holy Spirit brooded, as it were, on the waters to bring to life those substances which were to be quickened and adorned. For it is the office of the Holy Spirit to make alive.

And God said, "Let there be light," and there was light.

Genesis 1:3

The Speaker and the Word

For the first time Moses mentions the means and the instrument God used in doing His work, namely, the Word. . . . God is, so to speak, the Speaker who creates; nevertheless, He does not make use of matter, but He makes heaven and earth out of nothing solely by the Word which He utters. Now compare with this the Gospel of John (1:1): "In the beginning was the Word." He is in proper agreement with Moses. He says: "Before the creation of the world there was not a single one of the creatures, but God nevertheless had the Word." What is this Word, or what did He do? Listen to Moses. The light, he says, was not yet in existence; but out of its state of being nothing the darkness was turned into that most outstanding creature, light. Through what? Through the Word. Therefore in the beginning and before every creature there is the Word, and it is such a powerful Word that it makes all things out of nothing. From this follows without possibility of contradiction what John expressly adds: "This Word is God and yet is a Person distinct from God the Father, just as a word and he who utters a word are separate entities." . . . These are difficult matters, and it is unsafe to go beyond the limit to which the Holy Spirit leads us. . . . This, therefore, is sufficient for the confirmation of our faith: that Christ is true God, who is with the Father from eternity, before the world was made, and that through Him, who is the wisdom and the Word of the Father, the Father made everything.

January 4

"Let there be light."

GENESIS 1:3

Reality Brought into Being

he words "Let there be light" are the words of God, not of Moses; this means that they are realities. For God calls into existence the things which do not exist (Romans 4:17). He does not speak grammatical words; He speaks true and existent realities. Accordingly, that which among us has the sound of a word is reality with God. Thus sun, moon, heaven, earth, Peter, Paul, I, you, etc.—we are all words of God, in fact, only one single syllable or letter by comparison with the entire creation. We, too, speak, but only according to the rules of language; that is, we assign names to objects which have already been created. But the divine rule of language is different, namely: when He says, "Sun, shine," the sun is there at once and shines. Thus the words of God are realities, not bare words. Here men have differentiated between the uncreated Word and the created word. The created word is brought into being by the uncreated Word. What else is the entire creation than the Word of God uttered by God? . . . Thus God reveals Himself to us as the Speaker who has with Him the uncreated Word, through whom He created the world and all things with the greatest ease, namely, by speaking.

"Let the waters under the heavens be gathered together into one place, and let the dry land appear." And it was so.

GENESIS 1:9

Our Passage on Dry Land

e calls the earth dry because the waters had been removed. So we see the ocean seething miraculously, as if it were about to swallow up the entire earth. . . . Thus it happens through divine power that the waters do not pass over us, and until today and until the end of the world God performs for us the well-known miracle which He performed in the Red Sea for the people of Israel. At that time He displayed that might of His in a unique manner by an obvious miracle, in order that He might be worshiped with greater zeal by the small nation. For what is our entire life on this earth but a passage through the Red Sea, where on both sides the sea stood like high walls? Because it is very certain that the sea is far higher than the earth, God, up to the present time, commands the waters to remain in suspense and restrains them by His Word lest they burst upon us as they burst forth in the deluge. But at times God gives providential signs, and entire islands perish by water, to show that the sea is in His hand and that He can either hold it in check or release it against the ungrateful and the evil.

And God said, "Let the earth sprout vegetation,
plants yielding seed, and fruit trees bearing fruit
in which is their seed, each according to its kind."

GENESIS 1:11

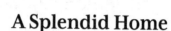

A Splendid Home

 prefer that we reflect on the divine solicitude and benevolence toward us, because [God] provided such an attractive dwelling place for the future human being before the human being was created. Thus afterward, when man is created, he finds a ready and equipped home into which he is brought by God and commanded to enjoy all the riches of so splendid a home. . . . There is a similar beneficence of God toward us in His spiritual gifts. Before we were brought to faith, Christ, our Redeemer, is above in the Father's house; He prepares mansions so that when we arrive, we may find a heaven furnished with every kind of joy (John 14:2). Adam, therefore, when he was not yet created, was far less able to concern himself with his future welfare than we are; for he was not yet in existence. We, however, hear these promises given us by the Word of God. Therefore let us look upon the first state of this world as a type and figure of the future world; and so let us learn the kindness of God, who makes us rich and gives us wealth before we are able to concern ourselves with ourselves.

Then God said, "Let Us make man in Our image,
after Our likeness."

GENESIS 1:26

By God's Special Plan

oses employs a new expression. He does not say: "Let the sea be set in motion," "Let the earth bring forth herbs," or "Let it bring forth." He says: "Let Us make." . . . Here Moses points out an outstanding difference between these living beings and man when he says that man was created by the special plan and providence of God. . . . Therefore the image of God, according to which Adam was created, was something far more distinguished and excellent, since obviously no leprosy of sin adhered either to his reason or to his will. Both his inner and his outer sensations were all of the purest kind. His intellect was the clearest, his memory was the best, and his will was the most straightforward—all in the most beautiful tranquility of mind, without any fear of death and without any anxiety. To these inner qualities came also those most beautiful and superb qualities of body and of all the limbs, qualities in which he surpassed all the remaining living creatures. . . . Therefore my understanding of the image of God is this: that Adam had it in his being and that he not only knew God and believed that He was good, but that he also lived in a life that was wholly godly; that is, he was without the fear of death or of any other danger, and was content with God's favor.

"Let Us make man in Our image, after Our likeness."

Genesis 1:26

In the Image of God

he Gospel brings it about that we are formed once more according to that familiar and indeed better image, because we are born again into eternal life or rather into the hope of eternal life by faith, that we may live in God and with God and be one with Him, as Christ says (John 17:21). And indeed, we are reborn not only for life but also for righteousness, because faith acquires Christ's merit and knows that through Christ's death we have been set free. From this source our other righteousness has its origin, namely, that newness of life through which we are zealous to obey God as we are taught by the Word and aided by the Holy Spirit. But this righteousness has merely its beginning in this life, and it cannot attain perfection in this flesh. Nevertheless, it pleases God, not as though it were a perfect righteousness or a payment for sin but because it comes from the heart and depends on its trust in the mercy of God through Christ. Moreover, this also is brought about by the Gospel, that the Holy Spirit is given to us, who offers resistance in us to unbelief, envy, and other vices that we may earnestly strive to glorify the name of the Lord and His Word, etc. In this manner this image of the new creature begins to be restored by the Gospel in this life, but it will not be finished in this life. But when it is finished in the kingdom of the Father, then the will will be truly free and good, the mind truly enlightened, and the memory persistent.

January 9

So God created man in His own image, in the image of God
He created him; male and female He created them.

GENESIS 1:27

A World in Miniature

I n the remaining creatures God is recognized as by His footprints; but in the human being, especially in Adam, He is truly recognized, because in him there is such wisdom, justice, and knowledge of all things that he may rightly be called a world in miniature. He has an understanding of heaven, earth, and the entire creation. And so it gives God pleasure that He made so beautiful a creature. But without a doubt, just as at that time God rejoiced in the counsel and work by which man was created, so today, too, He takes pleasure in restoring this work of His through His Son and our Deliverer, Christ. It is useful to ponder these facts, namely, that God is most kindly inclined toward us and takes delight in His thought and plan of restoring all who have believed in Christ to spiritual life through the resurrection of the dead.

And on the seventh day
God finished His work that He had done, and He rested.

GENESIS 2:2

God Rested?

 his passage] does not denote that God gave up preserving and governing the heaven and the earth which had already been created. . . . God rested from His work, that is, He was satisfied with the heaven and earth which had then been created by the Word; He did not create a new heaven, a new earth, new stars, new trees. And yet God works till now—if indeed He has not abandoned the world which was once established but governs and preserves it through the effectiveness of His Word. He has, therefore, ceased to establish; but He has not ceased to govern. . . . Until today there abides the Word which was pronounced over the human race: "Grow and multiply"; there abides the Word: "Let the sea bring forth fish and birds of the heaven." Almighty, therefore, is the power and effectiveness of the Word which thus preserves and governs the entire creation.

God blessed the seventh day and made it holy.

GENESIS 2:3

Why We Have the Sabbath

t is also shown here that man was especially created for the knowledge and worship of God; for the Sabbath was not ordained for sheep and cows but for men, that in them the knowledge of God might be developed and might increase. Therefore although man lost his knowledge of God, nevertheless God wanted this command about sanctifying the Sabbath to remain in force. On the seventh day He wanted men to busy themselves both with His Word and with the other forms of worship established by Him, so that we might give first thought to the fact that this nature was created chiefly for acknowledging and glorifying God. Moreover, this is also written that we might preserve in our minds a sure hope of the future and eternal life. All the things God wants done on the Sabbath are clear signs of another life after this life. Why is it necessary for God to speak with us through His Word if we are not to live in a future and eternal life? If we are not to hope for a future life, why do we not live like people with whom God does not speak and who do not know God? But because the divine Majesty speaks to man alone and man alone knows and apprehends God, it necessarily follows that there is another life after this life; to attain it we need the Word and the knowledge of God. For this temporal and present life is a physical life, such as all the beasts live that do not know God and the Word.

January 12

The Tree in the Midst of the Garden

 hen Adam had been created in such a way that he was, as it were, intoxicated with rejoicing toward God and was delighted also with all the other creatures, there is now created a new tree for the distinguishing of good and evil, so that Adam might have a definite way to express his worship and reverence toward God. After everything had been entrusted to him to make use of it according to his will, whether he wished to do so for necessity or for pleasure, God finally demands from Adam that at this tree of the knowledge of good and evil he demonstrate his reverence and obedience toward God and that he maintain this practice, as it were, of worshiping God by not eating anything from it. . . . This is a matter of theology that here this statement about the tree is put before Adam in order that he may also have some outward physical way of indicating his worship of God and of demonstrating his obedience by an outward work. In a similar way the Sabbath, of which we spoke above, has to do chiefly with demonstrating inner and spiritual worship, with faith, love, prayer, etc. . . . This tree of the knowledge of good and evil was Adam's church, altar, and pulpit. Here he was to yield to God the obedience he owed, give recognition to the Word and will of God, give thanks to God, and call upon God for aid against temptation.

The Lᴏʀᴅ God commanded the man, saying,
"You may surely eat of every tree of the garden, but of the tree
of the knowledge of good and evil you shall not eat."

Gᴇɴᴇsɪs 2:16–17

Worship in a Purer Form

 t is useful to note also that God gave Adam Word, worship, and religion in its barest, purest, and simplest form, in which there was nothing laborious, nothing elaborate. For He does not prescribe the slaughter of oxen, the burning of incense, vows, fastings, and other tortures of the body. Only this He wants: that he praise God, that he thank Him, that he rejoice in the Lord, and that he obey Him by not eating from the forbidden tree. We have the remnants of this worship, since Christ has restored it in some measure amid this weakness of our flesh; for we also praise God and thank Him for every spiritual and bodily blessing. But these are truly nothing but remnants. After this wretched life, however, when we join the choirs of the angels, then we shall offer this worship in a holier and purer form.

"In the day that you eat of it you shall surely die."

GENESIS 2:17

Spiritual Disaster

riginal sin really means that human nature has completely fallen; that the intellect has become darkened, so that we no longer know God and His will and no longer perceive the works of God; furthermore, that the will is extraordinarily depraved, so that we do not trust the mercy of God and do not fear God but are unconcerned, disregard the Word and will of God, and follow the desire and the impulses of the flesh; likewise, that our conscience is no longer quiet but, when it thinks of God's judgment, despairs and adopts illicit defenses and remedies. These sins have taken such deep root in our being that in this life they cannot be entirely eradicated. . . . Original sin is the loss of original righteousness, or the deprivation of it, just as blindness is the deprivation of sight. . . . In the case of the soul the outstanding fact is this: that the knowledge of God has been lost; that we do not everywhere and always give thanks to Him; that we do not delight in His works and deeds; that we do not trust Him; that when He inflicts deserved punishments, we begin to hate God and to blaspheme Him; that when we must deal with our neighbor, we yield to our desires and are robbers, thieves, adulterers, murderers, cruel, inhuman, merciless, etc. The passion of lust is indeed some part of original sin. But greater are the defects of the soul: unbelief, ignorance of God, despair, hate, blasphemy. Of these spiritual disasters Adam, in the state of innocence, had no knowledge.

January 15

Then the LORD God said, "It is not good that the man
should be alone; I will make him a helper fit for him."

GENESIS 2:18

No Longer Alone

od makes a husband of lonely Adam and joins him to a wife, who was needed to bring about the increase of the human race. Just as we pointed out above in connection with the creation of man that Adam was created in accordance with a well-considered counsel, so here, too, we perceive that Eve is being created according to a definite plan. Thus here once more Moses points out that man is a unique creature and that he is suited to be a partaker of divinity and of immortality. For man is a more excellent creature than heaven and earth and everything that is in them. But Moses wanted to point out in a special way that the other part of humanity, the woman, was created by a unique counsel of God in order to show that this sex, too, is suited for the kind of life which Adam was expecting and that this sex was to be useful for procreation. . . . For so far Adam was alone; he still had no partner for that magnificent work of begetting and preserving his kind. Therefore "good" in this passage denotes the increase of the human race. . . . Hence the meaning is that Adam as the most beautiful creature is well provided for so far as his own person is concerned but still lacks something, namely, the gift of the increase and the blessing—because he is alone.

Bones and Flesh

t is most worthy of wonder that when Adam looks at Eve as a building made from himself, he immediately recognizes her and says: "This now is bone from my bones and flesh from my flesh." These are words not of a stupid or a sinful human being who has no insight into the works and creatures of God, but of a righteous and wise being, one filled with the Holy Spirit. He reveals a wisdom hitherto unknown to the world: that the effecting cause of the wife and of marriage is God, but that the final cause is for the wife to be a mundane dwelling place to her husband. This knowledge is not simply the product of intelligence and reason; it is a revelation of the Holy Spirit. The word "now" or "this time" or "at last" is not superfluous, as it appears to be; it expresses most beautifully the affection of a husband who feels his need for a delightful and full relationship or cohabitation in both love and holiness. . . . Adam's love was most pure and most holy and also pleasing to God. Impelled by this love, he says: "This now is bone from my bones, not from wood, not from stone, not from a clod of the earth. It concerns me more closely, for it is made from my bones and my flesh."

Now the serpent was more crafty than any other beast.

GENESIS 3:1

That the Godly Prevail

 t pleased the Lord that Adam should be tempted and should test his powers. So it still is today. When we have been baptized and brought into the kingdom of Christ, God does not want us to be idle; He wants us to use His Word and gifts. For this reason He allows us weak beings to be sifted by Satan (Luke 22:31). Thus we see the Church, which has been cleansed by the Word, still exposed to continual danger. The Sacramentarians rise up; so do the Anabaptists and other fanatical teachers, who greatly trouble the Church with their various temptations. In addition, there are internal troubles. These God allows to happen this way, not because He has decided either to abandon the Church or to want it to perish; but, as Wisdom says (Wisdom 10:12), those conflicts befall the Church and the godly that the Church and the godly may prevail and learn by experience itself that wisdom is more powerful than everything else.

He said to the woman, "Did God actually say,
'You shall not eat of any tree in the garden'?"

A Sure Guide for Faith

he serpent directs its attack at God's good will and makes it its business to prove from the prohibition of the tree that God's will toward man is not good. Therefore it launches its attack against the very image of God and the most excellent powers in the uncorrupted nature. The highest form of worship itself, which God had ordained, it tries to destroy. . . . Eve is simply urged on to all sins, since she is being urged on against the Word and the good will of God. Accordingly, Moses expresses himself very carefully and says: "The serpent said," that is, with a word it attacks the Word. The Word which the Lord had spoken to Adam was: "Do not eat from the tree of the knowledge of good and evil." For Adam this Word was Gospel and Law; it was his worship; it was his service and the obedience he could offer God in this state of innocence. These Satan attacks and tries to destroy. Nor is it only his intention, as those who lack knowledge think, to point out the tree and issue an invitation to pick its fruit. He points it out indeed; but then he adds another and a new statement, as he still does in the Church. For when the Gospel is preached in its purity, men have a sure guide for their faith and are able to avoid idolatry. But then Satan makes various efforts and trials in an effort either to draw men away from the Word or to corrupt it.

And the woman said to the serpent, "We may eat of the fruit
of the trees in the garden, but God said, 'You shall not eat
of the fruit of the tree that is in the midst of the garden,
neither shall you touch it, lest you die.'"

GENESIS 3:2–3

Hold to the Word

o far as the passage before us in Moses is concerned, the words were most simple: "From the tree in the midst of Paradise you shall not eat." But reason did not understand the purpose of these words, why God wanted it to be so. Therefore Eve perishes while she investigates too inquisitively and refuses to be satisfied with what she had heard the Lord command. Thus this temptation is a true pattern of all temptations with which Satan assails the Word and faith. Before the desire to eat of the fruit arose in Eve, she lost the Word which God spoke to Adam. If she had adhered to this Word, she would have continued in the fear and faith of God. Where the opposite happens and the Word is lost, there is contempt of God and obedience to the devil. All this is useful, that we may learn, as Peter says (1 Peter 5:9), to stand undaunted in temptation and to resist the tempter while holding on to the Word with a firm faith and closing our ears so as not to grant admittance to what is foreign to the Word. For truly, these afflictions of Eve and Adam are lessons for us, in order that we may not have the same experiences by being drawn away from the Word and from faith.

They heard the sound of the Lord God walking in the garden in the cool of the day, and the man and his wife hid themselves.

GENESIS 3:8

The Growth of Sin

 t is worthwhile to note how sin gradually grows until it becomes exceedingly sinful sin, as Paul is wont to call it (Romans 7:13). First man falls from faith into unbelief and disobedience. Then fear, hatred, and avoidance of God follow unbelief, and these bring with them despair and impenitence. For where should the heart in its fright flee from the presence of God? To the devil? This is neither an advantageous nor an advisable thing to do, and yet it turns out this way. And so this account shows that God created man and made him lord of all, and yet man avoids Him and considers nothing either more hateful or more unbearable than God. Otherwise he would not have turned away from God; he would not have avoided Him; and he would not have trembled at the voice of God when He was coming, not at night, not with lightning and thunder, as at Sinai, but in the clear light of day, while a light and delightful breeze was blowing and the leaves of the trees were gently stirring. Thus there is nothing more grievous, nothing more wretched, than a conscience frightened by the Law of God and by the sight of its sins.

But the LORD God called to the man and said to him,
"Where are you?" And he said, "I heard the sound of You
in the garden, and I was afraid."

GENESIS 3:9–10

God Is Not Silent

I urge you with all diligence to consider the teaching of the Gospel a matter of the utmost importance. For we see from this passage what happens in the case of Adam and Eve when sin is present and this knowledge of the promise and of grace is lacking. . . . [Adam] is called to account that he might acknowledge his sin and, after he is thoroughly frightened by his sin, be given courage through the promise of the remission of sins. . . . God comes in a very soft breeze to indicate that the reprimand will be fatherly. He does not drive Adam away from Himself because of his sin, but He calls him and calls him back from his sin. Yet Adam does not understand or see this fatherly concern, since he is overwhelmed by his sin and terror. He does not notice that God deals far differently with the serpent. He does not call the serpent. Nor—in order in this way to call it to repentance—does He ask the serpent about the sin that has been committed. He condemns it immediately. This shows that even then Christ, our Deliverer, had placed Himself between God and man as a Mediator. It is a very great measure of grace that after Adam's sin God does not remain silent but speaks.

The Lord God said to the serpent, . . .
"I will put enmity between you and the woman,
and between your offspring and her offspring."

From the Midst of Sin

ho does not realize that the statement before us deals specifically with Satan, whom the Son of God resists in such a way that he cannot undertake anything with open force as though he had no antagonist? Under this protection the Church is safe; Satan not only cannot attack the Church with open force, but also in other respects his tyranny and his malevolence have been broken. . . . Moreover, this, too, ought to be noted here: that these words are not spoken by God for the devil's sake. God does not regard him worthy of His condemnation, but it is enough that his own conscience condemns Satan. These words are spoken for the sake of Adam and Eve that they may hear this judgment and be comforted by the realization that God is the enemy of that being which inflicted so severe a wound on man. Here grace and mercy begin to shine forth from the midst of the wrath which sin and disobedience aroused. Here in the midst of most serious threats the Father reveals His heart; this is not a father who is so angry that he would turn out his son because of his sin, but one who points to a deliverance, indeed one who promises victory against the enemy that deceived and conquered human nature.

Head and Heel

ee how uneven the outcome of the battle is. The human being's heel is in danger, but his head is uninjured and undefeated. On the other hand, it is not the tail and not the belly of the serpent but the head itself that is to be crushed and trodden underfoot by the Seed of the woman. But this victory will also be given to us as a gift, as Christ clearly states (Luke 11:22): "The spoils are divided after the defeat of the mighty one." By faith the Christian is made the victor over sin, over the Law, and over death, so that not even the gates of hell can prevail against him (Matthew 16:18). This first comfort, this source of all mercy and fountain-head of all promises, our first parents and their descendants learned with the utmost care. They saw that without this promise procreation would indeed continue to go on among people as well as among the other living beings, but that it would be nothing else than a procreation to death. And so that gift which was given by God to our nature is here made greater, nay, even made sacred; for there is hope of a pro-creation through which the head of Satan would be crushed, not only to break his tyranny but also to gain eternal life for our nature, which was surrendered to death because of sin.

The Lord God said to the serpent, . . .
"I will put enmity between you and the woman,
and between your offspring and her offspring;
He shall bruise your head, and you shall bruise His heel."

GENESIS 3:15

From Death to Life

his, therefore, is the text that made Adam and Eve alive and brought them back from death into the life which they had lost through sin. Nevertheless, the life is one hoped for rather than one already possessed. . . .

Through Baptism we are restored to a life of hope, or rather to a hope of life. This is the true life, which is lived before God. Before we come to it, we are in the midst of death. We die and decay in the earth, just as other dead bodies do, as though there were no other life anywhere. Yet we who believe in Christ have the hope that on the Last Day we shall be revived for eternal life. Thus Adam was also revived by this address of the Lord—not perfectly indeed, for the life which he lost he did not yet recover; but he got the hope of that life when he heard that Satan's tyranny was to be crushed.

Therefore this statement includes the redemption from the Law, from sin, and from death; and it points out the clear hope of a certain resurrection and of renewal in the other life after this life. If the serpent's head is to be crushed, death certainly must be done away with. If death is done away with, that, too, which deserved death is done away with, that is, sin.

January 25

If sin is abolished, then also the Law. And not only this, but at the same time the obedience which was lost is renewed. Because all these benefits are promised through this Seed, it is very clear that after the fall our human nature could not, by its own strength, remove sin, escape the punishments of sin and death, or recover the lost obedience. These actions call for greater power and greater strength than human beings possess.

And so the Son of God had to become a sacrifice to achieve these things for us, to take away sin, to swallow up death, and to restore the lost obedience. These treasures we possess in Christ, but in hope. In this way Adam, Eve, and all who believe until the Last Day live and conquer by that hope. Death is indeed an awful and undefeated tyrant; but God's power makes nothing out of that which is everything, just as it makes all things out of that which is nothing. Look at Adam and Eve. They are full of sin and death. And yet, because they hear the promise concerning the Seed who will crush the serpent's head, they have the same hope we have, namely, that death will be taken away, that sin will be abolished, and that righteousness, life, peace, etc., will be restored. In this hope our first parents live and die, and because of this hope they are truly holy and righteous. . . .

By hope we hold fast to both life and righteousness, things which are hidden from our eyes and our understanding, but will be made manifest in due time. Meanwhile our life is a life in the midst of death. And yet, even in the midst of death, the hope of life is kept, since the Word so teaches, directs, and promises.

> *To the woman [God] said,*
> *"I will surely multiply your pain in childbearing."*
> **GENESIS 3:16**

Momentary Affliction

ve had a heart full of joy even in an apparently sad situation. Perhaps she gave comfort to Adam by saying: "I have sinned. But see what a merciful God we have. How many privileges, both temporal and spiritual, He is leaving for us sinners! Therefore we women should bear the hardship and wretchedness of conceiving, of giving birth, and of obeying you husbands. His is a fatherly anger, because this stands: that the head of our enemy will be crushed, and that after the death of our flesh we shall be raised to a new and eternal life through our Redeemer. These abundant good things and endless kindnesses far surpass whatever curse and punishments our Father has inflicted on us." These and similar conversations Adam and Eve undoubtedly carried on often in order to mitigate their temporal adversities. Similarly we also ought to reflect often on the inexpressible treasures of the future life and by such thoughts make light the hardships of the flesh. We see Paul doing this in 2 Corinthians 4:17. "Our affliction," he says, "is for a moment and light; for it works in us an eternal weight of glory if we look not at those things which are seen but at those which are not seen. For the things that are seen are temporal, but those which are not seen are eternal."

To Adam [God] said, . . . "By the sweat of your face you shall
eat bread, till you return to the ground, for out of it you were
taken; for you are dust, and to dust you shall return."

GENESIS 3:17, 19

Hope Remains

 e must comfort ourselves in the face of such troubles and teach our hearts to be patient; for we see that these misfortunes are placed even upon the elect, who have the hope of resurrection and eternal life. Furthermore, since this hope remains for these very wretched people, we ought to have courage and overcome these evils through hope; for we shall not remain here forever. . . . Therefore let misfortunes come as the Lord passes them out to each, whether in the household or in the state and church. We shall not allow ourselves to be driven to impatience. We shall not let them divert us from our concern for the state, the household, or the church. . . . But this we shall be able to do if we compare the troubles of the present time with the hope of resurrection and eternal life. Just as no one would be willing to lose this hope, so each individual must be convinced that he should not abandon the position into which God has placed him. . . . Let us, who carry on this hard work, each in his own situation, keep in mind that even if we must endure something painful, these hardships will have their end.

What Is in a Name?

The name which Adam gives his wife is a very pleasing and delightful name. For what is more precious, better, or more delightful than life? . . . Moreover, Adam adds the reason: "Because she is the mother of all living." It is clear from this passage that after Adam had received the Holy Spirit, he had become marvelously enlightened, and that he believed and also understood the saying concerning the woman's Seed who would crush the head of the serpent. Moreover, he wanted to give an outward indication of this faith of his and lend distinction to it by means of his wife's name. He gave it to no other creature. By this designation of his wife he gave support to the hope in the future Seed, strengthened his own faith, and comforted himself with the thought that he believed in life even when all nature had already been made subject to death. If Adam had not been aware of the future life, he would not have been able to cheer his heart; nor would he have assigned so pleasing a name to his wife. But by assigning this name to his wife he gives clear indication that the Holy Spirit had cheered his heart through his trust in the forgiveness of sins by the Seed of Eve. He calls her Eve to remind himself of the promise through which he himself also received new life, and to pass on the hope of eternal life to his descendants.

*The L*ORD *God said, . . . "Behold, the man has become like one*
of Us in knowing good and evil. Now, lest he reach out his hand
and take also of the tree of life and eat, and live forever—"
*therefore the L*ORD *God sent him out of the garden of Eden.*

Mercy and a Warning

hy does God deal so harshly with wretched Adam? Why, after being deprived of all his glory and falling into sin and death, is he further vexed by his Creator with such bitter scorn? . . . My answer is: Adam had the promise of mercy; with this he ought to have lived content. But to make him fear future sin and beware of it, this harsh reminder is given him. . . . By His very Word, God calls attention to both past and future evils. It is not as though He were pleased by so sad a fall, for then He would not warn Adam in this way but would keep silence. What He wants is that man should long for the lost image of God and begin to hate sin as the cause of this great evil, and that Adam should warn his descendants about what followed after sin, namely, that when he was deprived of his mind by Satan and believed that he would be like God, he became like Satan himself. . . . So in this passage Adam and all his descendants are warned in various ways; after receiving the hope of life through the promise of the Seed, they should be on their guard lest they sin and lose it again.

January 29

At the east of the garden of Eden
He placed the cherubim and a flaming sword
that turned every way to guard the way to the tree of life.

GENESIS 3:24

The Tree of Life

hat else can the closed Paradise and the cherubim with their swords, stationed to guard Paradise, signify than that without faith in Christ man can endure neither the Law nor the Gospel? Paul speaks this way when he says that the Jews were unable to look at Moses' shining face and that Moses was compelled to place a veil before his face (2 Corinthians 3:7). The tree of death is the Law, and the tree of life is the Gospel, or Christ. Those who do not believe in Christ cannot draw near to these trees. They are prevented by the sword of the angel, who cannot put up with hypocrisy and corrupt righteousness. But for him who acknowledges his sin and believes in Christ, Paradise remains open. He brings with him not his own righteousness but Christ's, which the Gospel announces to all so that we all may place our reliance on it and be saved.

Now Adam knew Eve his wife,
and she conceived and bore Cain. . . .
And again, she bore his brother Abel.

GENESIS 4:1–2

The Name of "Son"

 ere the question arises why Moses says: "She bore Cain" and not rather, as below, "She bore her son Seth" [cf. Genesis 4:25]. Yet Cain and Abel were also sons. Why, then, are they not called sons? The answer is that this happens on account of their descendants. Abel, who was slain by his brother, perished physically; but Cain perished spiritually through his sin, and he did not propagate that nursery of the Church and of the kingdom of Christ. All his posterity perished in the flood. Therefore neither blessed Abel nor cursed Cain has the name of son; but it was Seth from whose descendants Christ, the promised Seed, would be born. And so Seth was the first who received the name of son.

In the course of time Cain brought to the Lord an offering of the fruit of the ground, and Abel also brought of the firstborn of his flock and of their fat portions.

GENESIS 4:3–4

Signs of Grace

t was a great comfort for Adam that, after he had lost Paradise, the tree of life, and the other privileges which were signs of grace, there was given to him another sign of grace, namely, the sacrifices, by which he could perceive that he had not been cast off by God but was still the object of God's concern and regard. This is what God was indicating when He kindled and consumed the sacrifices and offerings with fire from heaven, as we read about the sacrifice of Moses (Leviticus 9:24) and of Elijah (1 Kings 18:38). These were true manifestations of the divine mercy which the wretched people needed in order not to be without some light of the grace of God. In the same way the very Word, Baptism, and the Eucharist are our light-bearers today, toward which we look as dependable tokens of the sun of grace. We can state with certainty that where the Eucharist, Baptism, and the Word are, there are Christ, forgiveness of sins, and eternal life. . . . It is not the worth of the work itself that is of value in the sacrifice; it is the mercy and power of the divine promise, because God prescribes this form of worship and promises that it will be pleasing to Him. Therefore what Baptism and the Lord's Supper are for us, sacrifice and offering was for Adam after the promise.

February 1

And the L<small>ORD</small> had regard for Abel and his offering,
but for Cain and his offering He had no regard.

G<small>ENESIS</small> 4:4–5

The Lord's Regard

bel acknowledges that he is an unworthy and poor sinner. Therefore he takes refuge in God's mercy and believes that God is gracious and willing to show compassion. And so God, who looks at the heart, judges between the two brothers who are bringing their offerings at the same time. He rejects Cain, not because his sacrifice was inferior (for if he had brought the shell of a nut in faith as a sacrifice, it would have been pleasing to God), but because his person was evil, without faith, and full of pride and conceit. By contrast, He has regard for Abel's sacrifice because He is pleased with the person. Accordingly, the text distinctly adds that first He had regard for Abel and then for his sacrifice. For when a person pleases, the things he does also please, while, on the contrary, all things are displeasing if you dislike the person who does them. Therefore this passage is an outstanding and clear proof that God does not have regard for either the size or the quantity or even for the value of the work, but simply for the faith of the individual.

February 2

The LORD said to Cain,
"Where is Abel your brother?"

GENESIS 4:9

Precious Death

od does not inquire after sheep and cattle that have been slaughtered, but He does inquire after men who have been killed. Therefore men have the hope of resurrection and a God who leads them out of bodily death to eternal life, who inquires after their blood as after something precious, just as the psalm also says (116:15): "Precious is the death of His saints in His sight." This is the glory of the human race, which was won by the Seed when He crushed the serpent's head. This is the first example of that promise given to Adam and Eve, by which God shows that the serpent does not harm Abel even though it succeeds in having Abel killed. This is indeed why the serpent lies in wait for the heel of the woman's Seed. But while it bites, its head is crushed. Because of Abel's trust in the promised Seed, God inquired after Abel's blood when he was dead and showed that He is his God.

The LORD said, "What have you done? The voice of your brother's blood is crying to Me from the ground."

GENESIS 4:10

The Voice of Our Blood

e must not assume that God is disregarding our blood. We must not assume that God has no regard for our afflictions. "Our tears, too, He gathers into His bottle," as Psalm 56:8 says. And the cry of the blood of the godly penetrates the clouds and heaven until it arrives at God's throne and urges Him to avenge the blood of the righteous (Psalm 79:10). Just as these words have been written for our comfort, so they have been written to fill our adversaries with terror. What, in your opinion, is more awe-inspiring for those tyrants to hear than that the blood of those whom they have slain cries and incessantly accuses them before God? God is indeed long-suffering, especially now near the end of the world. Therefore sin reposes for a longer time. Vengeance does not follow immediately. But it surely is true that God is most profoundly outraged by this sin and will never allow it to go unpunished.

To Seth also a son was born, and he called his name Enosh.
At that time people began to call upon the name of the LORD.

GENESIS 4:26

Call upon the Name of the Lord

ere a most excellent definition is given of what it means to worship God, namely, to call upon the name of the Lord, a work or act of worship in the First Table, which contains the commandments about the true worship of God [Exodus 20:3–8]. But calling upon the name of the Lord includes the preaching of the Word, faith or trust in God, confession, etc. . . . Thus after the commotion occasioned by Cain in Adam's household the generation of the godly gradually increases, and a small church is formed in which Adam, as high priest, rules everything by the Word and sound doctrine. . . . Furthermore, the fact that Moses does not say "calling upon the Lord was begun" but "upon *the name* of the Lord" is correctly regarded as a reference to Christ. . . . From this arises the excellent thought that at that time men began to call upon the name of the Lord, that is, that Adam, Seth, Enosh exhorted their descendants to wait for their redemption, to believe the promise about the woman's Seed and through that hope to overcome the treachery, the crosses, the persecutions, the hatreds, the wrongs, etc., of the Cainites; not to despair about their salvation but rather to thank God, who one day would deliver them through the woman's Seed.

February 5

This is the book of the generations of Adam. . . .
Enoch walked with God, and he was not, for God took him.

GENESIS 5:1, 24

The Light of Immortality

 n this series [of names] there shines forth like a star the most charming light of immortality, when Moses relates about Enoch that he was no longer among men and yet had not died but had been taken away by the Lord. Moses is indicating that the human race has indeed been condemned to death because of sin, but that there has still been left the hope of life and immortality, and that we shall not remain in death. . . . Therefore it is stated about the individual patriarchs: "So many years he completed and died," that is, he bore the punishment of sin, or he was a sinner. But about Enoch Moses does not make this statement, not because he was not a sinner but because even for sinners there is left the hope of eternal life through the blessed Seed. And so also the patriarchs who died in the faith of this Seed clung to the hope of eternal life. Thus this is the second example which proves that God intends to give us eternal life after this life. For the Lord says that Abel is alive and cries even though he was killed by his brother (Genesis 4:10), and Enoch was taken away by the Lord Himself. . . . We have the hope concerning the divine plan and providence that God plans to do away with this death, just as He has begun to do through the promise of the blessed Seed; and the examples of Abel and Enoch point in the same direction.

February 6

Enoch walked with God,
and he was not, for God took him.

GENESIS 5:24

Walking with God

 his is the special jewel which Moses wants to be particularly prominent in this chapter: that Almighty God takes to Himself not geese, not cows, not pieces of wood, not stones, and not the dead, but Enoch in person, in order to show that there has been prepared and set aside for men another and also a better life than this present life which is replete with so many misfortunes and evils. Granted that Enoch, too, is a sinner, nevertheless he departs this life in such a way that God grants him another life, an eternal life. Inasmuch as he is living with God, God is also taking him to Himself. Thus Enoch walked with God; that is, in this life he was a faithful witness that after this life men would live an eternal life, thanks to the promised Seed. For this latter is the life with God; it is not that former life, which is physical and subject to corruption. And just as Enoch steadfastly preached this truth, so God fulfills and proves this message true in his person, in order that we may believe and maintain with assurance that Enoch, a human being like us, born of flesh and blood from the carnal Adam, as we are, was taken away to God and now lives the life of God, that is, the eternal life.

When man began to multiply on the face of the land . . .
the LORD saw that the wickedness of man was great in the earth.

GENESIS 6:1, 5

The Lord Sees

I n this conglomeration of people who were becoming progressively worse and were departing from the godliness and virtue of their ancestors, saintly Noah lived, utterly despised and hated by all. How could he approve of this lust of the decadent generation? But they on their part were most intolerant of any censure. While his example shines brightly and his saintliness fills all the lands, the world becomes worse day by day; the greater Noah's saintliness and chastity is, the greater the world's madness becomes through lust. These are the initial stages that always precede destruction. When God raises up holy men full of the Holy Spirit, to instruct and reprove the world, the world, intolerant of sound doctrine, indulges in sins with greater zeal and continues in them even more persistently. This was what happened at the beginning of the world, and we see that the same thing is happening now at the end of the world.

February 8

The LORD saw that the wickedness of man was great
in the earth, and that every intention of the thoughts
of his heart was only evil continually.

GENESIS 6:5

The Intentions of the World

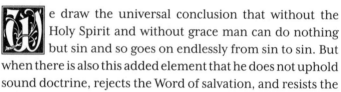 e draw the universal conclusion that without the Holy Spirit and without grace man can do nothing but sin and so goes on endlessly from sin to sin. But when there is also this added element that he does not uphold sound doctrine, rejects the Word of salvation, and resists the Holy Spirit, then, with the support of his free will, he also becomes an enemy of God, blasphemes the Holy Spirit, and completely follows the evil desires of his heart. . . . Or is not Psalm 14:2–3 general enough when it says: "The Lord looks down from heaven upon the children of men, to see if there are any that act wisely, that seek after God. They have all gone astray." [See also Romans 3:10; Psalm 116:11; Romans 11:32.] All these passages are very general and most emphatically conclude in our favor that without the Holy Spirit, whom Christ alone bestows, man can do nothing else than err and sin. . . . This is also the reason why it is the office of the Holy Spirit to reprove the world (John 16:8), namely, that He might recall the world to repentance and to a recognition of this fault. But the world remains the same; even when it is reprimanded by means of the Word of God, it does not listen.

*The L*ORD *was sorry that He had made man on the earth,*
and it grieved Him to His heart.

GENESIS 6:6

The Lord Grieves

 his grief is particularly the grief of the Holy Spirit, as St. Paul states in Ephesians 4:30: "Do not grieve the Holy Spirit of God, in whom you were sealed for the day of redemption." It means that the Holy Spirit is grieved when we wretched men are bewildered and tormented by the wickedness of the world, which despises the Word we preach in the Holy Spirit. . . . But what need, someone will say, has God of such a complaint? Can He not suddenly destroy the entire world when He wants to do so? Certainly He can, but He does not do it gladly, as He says (Ezekiel 33:11): "I have no pleasure in the death of the wicked, but that the wicked turn from his way and live." This disposition proves that God is ready to pardon, to forbear, and to forgive sins if only people were willing to come to their senses. But because they continue to be stubborn and to reject every remedy, He is tortured, as it were, by their wickedness.

The Lord was sorry . . . and it grieved Him to His heart.

GENESIS 6:6

Images of God

That Scripture thus assigns to God the form, voice, actions, emotions, etc., of a human being not only serves to show consideration for the uneducated and the weak, but we great and learned men, who are versed in the Scriptures, are also obliged to adopt these simple images because God has presented them to us and has revealed Himself to us through them. . . . This is the simplest procedure for dealing with passages of this kind, for we cannot define what God is in His nature. Yet we can define what He is not, namely, that He is not a voice, not a dove, not water, not bread, and not wine. Nevertheless, He presents Himself to us in these visible forms, deals with us, and puts these forms before us to keep us from degenerating into erratic and vagabond spirits who indeed carry on discussions about God but are profoundly ignorant of Him as of one who cannot be comprehended in His unveiled majesty. God sees that this way of knowing God is impossible for us; for, as Scripture states (1 Timothy 6:16), He dwells in unapproachable light, and He has made known what we can grasp and understand. Those who adhere to this truly understand God while those who boast of visions, revelations, and enlightenments and follow them are either overwhelmed by God's majesty or remain in utter ignorance of God.

Noah walked with God.
And Noah had three sons.
GENESIS 6:9–10

Faith in the Midst of Wickedness

After the verdict has been rendered about the destruction of the world, [Noah] obeys God, who calls upon him to marry, and believes God, that even if the entire world should perish, he himself will be saved together with his children. This is an outstanding faith, one worthy of our reflection. In the first place, he had that common faith about the Seed who would crush the head of the serpent, a faith which the other patriarchs also had. Moreover, it was a rare virtue to maintain this confidence in the face of so many corrupting influences and not to depart from God. Added to this faith there was, in the second place, particular faith, namely that he believed God both when He threatened destruction to all the rest of the world and when He promised deliverance to Noah himself and his sons. . . . This faith taught him to disdain the smugness of the world, which scoffed at him as at a deranged old man. This faith urged him to keep busy with the building of the ark, a structure which those notorious giants undoubtedly ridiculed as the utmost stupidity. This faith strengthened Noah to such an extent that he stood alone in the face of so many examples of the world and courageously despised the opinions of all people.

Noah found favor in the eyes of the LORD.

GENESIS 6:8

The Lord's Favor

hese are words that restored Noah's courage and life. Such great wrath of the divine Majesty would have slain him if God had not added the promise to preserve him. Nevertheless, it is likely that his faith was still troubled even though he heard this promise. It is unbelievable how much the contemplation of the wrath of God depresses the heart. Furthermore, here there is a new expression of the Holy Spirit—an expression which the heavenly messenger Gabriel also employs when addressing the Blessed Virgin (Luke 1:30): "You have found favor with God." This expression very clearly rules out any merit and gives praise to faith, by which alone we are justified before God, that is, are acceptable to God and please Him.

Noah was a righteous man,

blameless in his generation.

GENESIS 6:9

Righteous and Blameless

 oah is declared "righteous" in relation to the First Table [Exodus 20:3–8] and "perfect" ["blameless"] in relation to the Second Table [Exodus 20:12–17]. He is declared righteous through his faith in God, because he believed first the universal promise about the Seed of the woman and later on also the special one about the destruction of the world by the flood and about the preservation of his descendants. He is declared perfect because he walked in the fear of God and carefully avoided murder and the other sins with which the ungodly were polluting themselves in violation of their conscience; and he was in no way influenced by the many offenses of the most distinguished, the wisest, and, in appearance, the holiest men. . . . To be righteous and perfect is evidence of personal excellence; but to walk with God is something public, namely, to carry on God's business before the world, to occupy oneself with His Word, and to teach His worship. Noah was not only righteous and holy so far as his own person was concerned, but he was also a confessor. He informed others of the promises and threats of God, and in that most wicked and depraved age he carried out and suffered everything that is the obligation of a person in a public position.

[God said to Noah,] "I will establish My covenant with you."

GENESIS 6:18

The Importance of God's Covenant

his consolation Moses had already indicated above, when he said that Noah had found favor. There was need of this, not only to keep Noah from despairing before such a terrible wrath but also in order that his faith might be strengthened amid the punishment that was about to rage. It was not easy to believe that the entire human race would perish. The world regarded Noah as exceedingly stupid for believing such things; it derided him and without a doubt also made his structure the object of ridicule. In order to encourage him in such trying circumstances, God speaks with him several times and now reminds him of the covenant. . . . In my opinion, however, the text speaks of the spiritual covenant or of the promise of the Seed who would crush the head of the serpent. . . . God confirms this covenant that [Noah] may firmly believe that Christ will be born from his descendants and that God, in His great wrath, will let a seedbed of the Church remain. Accordingly, this covenant includes not only physical protection . . . but also eternal life. Hence the meaning is: "I shall punish those who insolently despise the threats and promises. . . . But I shall convey this covenant to you, that you may be saved not only from the violence of the water but also from eternal death and damnation." God expressly says: "With you." . . . This, then, is the second promise of Christ, and it is taken away from all the other descendants of Adam and bestowed upon Noah alone.

February 15

"Take with you every sort of food that is eaten, and store it up."

GENESIS 6:21

God's Providence

n this passage we observe the providence of God, according to whose counsel the ungodly are punished but the good are preserved. . . . It would have been easy for God to preserve Noah and the animals for an entire year even without food, as He preserved Moses, Elijah, and Christ for forty days without any food, yes, even as He made everything out of nothing, which is greater and more amazing. Nevertheless, as Augustine learnedly states, God governs the things He has created in such a way that He allows them to function with their distinctive activities; that is (applying Augustine's statement to the instance before us), God makes use of definite means and tones down His miracles in such a manner that He makes use of the service of nature and of natural means. And He demands from us too that we do not waste the products of nature (for that would be tempting God), but that we use with thanksgiving the means He has provided and offered. It would be a sin to expect food from heaven when one is hungry and not rather to provide it in some other manner or ask for it. Christ commands the apostles to eat what is set before them (Luke 10:7). Thus in this passage Noah receives the command to make use of the regular means of gathering food; he is not ordered to wait in the ark for some miraculous method of supplying food from heaven.

Noah did this; he did all that God commanded him.

GENESIS 6:22

Faithful Obedience

his is the first passage in which obedience toward God is praised in these words. Later on, however, it is repeated more frequently: "Moses or the people did according to all that the Lord had commanded them, etc." Noah is praised as an example for us because he did not have a dead faith, which is actually no faith at all, but a living and active faith. He is obedient when God gives him a command; and because he believes God both when He gives a promise and when He utters a threat, he painstakingly carries out God's direction in regard to the ark, the gathering of the animals, and the food. The particular praise of Noah's faith is that he stays on the royal road; he adds nothing, changes nothing, and takes nothing away from God's directive but abides completely by the command he hears. . . . This is giving glory to God for His wisdom and goodness. He did not argue about the task, as Adam, Eve, and Saul did to their great misfortune. He complied with the majesty of Him who gave the command; this was sufficient for him, even though he was commanded to do things that were preposterous, impossible, and inconvenient. He passes by all these offenses as if with closed eyes and relies on this one fact, that it was God who had given the command.

The LORD said to Noah, "Go into the ark,
you and all your household, for I have seen
that you are righteous before Me in this generation."

GENESIS 7:1

The Object of God's Care

ow that the extraordinary structure of the ark was completed, the Lord commanded Noah to enter it; for the time of the flood, about which the Lord had given advance warning one hundred and twenty years before, was now at hand. The purpose of all this was that Noah should realize that he was the object of God's care; and not this alone but, as Peter (2 Peter 1:19) expresses it, also that he might have a rich and abundant Word by which his faith would be supported and strengthened in such great trouble. Since he had foretold the flood for more than a hundred years, the world undoubtedly made him the object of various kinds of attacks. . . . The command to enter the ark is the same as though the Lord were to say: "Have no doubts. It will surely happen, and the time to inflict punishment on the unbelieving world is already very close at hand. But do not be alarmed, and do not be afraid; for at times faith is very weak even in the saints. You will be an object of My care, you and your household." For us indeed this would have been impossible to believe, although we must conclude that it is possible for God to do anything.

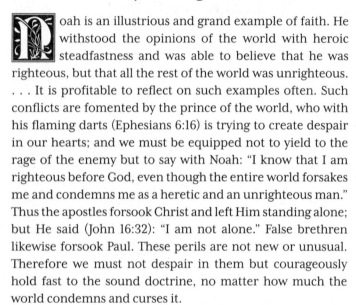

Unyielding Faith

oah is an illustrious and grand example of faith. He withstood the opinions of the world with heroic steadfastness and was able to believe that he was righteous, but that all the rest of the world was unrighteous. . . . It is profitable to reflect on such examples often. Such conflicts are fomented by the prince of the world, who with his flaming darts (Ephesians 6:16) is trying to create despair in our hearts; and we must be equipped not to yield to the rage of the enemy but to say with Noah: "I know that I am righteous before God, even though the entire world forsakes me and condemns me as a heretic and an unrighteous man." Thus the apostles forsook Christ and left Him standing alone; but He said (John 16:32): "I am not alone." False brethren likewise forsook Paul. These perils are not new or unusual. Therefore we must not despair in them but courageously hold fast to the sound doctrine, no matter how much the world condemns and curses it.

"Every living thing that I have made
I will blot out from the face of the ground." . . .
And rain fell upon the earth forty days and forty nights.

GENESIS 7:4, 12

Humbly Receive His Word

his account is sure evidence that even though God is long-suffering and patient, nevertheless He will finally punish the ungodly. Peter states (2 Peter 2:5): "If He did not spare the original world." . . . How much less will He spare us when we desecrate His name, when we lead an unworthy life in our vocation or profession, and when we sin daily against our conscience? Let us, therefore, learn to fear the Lord and with humility to receive His Word and to obey it; otherwise punishment will also overtake us, as Peter threatens.

On the very same day Noah and his sons,
Shem and Ham and Japheth, and Noah's wife
and the three wives of his sons with them entered the ark.

GENESIS 7:13

Entering the Ark

In what frame of mind do you suppose we would have been if we had been brought into the ark and had seen the waters rushing in from all sides with such force and the wretched mortals swimming in the water and wretchedly perishing without any help? We must keep in mind that Noah and his sons were also flesh and blood. . . . They sat in the ark for forty days before it was lifted from the earth. During these days whatever human beings and animals lived on the earth were destroyed. This disaster they saw with their own eyes. Who would doubt that they were profoundly shocked by it? . . . What loud cries there are, what grief, and what wailing when, from the shore, we observe a boat overturned and human beings perishing wretchedly! But in this instance not only one skiff but the entire world perished in the water. . . . Extraordinary indeed was the faith of Noah, who comforted himself and his people with the hope of the promised Seed and considered this promise of greater weight than the destruction of all the rest of the world.

All flesh died that moved on the earth. . . . Only Noah was left, and those who were with him in the ark.

GENESIS 7:21, 23

Only Those in the Ark

od remains truthful and preserves the Church, rules, and guides it, but in a manner that the world neither sees nor understands. . . . [The Church] God has chosen for Himself . . . receives the Word and shuns idolatry, although it is so hard pressed by cross and dishonor that it is not considered a church but a heretical body and a school of the devil. . . . In the same way man was given dominion over the world at the beginning of creation. In the flood this is taken away, not forever but for a time; and even then it is not taken away entirely. Even though the greater part of the world perishes, man nevertheless remains lord of the creatures; that lordship is preserved for him, if not in so large a multitude as the world believed and wanted, nevertheless in a few individuals, that is, eight souls, something that the world did not consider. God's promise [of the dominion over the earth by human beings], therefore, did not lie. God kept His promise, but He did not keep it in the manner in which the world wanted it kept. He destroyed the sinners; but He saved the righteous, even though they were few and were like seed that God increased later on in various ways.

But God remembered Noah . . .

GENESIS 8:1

The Beginning of the Fulfillment

fter the end of that awful wrath and after the destruction of all flesh, together with the earth, comes the
beginning of the fulfillment of the promise that the
Lord gave to Noah and his sons, that they would be the seed
of the human race. Undoubtedly they were looking forward
very eagerly to this promise. No life is more difficult than
one lived in faith, like the one Noah and his sons lived, whom
we see utterly dependent on heaven. Because the earth was
covered with water and they had no ground on which to set
foot, there was only the Word of the promise to give them
support as they drifted over that vast mass of water. . . . Look
at Noah, who was surrounded by water on all sides and was
all but overwhelmed by it. It is not works that preserve him,
but solely his reliance on the mercy of God, to which the
Word of the promise kept calling him. This difficult situation Moses describes by implication in the statement, "The
Lord remembered." He points out that Noah had drifted on
the waters for so long that God seemed to have completely
forgotten him. Men who live in such a conflict of thoughts—
when the rays of divine grace are withdrawn, and we find
ourselves in darkness or in a state of being forgotten by God—
discover that it is far more difficult to live by the Word alone
or by faith than to be a hermit or a Carthusian monk.

But God remembered Noah . . .

GENESIS 8:1

Our Example of Perseverance

ne must take into consideration the state of mind and the indescribable groaning of the heart when, in the very feeling of despair, a spark of faith still remains and overcomes the flesh. Just as Paul complains of the angel of Satan (2 Corinthians 12:7), so we must assume that Noah, too, felt similar barbs in his heart and often reasoned with himself: "You don't suppose that God loves only you this much, do you? You don't suppose, do you, that in the end God will save you, even though there is no limit to the waters and it seems that those immense clouds can never be emptied?" . . . It was no joke or laughing matter for them to live shut up in the ark for so long, to see the endless masses of rain, to be tossed about by the waves, and to drift. In these circumstances there was the feeling that God had forgotten them, as Moses indicates when he states that the Lord at last remembered Noah and his sons. Even though they overcame this feeling through faith, they did not overcome it without great annoyance to the flesh. . . . Let us, then, remember that this story sets before us an example of faith, perseverance, and patience, in order that those who have the divine promise may not only learn to believe it but may also realize that they need perseverance. But perseverance does not come without a great struggle. In the New Testament Christ calls on us to persevere when He says (Matthew 24:13): "He who endures to the end will be saved."

*God made a wind blow over the earth, and the waters
subsided. . . . Then God said to Noah, "Go out from the ark,
you and your wife, and your sons and your sons' wives with
you. Bring out with you every living thing that is with you."*

GENESIS 8:1, 15–17

Go Out from the Ark

 o far there has been only a factual account, or a
description of a divine work. Although God's works
are not mute but speak to us and, as it were, set
before our eyes a view of God's will, God nevertheless comforts us far more effectively when to His works He adds the
spoken Word, which the eyes do not see but the ears hear,
and which the heart understands as a result of the working
of the Holy Spirit. So far, by His work, God has shown that He
has been appeased and, as it were, has been changed from
an angry God to a merciful one, since He restrains the waters
and dries up the earth. Now He continues to strengthen this
comfort with His Word. He addresses Noah in a friendly
manner and commands Him, together with the rest of the
human beings and the animals, to leave the ark.

The LORD said in His heart,
"I will never again curse the ground because of man,
for the intention of man's heart is evil from his youth."

GENESIS 8:21

Our Heart's Intention

areful note must be taken of this passage, since it clearly shows that the nature of man is corrupt. This knowledge of our corrupt nature is necessary above all else; without it the mercy and grace of God cannot be properly understood. . . . Even though these inclinations can be corrected or restrained to some extent by discipline, they cannot be removed from the heart entirely, as their traces prove after we have grown up. The crude little verse is true: "In his old age the angelic child behaves like Satan." God indeed incites some men to natural drives that are good; but this happens beyond nature, as when Cyrus is incited to restore the worship of God and to preserve the Church (Ezra 1:2). These actions do not belong to human nature; for where God is with His Spirit, there is no longer the imagination of the human heart but the imagination of God. There God dwells through the Word and the Spirit of God. Of such things Moses is not speaking in this passage; he is speaking solely of men who lack the Holy Spirit. These are evil even when they are at their best.

February 26

"Neither will I ever again strike down every living creature as I have done. While the earth remains, seedtime and harvest, cold and heat, summer and winter, day and night, shall not cease."

GENESIS 8:21–22

While the Earth Remains

he simple meaning is that in this passage God promises Noah that the earth will be restored; that it will be possible again to sow the fields; that the destruction which the flood had brought about will come to an end; that the seasons will occur with customary regularity; and that in due order harvest will follow sowing, winter will follow summer, cold will follow heat. . . . The statement of the text, "while the earth remains," is not without purpose; for it implies that at some time the days of the earth will come to an end and other days—of heaven—will follow. As long as the days of the earth endure, the earth will endure, and the changes of the seasons will endure. But when these days of the earth come to an end, everything will come to an end, and there will follow days of heaven, that is, eternal days, which will be Sabbath after Sabbath, when we shall not be engaged in physical labors for our subsistence; for we shall be like the angels of God (Mark 12:25). Our life will be to know God, to delight in the wisdom of God, and to enjoy the presence of God. We attain this life through faith in Christ. May the eternal Father, through the merit of His Son and our Deliverer, Jesus Christ, mercifully preserve us in it through the guidance and direction of the Holy Spirit. Amen. Amen.

God blessed Noah and his sons and said to them,
"Be fruitful and multiply and fill the earth."

GENESIS 9:1

The Nursery of the Church

hese words were a truly necessary comfort after the entire human race had perished by the flood and only eight souls were saved. Noah realized that God is indeed favorably inclined toward him; for He is not satisfied with that first blessing with which He blessed the human race at the creation of the world, but He adds this new one in order that Noah may have no doubt whatever concerning the future increase of his progeny. This promise was all the more welcome because God had previously given the express promise that He would never again rage against the human race with so severe a punishment. For one thing, this chapter confirms marriage; for through His Word and command God joins the male with the female, and that for the definite purpose of filling the earth with human beings. Because before the flood God had been provoked to wrath by the sin of lust, it was necessary, on account of this awful expression of wrath, to show now that God does not hate or condemn the lawful union of a man and a woman but wants the human race to be propagated by it. This was a sure proof for Noah that God actually loves man, is well disposed toward him, and has now put away all wrath. . . . This passage, therefore, deals with the honorableness of marriage, which is the source of both the family and the state, and the nursery of the Church.

"Whoever sheds the blood of man,
by man shall his blood be shed."

GENESIS 9:6

The Authority of Humans

ere we have the source from which stem all civil law and the law of nations. If God grants to man power over life and death, surely He also grants power over what is less, such as property, the home, wife, children, servants, and fields. All these God wants to be subject to the power of certain human beings, in order that they may punish the guilty. In this connection the following difference must be maintained between the authority of God and that of human beings: even if the world should be unable to bring a charge against us and we should be guiltless before the world, God still has the power to kill us. For sin, with which we were born, makes us all guilty before God. But human beings have the power to kill only when we are guilty before the world and when the crime has been established. For this reason courts have been established and a definite method of procedure has been prescribed. . . . Therefore we must take careful note of this passage, in which God establishes government, to render judgment not only about matters involving life but also about matters less important than life. Thus a government should punish the disobedience of children, theft, adultery, and perjury. In short, it should punish all sins forbidden in the Second Table [Exodus 20:12–17]. For He who allows judgment in matters involving life also permits judgment in less important matters.

"For God made man in His own image."

GENESIS 9:6

Respect for the Image of God

his is the outstanding reason why He does not want a human being killed on the strength of individual discretion: man is the noblest creature, not created like the rest of the animals but according to God's image. Even though man has lost this image through sin, as we stated above, his condition is nevertheless such that it can be restored through the Word and the Holy Spirit. God wants us to show respect for this image in one another; He does not want us to shed blood in a tyrannical manner. But the life of one who does not want to show respect for the image of God in man but wants to yield to his anger and grief—his worst advisers, as someone has said—this life God turns over to the government, in order that his blood, too, may be shed. Thus this passage establishes civil government in the world.

March 1

"I establish My covenant with you, that never again shall all
flesh be cut off by the waters of the flood,
and never again shall there be a flood to destroy the earth."

GENESIS 9:11

Preservation of the Promise

 he flood is truly death and the wrath of God; nevertheless, the believers are saved in the midst of the flood. Thus death engulfs and swallows up the entire human race; for without distinction the wrath of God goes over the good and the evil, over the godly and the ungodly. . . . The difference becomes apparent in this: those who believe are preserved in the very death to which they are subjected together with the ungodly, but the ungodly perish. Noah, accordingly, is preserved because he has the ark, that is, God's promise and Word, in which he is living; but the ungodly, who do not believe the Word, are left to their fate. This difference the Holy Spirit wanted to point out in order that the godly might be instructed by this example to believe and hope for salvation through the mercy of God, even in the midst of death. For they have Baptism joined with the promise of life, just as Noah had the ark. Hence even though the death of the wise man and of the fool is the same (Ecclesiastes 2:16)—for Peter and Paul die no differently from the way Nero and other ungodly men die later on—they nevertheless believe that in death they will be preserved for eternal life. Nor is this an idle hope; for they have Christ to receive their spirits. On the Last Day He will revive also the bodies of believers for eternal life.

*"This is the sign of the covenant that I make between Me and
you and every living creature that is with you, for all future
generations: I have set My bow in the cloud, and it shall be a
sign of the covenant between Me and the earth."*

GENESIS 9:12–13

The Sign of the Covenant

oah and his people were in great need of such
comfort. . . . How much more difficult it is for a conscience that has experienced God's wrath and the
terrors of death to let comfort come in! These experiences
remain so firmly entrenched later on that a heart becomes
fearful and terrified even in the face of kindnesses and comforting words. It is for this reason that God shows Himself
benevolent in such a variety of ways and takes such extraordinary delight in pouring forth compassion. . . . We, too,
need this comfort today, in order that despite a great variety
of stormy weather we may have no doubt that the sluice
gates of the heavens and the fountains of the deep have been
closed by the Word of God. . . . This sign should remind us
to give thanks to God. For as often as the rainbow appears,
it preaches to the entire world with a loud voice about the
wrath which once moved God to destroy the whole world. It
also gives comfort, that we may have the conviction that God
is kindly inclined toward us again and will never again make
use of so horrible a punishment. Thus it teaches the fear of
God and faith at the same time, the greatest virtues.

March 3

Noah began to be a man of the soil,
and he planted a vineyard.
He drank of the wine and became drunk
and lay uncovered in his tent.

GENESIS 9:20–21

A Saint Falls

his is indeed a silly and altogether unprofitable little story if you compare it with the rest of Noah's outstanding achievements through the course of so many years. . . . But the intention of the Holy Spirit is familiar from our teaching. He wanted the godly, who know their weakness and for this reason are disheartened, to take comfort in the offense that comes from the account of the lapses among the holiest and most perfect patriarchs. In such instances we should find sure proof of our own weakness and therefore bow down in humble confession, not only to ask for forgiveness but also to hope for it. . . . Hence when we see saints fall, let us not be offended. Much less let us gloat over the weakness of other people, or rejoice, as though we were stronger, wiser, and holier. Rather let us bear with and cover, and even extenuate and excuse, such mistakes as much as we can, bearing in mind that what the other person has experienced today we may perhaps experience tomorrow. We are all one mass, and we are all born of one flesh. Therefore let us learn St. Paul's rule that "he who stands should take heed lest he fall" (1 Corinthians 10:12).

These are the clans of the sons of Noah,
according to their genealogies, in their nations, and from these
the nations spread abroad on the earth after the flood.

GENESIS 10:32

The Connecting Thread

ne must consider this chapter of Genesis a mirror in which to discern what we human beings are, namely, creatures so marred by sin that we have no knowledge of our own origin, not even of God Himself, our Creator, unless the Word of God reveals these sparks of divine light to us from afar. Then what is more futile than boasting of one's wisdom, riches, power, and other things that pass away completely? Therefore we have reason to regard the Holy Bible highly and to consider it a most precious treasure. This very chapter, even though it is considered full of dead words, has in it the thread that is drawn from the first world to the middle and to the end of all things. From Adam the promise concerning Christ is passed on to Seth; from Seth to Noah; from Noah to Shem; and from Shem to this Eber [see Genesis 10:21–25], from whom the Hebrew nation received its name as the heir for whom the promise about the Christ was intended in preference to all other peoples of the whole world. This knowledge the Holy Scriptures reveal to us. Those who are without them live in error, uncertainty, and boundless ungodliness; for they have no knowledge about who they are and whence they came.

"Come, let us build ourselves a city and a tower with its top
in the heavens, and let us make a name for ourselves."

Genesis 11:4

Beware the False Church

 mphasis lies on their saying: "Let us build *ourselves* a city and a tower," not for God, not for the Church of God, but to suppress the Church; and on the words: "Let us make a name for *ourselves*." These men who are gripped by such an intense desire to exalt their own name are surely not concerned that the name of God may be hallowed; and without a doubt they looked with profound contempt upon the humble cabins of the holy fathers and of their brothers, since they were building in such grand style. Nor is it without purpose when they declare that the top of the tower should reach to heaven. These words must not be applied to the height alone; they also denote that this was to be a place of worship. The implication was that God was dwelling very close to this tower. This is Satan's way. He adorns himself with the title of God and wants to have superstition regarded as religion. . . . Thus this account portrays the ungodliness, the schemes, the ambition, and the plots of all ungodly men, especially of the hypocrites who alone appear to themselves to be holy and very close to God and who want to rule the earth. . . . For the false church is always the persecutor of the true Church, not only spiritually, by means of false doctrine and ungodly forms of worship, but also physically, by means of the sword and tyranny.

March 6

*And the L*ORD* came down to see the city and the tower.*

GENESIS 11:5

The Lord Comes Down

ver against our weakness and the smugness of the ungodly, Scripture bears witness that finally God descends, punishes, and opens His eyes, ears, and mouth. This the godly believe, but with a feeble faith, while the ungodly smugly disregard it. Hence let us be warned by the example before us and learn this: the longer God puts up with idolatry and other sins, and the longer He pays no attention to them, the more intolerable will His wrath reveal itself to be later on. Therefore we ought to consider it a great kindness if He does not permit our sins to go unpunished for a long time. Psalm 30:5 exhorts the Church to give thanks because the wrath of the Lord is "for a moment" and because He loves life. It says: "Weeping may tarry for the night, but joy comes with the morning"; and Psalm 89:30, 32: "If his children forsake My Law and do not walk according to My ordinances, I will punish their transgression with the rod and their iniquity with scourges." This is a wrath of grace, when the punishment comes quickly and calls us back from sin.

"Come, let Us go down and there confuse their language."

GENESIS 11:7

Comfort through Confusion

his also serves to comfort the true Church, that God not only sees the enterprises, machinations, and counsels of the ungodly who oppose the Church but also laughs at them, as the second psalm (2:4) says: "He who sits in the heavens laughs; the Lord has them in derision." But it is a scornful laughter; for fury, wrath, and dispersion follow upon this laughter. "He will speak at some time in His wrath," says David, "and terrify them in His fury" (Psalm 2:5). . . . Thus the Holy Spirit comforts the true Church, which is being troubled by the church of Satan, lest it believe that God is paying no attention to it. He says: "The Lord sees what the ungodly are doing. And now He is getting ready to descend, that those who laugh smugly at all threats and mistakenly suppose that their power cannot be broken may become aware that their plans are not hidden from God." Yet God does not make use of battering-rams to break down walls, nor does He use other engines of war; He merely confuses their languages. This is truly an astounding method of conquering cities and of demolishing walls, but it is the surest and easiest of all.

March 8

*There the L*ORD *confused the language of all the earth.*

GENESIS 11:9

The Language Gap Defeated

herefore it is a great blessing and an outstanding miracle of the New Testament that by means of various languages the Holy Spirit on the day of Pentecost brought men of all nations into the one body of the one Head, Christ (Acts 2). Christ joins and unites all into one faith through the Gospel, even though the different languages remain; and He tears down the wall (Ephesians 2:14), not only by reconciling us to God through His death and speaking to us in a new language but also by bringing about outward harmony, so that different flocks are brought together under one Shepherd and are gathered into one fold (John 10:16). This is Christ's blessing; and since it is common to all, differences in outward life cause no offense. Let us, therefore, give Him the credit that through the Holy Spirit He has removed this most severe punishment, which was the beginning and seedbed of all evils and discords, and has brought us a holy harmony, even though the different languages remain.

March 9

These are the generations of Shem.

The Church Is Not a Place

 his list of the fathers teaches us the basic doctrine that God has never altogether abandoned His Church, even though on some occasions it was larger and on others smaller, just as also on some occasions its teaching was purer and on others less clear. Let us sustain ourselves with this hope against the great wickedness of the world and of the opponents of the Word. Christ also gives us the comfort (Matthew 24:22) that the days of the last time will be shortened for the sake of the godly, namely, that the Church will be preserved and Antichrist will not encompass everything with error and falsehood. These grandsons of Shem were heirs of the promise concerning Christ, and God wanted them preserved and defended, in order that there might be people among whom the Church or the Word might be found. For these cannot be separated: where the Word is, there the Church is, there the Spirit is, there Christ is, and everything. . . . The fathers had a physical succession, just as later on in the Law there was a physical succession to the priesthood. But in the New Testament there is no such physical succession. Christ did not beget sons according to the flesh. Therefore the Church is not confined to a place or to persons but is only where the Word is.

The Lord's Calling

hen Moses was describing Noah (Genesis 6:9), he called him a righteous and perfect man in his generation. No such title is bestowed on Abraham in this passage. No doubt this is because, as Joshua bears witness, Abraham, with his father and brothers, was an idolater and was righteous, not before God but before Nimrod, whose worship he was imitating (Joshua 24:2). Moses, therefore, says nothing about Abraham's person and has no praise for anything in him. For idolatry must be reproved, not praised. But he does praise God's mercy and extol Him because He did not allow this idolater to remain in idolatry any longer but called him out of the church of the ungodly to another place. . . . This blessing of deliverance from idolatry has its source, not in [Abraham's] own merits or powers but solely in a God who pities and calls him. Similarly, Moses reminds his people that they were chosen by the Lord, not because they had deserved this but because the Lord had loved them and was keeping the oath that had been given to their fathers. In this passage we see that the beginnings are in agreement with the end. For what is Abraham except a man who hears God when He calls him, that is, a merely passive person and merely the material on which divine mercy acts?

March 11

"I will make of you a great nation, and I will bless you
and make your name great, so that you will be a blessing."

GENESIS 12:2

Firm in Faith

braham saw none of these things. In fact, he had abundant reason not to believe them if he had wanted to follow his flesh; for his marriage was childless. . . . Thus the faith of this holy man was outstanding, because he believed these things as though he were already seeing them before his eyes and had no doubts about the promises that were given to him. With this great faith let us compare our own lack of faith. We know that Christ will come on the Last Day and will destroy all His enemies . . . and whatever ungodly men there are, who either persecute the Word or proudly despise and disregard it. We also know that meanwhile Christ will be with His Church and will preserve sound doctrine and the true forms of worship. But if we firmly believed what we know, do you think that it would be possible for any misfortune to perturb us? Or do you think that in our hearts there would arise the smugness we feel in ourselves, as though we were sure that the day of the Lord is a thousand years away? If, then, we believe at all, our faith is surely weak. We are truly people of little faith and can in no wise compare ourselves to holy Abraham, who receives these invisible things with a firm faith, as though he were already holding them in his hands and touching them.

"I will make of you a great nation, and I will bless you."

GENESIS 12:2

Blessed to Be a Great Nation

he first gift is that Abraham will be "a great nation," that is, that his descendants will have a kingdom, power, wealth, laws, ceremonies, a church, etc. For this is what is properly called a nation. But the second gift is that this nation will endure, as Psalm 89:30–33 explains uncommonly well: "If his children forsake My Law and do not walk according to My ordinances, if they violate My statutes and do not keep My commandments, then I will punish their transgressions with the rod and their iniquity with scourges; but I will not remove from him My steadfast love, or be false to My faithfulness." Truly, that people was often afflicted. The tribe of Benjamin was almost entirely slain. The kingdom of Israel was utterly destroyed. The tribe of Judah, too, was weakened in various ways by the Babylonian kings and then by the Syrians and the Egyptians. And yet that people was preserved by God until the promise concerning Christ would be fulfilled. Then began the real blessing and the real increase, because in place of the few unbelieving Jews the fullness of the Gentiles came in, and the seed of Abraham truly became like the sand of the sea and the stars of the heavens (Genesis 22:17). Therefore it endures to this day and will endure until the end of the world.

"And I will make of you a great nation . . . and in you all the families of the earth shall be blessed."

GENESIS 12:2–3

Called from Idolatry to Be a Blessing

It is a great and inexpressible gift that Abraham is physically the father of the Son of God. But what is the beginning of this honor? That Abraham is an idolater and a very great sinner, who worships a God he does not know! The Son of God wants this ancestor in His line of descent to be exalted, just as other ancestors of Christ are noted for their great sins. Why should this be the case? In the first place, in order to show that He is the Savior of sinners. In the second place, to inform us of His limitless kindness, lest we be overwhelmed by our sins and plunged into despair. In the third place, to block the road to haughtiness and pride. For when Abraham has been called in this way, he cannot say: "I have deserved this; this is my work." Even though he was guiltless before men so far as the Second Table [Exodus 20:12–17] is concerned, yet he was an idolater. He would have deserved eternal death had it not been for the call by which he was delivered from idolatry and finally granted the forgiveness of sins through faith. Therefore the statement stands (Romans 9:16): "It depends not upon man's will or exertion but upon God's mercy."

"In you all the families of the earth shall be blessed."

Christ Brings the Blessing

here follows that promise which should be written in golden letters and should be extolled in the languages of all people, for it offers eternal treasures. For it cannot be understood in a material sense, namely, that it would be confined to this people only, as the previous blessings were. But if, as the words clearly indicate, this promise is to be extended to all nations, or families of the earth, who else, shall we say, has dispensed this blessing among all nations except the Son of God, our Lord Jesus Christ? Therefore the simple, true, and incontrovertible meaning is this: "Listen, Abraham, I have given you and your descendants grand promises; but this is not yet enough. I shall distinguish you also with a blessing that will overflow to all the families of the earth." Abraham understood this promise well. For he reasoned thus: "If all the families of the earth are to be blessed through me, then of necessity this blessing must not depend on my person. For I shall not live till then. Furthermore, I am not blessed through myself, but through the mercy of God the blessing has come to me too. Therefore all nations will not be blessed because of my person or through my power. But from my posterity will be born One who is blessed in His own person and who will bring a blessing so long and wide that it will reach all the families of the earth. He must necessarily be God and not a human being, although He will be a human being and will take on our flesh so that He is truly my seed."

March 15

"In you all the families of the earth shall be blessed."

GENESIS 12:3

Blessing upon Blessing

ut of this promise flowed all the sermons of the prophets concerning Christ and His kingdom, about the forgiveness of sins, about the gift of the Holy Spirit, about the preservation and the government of the Church, about the punishments of the unbelievers, etc. They saw that these conclusions were definitely implied: If the Seed of Abraham does this, He must necessarily be a true human being by nature; on the other hand, if He blesses others, even all the families of the earth, He must necessarily be something greater than the seed of Abraham, because the seed of Abraham itself stands in need of this blessing on account of its sin. In these few simple words the Holy Spirit has thus encompassed the mystery of the incarnation of the Son of God. The holy patriarchs and prophets explained this more fully later on in their sermons, namely, that through the Son of God the entire world would be made free, hell and death would be destroyed, the Law would be abrogated, sins would be forgiven, and eternal salvation and life would be given freely to those who believe in Him. This is the day of Christ about which He discourses in John (8:56), the day which Abraham did not see with his bodily eyes but did see in the spirit, and was glad. To the flesh these things were invisible, impossible, and for this reason incredible.

March 16

So Abram went, as the LORD had told him.

GENESIS 12:4

Promise and Faith

romise and faith belong together naturally and inseparably. For what is the use of making any promise if there is no one to believe it? On the other hand, what would be the advantage of faith if there should be no promise? . . . But when God makes a promise of some kind, faith wrestles much and long; for reason, or flesh and blood, regards God's promise as altogether impossible. Therefore faith must wrestle with doubt and against reason. . . . Faith is a vigorous and powerful thing; it is not idle speculation. . . . But just as water that has been heated, even though it remains water, is no longer cold but is hot and an altogether different water, so faith, the work of the Holy Spirit, fashions a different mind and different attitudes, and makes an altogether new human being. Therefore faith is an active, difficult, and powerful thing. If we want to consider what it really is, it is something that is done to us rather than something that we do; for it changes the heart and mind. And while reason is wont to concern itself with the things that are present, faith apprehends the things that are not present and, contrary to reason, regards them as being present. This is why faith does not belong to all men, as does the sense of hearing; for few believe. The remaining masses prefer to concern themselves with the things that are present, which they can touch and feel, rather than with the Word.

So Abram went, as the Lord had told him.

GENESIS 12:4

Our Chief Concern

rue obedience is not to do what you yourself choose or what you impose upon yourself, but what the Lord has commanded you through His Word. . . . The Lord, it says, has spoken, and He has told Abraham that he should go out. Therefore this going out was a most sacred work, an obedience that was most pleasing to God. One must note, however, that the Lord also speaks to us through human beings. . . . Let us, therefore, remember this brief statement: "Abraham went, as the Lord had told him," and write it above all the activities that we carry on, whether at home or abroad, whether in war or in peace, whether during a plague or in any other danger. Then it follows that even if we have to die, we may comfort ourselves that we continued steadfast in our obedience to God. . . . Obedience deserves to be praised as obedience only if it proceeds from the promises or from the commands of God. Without these nothing has the right to be called obedience, unless perhaps one would want to call it the obedience of Satan; for not to obey God and His Word is to obey Satan. Therefore let the Word, or the call, be our chief concern. For this alone produces true obedience and worship that is pleasing to God; and if we render this, we are able not only to defend ourselves with the witness of our conscience but also to look for help from God, whose voice we follow even in real danger.

Let Nothing Terrify You

t is not merely because of her wifely affection that [Sarai] follows her husband. She was aided by the Holy Spirit, who moved her womanly heart so that she also, disregarding everything else, followed God when He called, since she also desired to be saved and not be condemned with the idolaters. Peter, therefore, properly praises this obedience in 1 Peter 3:6 and wants wives to imitate this extraordinary virtue of Sarah. "You are," he says, "her children if you do right and let nothing terrify you."

March 19

Abram took Sarai his wife, and Lot his brother's son . . . and the
people that they had acquired in Haran.

GENESIS 12:5

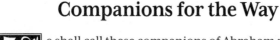

Companions for the Way

e shall call these companions of Abraham not simply his household but the true and holy Church, in which Abraham was the high priest. He instructed it concerning God's mercy, which would be revealed through His Son, who would first rule and bless the descendants of Abraham and all who allied themselves with him, and secondly would take on flesh in His time and transfer the wrath and curse from His people to Himself, so that they would be rid of all their sins and escape the punishment of eternal death. Sarai, Lot's wife, Lot's daughters, and the servants of both believed this preaching of Abraham. Therefore they followed the holy head of the household with the utmost joy, preferring to endure want, danger, and all kinds of harm to forfeiting the possession of such great promises—even though the possession was not yet a reality but merely a hope. In this manner the Lord comforted Abraham himself; for it was indeed a blessing of God that he could find companions for his exile, and such good and godly ones at that, who also held the Word in high esteem and followed it.

Abram passed through the land to the place at Shechem, to the
oak of Moreh. At that time the Canaanites were in the land.
Then the LORD appeared to Abram and said,
"To your offspring I will give this land."

GENESIS 12:6–7

A Definite Place

he fact that Moses adds that the Canaanites were in the land serves to remind us of the wretched exile in which the holy patriarch lived. For [Abraham] dwelt not among friends but in the midst of enemies and among men who were different in their worship and religion. By the will of Noah this region had indeed been assigned to the godly Shem, but the children of Nimrod had poured out of both Arabias and had taken possession of it by force. Thus you see that in all ages the lot of the Church is the same: it is the prey of the ungodly, and yet the Lord preserves it in a marvelous manner, even against the gates of hell (Matthew 16:18). After Abram, the exile, has been annoyed and troubled among the Canaanites long enough and in various ways, he finds great comfort in his trials, to keep him from being overcome by impatience. For it is true that no flesh would be saved (Matthew 24:22) unless at that time the days were shortened and comfort followed. He who perseveres in faith will surely experience in the end that God does not forsake His own. . . . Now at last a definite place is pointed out where the descendants of Abraham should settle.

And Abram journeyed on.

GENESIS 12:9

The Lord's Leading

 his is [Abraham's] third migration within the land of Canaan. So it is clear what a welcome guest he was to the people of that land. . . . This example of extraordinary faith the Holy Spirit here sets before our eyes. Previously, in our discussion of Cain's sin and punishment, we stated that he had to be a wanderer on the earth. But Abraham is holy through faith. Besides, he has the promise of an excellent blessing. Compare these facts with his lot, and you will realize that he is enduring punishment similar to Cain's. Like one who is cursed, he is wandering about in the land that has been promised to him, and not alone at that, but with his wife, his nephew by his brother, and all his domestics. Thus "the Lord leads His saints in a wonderful manner" (Psalm 4:3); and if they persevere in the faith, they ultimately receive what they believe. Let us, therefore, prepare ourselves for such conflicts and steadfastly persevere in the faith. For this is the purpose for which these accounts are written.

Now there was a famine in the land.
So Abram went down to Egypt to sojourn there.
GENESIS 12:10

Faith in the Face of Famine

 braham roamed about in the land, and nowhere did he find a place at which he could remain for any length of time. Finally came the misfortune that he was compelled to leave this promised land and on account of famine to migrate to Egypt with his entire household. Was this not a severe trial of his faith? . . . These things happen by a definite counsel of God, in order to test the faith of the saints. But they happen for a time; later there follows not only an earthly compensation, as Abraham became very rich, but also an increase of faith and a deeper sense of God's mercy. Therefore Paul states (Romans 5:3) that even though the saints sigh, complain, and wail when they are afflicted, they nevertheless also glory in their cross or tribulation, since they are aware of the amazing governance of God. . . . [First, Abraham] considers the spiritual promise about the eternal kingdom through the Son of God, and with this he comforts himself. In the second place, he does not discard his confidence in the physical promise either. . . . Hence you see here an outstanding example how faith is tried in the saints; and yet holy Abraham does not succumb, as do the ungodly, who are immediately offended at the first sensation of a trial and shrink back. . . . But the godly seize the Word and support themselves against temptation with it as with a staff, lest they be overcome.

March 23

Now Abram was very rich in livestock,
in silver, and in gold.

GENESIS 13:2

God Is Faithful

ere Moses mentions for the first time that Abraham was very rich and well supplied with gold and silver. This is comforting to exiles and strangers. For sometimes God is wont to pursue such a course and even in the midst of misfortunes to enrich His own with temporal goods. If there were perpetual struggles and perplexities when trials come, and no intervals of comfort, faith would be shaken. For this reason God sometimes allows us a breathing spell and assuages cares and misery with some comfort, just as we use a potion or spices to revive those who are exhausted by trouble or grief and to keep them from dying. We should keep this example in mind in our perils, that we may bear patiently the adversities facing us and wait for comfort in faith. God is faithful, and with the trial He provides also an escape (1 Corinthians 10:13). Of course, the real deliverance takes place only when we are rid of this flesh and leave this life. But prior to this perfect deliverance He often comforts our troubled hearts, granting also earthly advantages, which prove both that God does not forget His own and that the rewards of godliness are sure.

Now Abram was very rich in livestock,
in silver, and in gold.

The Godly Use of Wealth

t was a famous maxim, not only in the schools of the philosophers but also among the theologians: "What is outside us does not concern us." Money and similar things are outside us; hence they do not concern us. This sophistry sounds good, but it is harmful and ungodly. You must rather say: "The things that are outside us concern us very much." For God said (Genesis 1:28): "Have dominion over the fish of the sea and over the birds of the air and over the earth with everything that it contains." Among these gifts are also gold and silver. Make use of these, but in such a way that your heart is good, that is, without greed and without harm to anyone else. In the first place, provide for the livelihood of the people of your household, "so that you may not be worse than a heathen" (1 Timothy 5:8). In the second place, use these things for the advantage of others. Be on your guard, as against a plague that is sure to occur, lest, like foolish Crates, you throw your possessions away or, like Epictetus and the Stoics, do not consider them good and useful. . . . Reform your mind, and use these things with a sincere heart. If God has given you wealth, give thanks to God, and see that you make the right use of it; if He has not given it, do not seek it greedily. Have patience, and trust God to give you daily bread.

And he journeyed on . . .
to the place where he had made an altar at the first;
and there Abram preached the name of the Lord.

GENESIS 13:3–4 (according to Luther's translation)

Preaching and Prayer

n the Hebrew there is a clear difference between these two: to call *on* the name of the Lord and to call *in* the name of the Lord. The first is used for what we express by "to seek something from God," to ask of God through prayer, etc. But in its strict sense to call *in* the name of the Lord is to preach, teach, read, and whatever else there is that pertains to the ministry of teaching. . . . If someone should maintain that they mean the same thing, I shall not quarrel with him; for by their nature preaching and prayer are connected with each other. It is impossible to pray unless one has first instructed the people concerning God. In fact, you will never pray successfully in private unless you have preached to yourself either the Creed or some other passage of Scripture that draws your attention to the goodness of God as the one who has not only commanded you to pray but has also added the promise that He will hear you. Through this private sermon, which you direct to yourself, your heart is impelled to pray. The same thing takes place publicly in our churches. We have no silent forms of worship, but the voice of the Gospel is always heard. Through it men are taught about the will of God. And to the sermons we add prayers or thanksgivings.

The Nature of the Word

t is not the stones, the construction, and the gorgeous silver and gold that make a church beautiful and holy; it is the Word of God and sound preaching. For where the goodness of God is commended to men and hearts are encouraged to put their trust in Him and to call upon God in danger, there is truly a holy church. Whether it is a dark nook or a bare hill or a barren tree, it is truthfully and correctly called a house of God and a gate of heaven, even though it is without a roof, under the clouds and the open sky. Therefore one must pay primary attention to the character of the teaching and prayer, not to the character of the building. What God demands is that people be converted and He be glorified, but this is achieved solely through the Word and prayer. When Abraham spoke the Word here, he undoubtedly experienced the troubles that accompany it. For Satan, the adversary of Christ, was alive at that time too. Therefore he plagued Abraham with the countless evils that usually follow the Word—persecution, hatred, contempt, antipathy, and countless perils. These rewards of his godliness Abraham surely endured. Even though they are not recorded, we know that the nature of the Word is such that wherever it is taught, the prince of the world is infuriated. These are the two principal effects the Word brings about: it glorifies God, and it judges and condemns the prince of the world together with the flesh and sin.

March 27

Abram said to Lot, "Let there be no strife
between you and me . . . for we are kinsmen."

GENESIS 13:8

The Purpose of Earthly Law

hat could Abram have said that was more proper and more conducive to peace? He puts himself on the same level with Lot and says: "Behold, we are kinsmen." Next he even lowers himself beneath Lot by letting him have the choice of where he would most like to go. Thus the uncle yields to the nephew, the older to the younger, the prophet and priest of God to the pupil—and all this to keep their love from being destroyed and to avoid giving occasion for strife. This account is worthy of our careful attention, for it teaches how all laws and rights are to be dealt with. The purpose of all earthly laws is peace, harmony, and quiet, or, as we theologians express it, love. . . . You should realize that this is being said about our laws and this earthly life, not about the laws of God, His promises, or the Sacraments. For there extreme justice should prevail, in accordance with the statement (Matthew 10:37): "He who loves father or mother more than Me is not worthy of Me." But in those things which people command us to do allowance is made for love, the moderator of the law and of all court actions; it is the main thing to be considered and followed. Therefore in order to preserve it, Abram, with extreme sorrow, sends his nephew away. Physically they were separated, but in spirit they were most closely united; this was something greater and more delightful for him than all his wealth.

March 28

The Lord said to Abram . . .

Genesis 13:14

Sacred Accounts

Now comes the third passage in which it is written: "The Lord spoke with Abraham." I have often exhorted that . . . this chief feature of the account must be particularly observed, namely, the Word of God. In all ages God has done great things and wonderful works through His saints. These works are impressive and strike the eye; but for us who teach as well as learn the Holy Scriptures, God's own utterance must be especially resplendent. This, above all, adorns the legends of the saints and distinguishes them from the accounts of the heathen. They are called "sacred" accounts because the Word of God shines in them. . . . The account of Abraham is most excellent because it is replete with the Word of God, with which everything that he did is embellished. Everywhere he is led by the Word of God, who promises, commands, comforts, and admonishes, so that it is evident that Abraham is an extraordinary friend and intimate of God. . . . What are the glorious victories and triumphs of kings in comparison with this friendship that Abraham has with the divine Majesty—that he has God close by, to converse with him, direct him, love him, and preserve him? . . . The heathen have countless volumes of their achievements, written in all languages; but we have the sacred accounts, authenticated by the Word of God. We hear God speaking intimately with human beings; we see God governing human affairs in a wonderful manner and preserving His own in the midst of dangers.

March 29

The LORD said . . . .

GENESIS 13:14

God Still Speaks

f we Christians also realized this great gift of ours, we would truly be blessed, as Christ says in Luke 10:23–24: "Blessed are the eyes which see what you see! Many kings desired to see what you see, and did not see it." Indeed, I would go even further and say that just as we now praise Abraham because of this gift, so he would praise us in the New Testament even more; for he saw the day of Christ, as John 8:56 states. But he saw it only in faith and in the spirit. But we see this glory face to face. We hear God speaking with us and promising forgiveness of sins in Baptism, in the Supper of His Son, and in the true use of the Keys. These Abraham did not have, but he saw in the spirit and believed. Therefore our glory is greater. . . . Thus the Church is the pupil of Christ. It sits at His feet and listens to His Word, that it may know how to judge everything—how to serve in one's vocation and to fill civil offices, yes, how to eat, drink, and sleep—so that there is no doubt about any area of life, but that we, surrounded on all sides by the rays of the Word, may continually walk in joy and in the most beautiful light.

"Arise, walk through the length and breadth of the land,
for I will give it to you."

GENESIS 13:17

Looking Forward

ou observe that Abraham, who, according to the promise, is the lord of the land of Canaan, is merely a guest and has no definite place to come to rest with his people; for he is commanded to migrate from one place to another. And this is the reason why the fathers regarded also their material promises with a spiritual understanding. Thus the Letter to the Hebrews (11:9–10) states very beautifully: "By faith Abraham sojourned in the Land of the Promise, as in a foreign land, living in tents with Isaac and Jacob, heirs with him of the same promise. For he looked forward to the city which has foundations, whose Builder and Maker is God." Through this faith Abraham overcame a long and troublesome exile; nor did it offend him that Lot had an abode that was both definite and very comfortable.

So Abram moved his tent and came and settled
by the oaks of Mamre, which are at Hebron,
and there he built an altar to the Lord.

GENESIS 13:18

Establishing the Church

oses takes special care to mention that there [Abraham] built an altar to the Lord; that is, as I stated above, Abraham preached at that place and gave instruction about the true worship of God. But this is no small comfort, that God gathers remnants from the heathen and lets them partake of the blessing of Abraham. Unless Mamre had been a godly and pious man and, like Abraham, had believed in the true God and had heard His Word from Abraham, he would not have received Abraham hospitably; nor would Abraham have gone to him. Even at that time, therefore, God had His worshipers among the heathen, worshipers whom He called in a marvelous manner through the holy patriarch, in accordance with the promise given him above in chapter 12:3: "You will be a blessing"; that is, "The blessing is so inherent in you that wherever you may come, others will also receive a blessing through your ministry." . . . The holy patriarchs were especially zealous in endeavoring to bring as many as possible to the knowledge of God. Therefore Abraham not only takes care of his household, but he also builds an altar. There he teaches the true religion; there he calls upon God; there he publicly practices the outward forms of worship. The Amorite Mamre and his brothers join him, and so a large church is established.

April 1

The enemy took all the possessions of Sodom and Gomorrah.

. . . They also took Lot.

Apparent Defeat

oses reveals his true reason for presenting such a detailed account of this war [Genesis 14:1–12], namely, in order to impress on us the great miracle that follows, Abraham's glorious victory. This passage is too rich and too lofty for me to be able to explain all its sections as they deserve. The main point and chief content of the lesson is to have you see this: God places His own under the cross; and although He delays their deliverance, nevertheless in the end He gloriously snatches them out of their dangers and makes them victors, but only after they have first been greatly vexed and have been wearied to despair by sundry conflicts. To be aware of this divine procedure with which God rules us is profitable and necessary. Thus we learn to show patience in adversity, to trust in God's goodness, and to hope for salvation, but in prosperity to humble ourselves and give the glory to God. For it is His custom to do both: to bring down to hell and to bring back, to afflict and to comfort, to kill and to make alive. This is the game, with its continual changes, that He plays with His saints. For there is no perfect joy in this life, as there will be in the life to come. Sometimes, like an angry father, He inflicts punishments; sometimes, like an affectionate father, He fosters and comforts His children.

Then [Abram] brought back all the possessions,
and also brought back his kinsman Lot with his possessions,
and the women and the people.

GENESIS 14:16

Clear Victory

braham makes use of a military stratagem both when he attacks the enemy at night and when he attacks with a divided army . . . so the enemy, thrown into disorder by fear and danger, suppose that a countless multitude is present and turn to flight. The weapons frighten them, but it is actually the faith of Abraham and of his people that defeats them and puts them to flight. . . . Just as many people were saved through Abram and because of Lot . . . so it still happens that whatever good thing the world has, it has solely thanks to the saints on earth and because of them. Hence when you see God's blessing, you would be doing the right thing if you encouraged yourself and reflected that there is still a Church on earth and that the holy seed has not perished altogether, even though it is small in number, and that because of it God shows kindness to all the rest of the world. . . This account also serves to make you see how the pious are always being trained by their own adversities, that they may be cleansed more and more and daily become more pious. For the elect all things work together for good (Romans 8:28), even the rod and the cross. The flesh is mortified, faith is strengthened, and the gift of the Holy Spirit is increased.

[Melchizedek king of Salem] blessed him and said,
"Blessed be Abram by God Most High,
Possessor of heaven and earth."

GENESIS 14:19

Public Blessing

he text separates the worship and profession of Abraham from the forms of worship of all the heathen; and it confirms what was said above in chapter 12:3, that not only Abraham himself was blessed, but that he would be a blessing also for others. For through him had come rescue and blessing for his adversaries, who were under the curse and wrath of God and were paying the deserved penalties for their sins by a harsh captivity. All this serves to comfort Abraham and to strengthen him in faith and patience. Abram had given glory to God among the heathen when he professed the true doctrine publicly. Therefore, God exalts him in turn, in the sight of the heathen by this glorious victory. . . . Through this sermon of Melchizedek Abraham is set apart from all the other fathers, and his house or family is marked with this most glorious distinction: that the blessing of God must surely be expected from it, and that there is no Church anywhere except in the house of Abraham and among those who ally themselves with Abraham.

"Blessed be Abram by God Most High,
Possessor of heaven and earth."

GENESIS 14:19

God Most High

he name of God is explained more fully by what the text adds about the Possessor of heaven and earth. . . . It points out the God who has heaven and earth under His control as His property and possession. In this way, therefore, it excludes all false gods, yes, even angels, kings, the holy fathers, etc. To this one Most High it ascribes being the Head of the family, whose abode is the heaven and the earth, and who, like the head of a household, directs and rules whatever there is anywhere—angels, devils, human beings, tyrants, slaves, saints, and wicked men. All these are in the household of God and are forced to acknowledge Him as the Head of the household and to obey His will. . . . Melchizedek praises the divine Majesty as the only and supreme God, who has everything in His hand and controls it with power and dispatch; for He gave the four kings into the hands of Abraham, a beggar and sojourner. "Why, then, do you deceive yourselves and worship stones and wood, the works of your own hands? Why do you not turn to the God of Abraham, who has revealed to you so clearly that He alone controls and possesses the heaven and the earth?" He praises the God who bestows blessings, and at the same time he instructs the Church and calls the heathen away from their idolatry to the true knowledge of God.

The king of Sodom said to Abram, "Give me the persons,
but take the goods for yourself."
But Abram said . . . , "I will take nothing."

GENESIS 14:21, 24

Attached to God

ecause Abraham is sure of the Lord's benevolence and certain that because of His blessing he would have more lands and wealth than the king of Sodom or anyone else could give him, he does the right thing when he declines this gift. "Do not," he says, "cause me this disgrace, and do not impose this ignominy on me, that you, the king of Sodom, made me rich, and that if Abraham had not had you, he would have nothing. Take your booty and go, but do not impair my glorying in the only God, the kindly one who gives promises. He is the Possessor of heaven and earth, while you are only the possessor of Sodom. I shall hold fast to that Giver, Blesser, and Savior." . . . Thus Abraham is described to us here as full of faith and of hope concerning eternal life. He makes use of this earthly victory as of a field or any other thing that serves only to exercise the body but does not give the heart cause for worry. His heart he keeps attached to the mercy of God and to the promise of the future Seed, in accordance with the statement of the psalm (62:10): "If riches increase, set not your heart on them." He has a wife, servants, and maids; but he has all these as though he did not have them. He is a true monk; for he truly despises the pleasures, glories, and riches of the world, and with his whole heart he is engaged in waiting for the promise concerning Christ.

April 6

"Fear not, Abram, I am your shield;
your reward shall be very great."

GENESIS 15:1

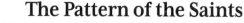

The Pattern of the Saints

hen God addresses Abraham in these words and commands him not to be afraid, these words are not without a reason. Elated and victorious a little while ago, Abraham was now surrounded by new dangers, cares, and terrors. . . . This is the usual way of training saintly and godly men. For this reason Psalm 4:3 states that God rules His saints in a wonderful manner. Encouraged now by his miraculous victory, Abraham feels such joy of spirit and such a boundless sense of security with regard to God's goodness that he says in his heart: "I shall never be shaken." But immediately everything is reversed. . . . Why or how does God rule in this manner? Why does He not make this joy complete and lasting for His saints? I do not know, except for the fact that I observe this pattern and common example in all the saints, even in Christ Himself, their Head, who sometimes rejoices in spirit and joyfully gives thanks to God in the Holy Spirit. Afterward He is again troubled in spirit, prays for protection, and laments that He has been forsaken in the hour of death, as one can see in Psalm 8:5 and in Psalm 22:1. Therefore one should learn this example and this pattern of the saints, yes, this method by which God governs His saints.

"Fear not, Abram, I am your shield;
your reward shall be very great."
GENESIS 15:1

A Future Reward

God indeed gives great gifts to those who are His, just as here He gave Abraham a glorious victory. Nevertheless, He does not yet pour out all His gifts; nor does He give Himself completely. Although you may have greater gifts than either Abraham or Moses, still you do not yet have the Lord Himself. He withholds and, as it were, removes Himself from us, evidently in order that when we are not being tried and all is serene and quiet, we may still fear Him and not say, as the smug do: "I shall never be shaken." For if we sing this song, the words "Thou didst hide Thy face, I was dismayed" follow at once. Therefore those who consider themselves invincible when they are not afflicted are struck with boundless fear when they are in the clutches of a trial. But this is not because God may have changed His mind, as though He had withdrawn His grace and were refusing to grant forgiveness of sins. His will to save us through His Son, to whose kingdom He has called us, remains steadfast and unchangeable; but the awareness of this mercy is removed for a time.

And [God] brought [Abram] outside and said,
"Look toward heaven, and number the stars,
if you are able to number them."

GENESIS 15:5

The Conversation of a Friend

hese accounts are outstanding because the voice of God is heard in them. Thus this very passage, because of God's extensive conversation with Abraham, deserves to be regarded as highly important. For God speaks with Abraham in a manner that is no different from the way a friend speaks with a close acquaintance and another friend. It is God's practice to do so, and this is His nature. After He has properly afflicted His own, He shows Himself most benevolent and pours Himself out completely.

And [Abram] believed the L{\sc ord},
and He counted it to him as righteousness.

G{\sc enesis} 15:6

For Our Sake

hen Moses adds that Abraham believed God, this is the first passage of Scripture which we have had until now about faith. For the others, which Moses mentioned previously—the passage about the Seed of the woman, for example, the command to build the ark, the threat of the flood, and the command to Abraham to leave his country, etc.—merely demand faith; they do not praise or recommend it. . . . Therefore this is one of the foremost passages of all Scripture. And Paul has not only expounded this passage most carefully; he also takes great pains to commend it to the Church when he adds this statement (Romans 4:23): "But the words 'it was reckoned to him' were written not for his [Abraham's] sake alone"—who later on died—but (Romans 15:4) "for our instruction, that . . . we might have hope." This is truly an instance of treating the Scriptures in an apostolic manner and of establishing the universal statement which is so dreadful and detestable to the very gates of hell: that all who believe the Word of God are just. . . . Read Paul, and read him most attentively. Then you will see that from this passage he constructs the foremost article of our faith—the article that is intolerable to the world and to Satan—namely, that faith alone justifies, but that faith consists in giving assent to the promises of God and concluding that they are true.

April 10

He counted it to him as righteousness.

GENESIS 15:6

Righteousness

f you should ask whether Abraham was righteous before this time, my answer is: He was righteous because he believed God. But here the Holy Spirit wanted to attest this expressly, since the promise deals with a spiritual Seed. He did so in order that you might conclude on the basis of a correct inference that those who accept this Seed, or those who believe in Christ, are righteous. . . . In this connection Paul learnedly stresses the matter of time: that in this chapter Moses is speaking about righteousness and a righteous or justified Abraham prior to the Law, prior to the works of the Law, yes, prior to the people of the Law and before Moses, the lawgiver, was born. . . . Then what? Is the Law useless for righteousness? Yes, certainly. But does faith alone, without works, justify? Yes, certainly. Otherwise you must repudiate Moses, who declares that Abraham is righteous prior to the Law and prior to the works of the Law, not because he sacrificed his son, who had not yet been born, and not because he did this or that work, but because he believed God who gave a promise. . . . How, then, did he obtain righteousness? In this way: God speaks, and Abraham believes what God is saying. Moreover, the Holy Spirit comes as a trustworthy witness and declares that this very believing or this very faith is righteousness or is imputed by God Himself as righteousness and is regarded by Him as such.

April 11

*And [Abram] believed the L*ORD*,*
and He counted it to him as righteousness.

GENESIS 15:6

Faith Is Never Alone

he chief and most important part of the doctrine is the promise; to it faith attaches itself, or, to speak more clearly, faith lays hold of it. Moreover, the confident laying hold of the promise is called faith; and it justifies, not as our own work but as the work of God. For the promise is a gift, a thought of God by which He offers us something. It is not some work of ours, when we do something for God or give Him something. No, we receive something from Him, and that solely through His mercy. Therefore he who believes God when He promises, he who is convinced that God is truthful and will carry out whatever He has promised, is righteous or is reckoned as righteous. After that there is also the Law; for God not only promises, but He also commands and enjoins. Moreover, it is the concern of the Law that you conform your will to it and obey God's commands. . . .

We know indeed that faith is never alone but brings with it love and other manifold gifts. For he who believes in God and is sure that God is graciously inclined toward us, since He gave His Son and with His Son the hope of eternal life, how could he not love God with all his heart? How could he not revere Him? How could he not strive to display a grateful heart for such great blessings and to obey God while bearing hardships? . . . Faith is the mother, so to speak, from whom that crop of virtues springs. If faith is not there first, you would look in vain for those virtues. If faith has not embraced the promises concerning Christ, no love and no other virtues will be there, even if for a time hypocrites were to paint what seem to be likenesses of them.

Therefore the promise must be distinguished from the Law. The promise requires faith; the Law, works. The promise is certain and reliable, and is surely carried out, because God carries it out. But the Law is not carried out, because we, who try to fulfill it, are human beings, that is, weak sinners. Accordingly, our righteousness does not depend on the Law and works, because we cannot perfectly fulfill the Law; it depends on the promise, which is sure and unalterable. Therefore this promise is surely carried out and fulfilled when faith takes hold of it; and it follows with infallible logic that faith alone justifies, inasmuch as faith alone accepts the promise. The Law and works do not justify; yet Law and works must be taught and performed, in order that we may become aware of our wretched state and accept grace all the more eagerly.

This theology did not originate with us. . . . St. Paul teaches it, and as a witness he quotes Moses, who says that Abraham believed God and that this was reckoned to him for righteousness, that is, that Abraham was reckoned as righteous when he believed the promise, since God had compassion on him. Furthermore, every promise of God includes Christ; for if it is separated from this Mediator, God is not dealing with us at all. Therefore the only difference between Abraham's faith and ours is this: Abraham believed in the Christ who was to be manifested, but we believe in the Christ who has already been manifested; and by that faith we are all saved.

"You shall go to your fathers in peace;
you shall be buried in a good old age."

GENESIS 15:15

A Peaceful Death

od declares that Abraham will die; yet He promises that He will be Abraham's reward [see Genesis 15:1]. How are we going to harmonize these statements unless we conclude that after this life there remains another life, one that is better and eternal, to which we shall be awakened out of the very dust of death by the Son of God? . . . "But these words—were written not for Abraham's sake alone," says Paul (Romans 4:23–24), "but for ours also," in order that we, too, may believe that there has been laid up a reward for us when we shall lie buried in the earth, and indeed such a reward that we may live with God as long as He Himself will live, that is, forever. With this hope Abraham is satisfied. Even though he does not obtain the promise of the land of Canaan, yet he is cheerful. He disregards and despises death, for he knows that he will live with God in all eternity. . . . These things, as we have said, were not written for Abraham's benefit. They are of service to us, in order that when we, with Abraham, believe in the woman's Seed, we may through this hope overcome death and no longer have a horror of departing from this life. Our bodies will indeed be buried in the earth; yes, they will decay in the earth and will be reduced to dust. But in due time the earth will return this deposit to Him who has promised that He will be our reward. This hope is sure and firm.

April 13

*The angel of the L*ORD *also said to [Hagar],*
"I will surely multiply your offspring
so that they cannot be numbered for multitude."

GENESIS 16:10

Divine Succession

 his is an extraordinary promise. By it the terrified Hagar is again encouraged. For these are the divine successions: Comfort follows affliction, hope follows despair, and life follows death. Satan has the habit of doing the opposite. First he makes glad, then he disturbs, and eventually despair follows complacency in sins. Therefore let no one be disturbed in his heart when he experiences terrors and dangers, but let him take courage to hope that the Lord will again give comfort and encouragement. Because the godly have this sure hope, they pray so diligently and fervently for deliverance.

And the angel of the Lord said to [Hagar], "Behold, you are pregnant and shall bear a son. You shall call his name Ishmael, because the Lord has listened to your affliction."

GENESIS 16:11

Comfort Follows Affliction

ow much more proper and profitable it would be for directing one's life to teach that God loves, and does a kindness to, those who know that He is chastising them! Hagar is being punished by her mistress Sarah, and Hagar does not bear this punishment calmly but tries to help herself through flight. Even though she sins by doing this, God nevertheless has regard for her affliction and comforts her. What could be called more benevolent? Therefore let us accustom ourselves to patience and calmly bear even lashes and blows—children from their parents, subjects from the magistrate, and pupils from the teacher. For if we allow ourselves to be disciplined, obedience is pleasing to God. But when nature feels the blows, it not only grumbles; it also despairs of the grace and mercy of God. These evils arise from ignorance of sacred matters. Those who know that they are being cared for by God when they are disciplined and afflicted either by their parents, by the head of the family, or by a magistrate will lighten their grief and sorrow with that hope and will wait for the Lord's blessing, which, as they see, came to Hagar even when she was wrongfully running away.

April 15

*So [Hagar] called the name of the L*ORD *who spoke to her,*
"You are a God of seeing."

GENESIS 16:13

The God of Seeing

he Word of God is never without fruit. Therefore the rebellious, proud, and disobedient Hagar is changed when the angel speaks; she returns to her mistress and patiently submits to her authority. And not only this; she acknowledges God's mercy, praises God, and calls upon Him by a new name, in order to proclaim abroad the kindness through which He had manifested Himself to her. Thus in the New Testament we call Christ the Redeemer because of the work through which He has manifested Himself to us. We call the Holy Spirit the Paraclete. Thus Hagar calls God the Seeing One because He had regard for her lowliness or affliction. . . . This is a most beautiful name for God. Would that we all could bestow it on Him, that is, conclude with certainty that He has regard for us and cares for us, especially when He seems to have forgotten us, when we think we have been forsaken by Him. For he who can say in affliction: "God sees me" has true faith and can do and bear everything, yes, he overcomes all things and is triumphant.

"Truly here I have seen Him who looks after me."

GENESIS 16:13

God's Eyes Are on Us

hese are words of one who is glad and filled with wonder. "Ah," says Hagar, "how incredulous I have been! I did not think that God was concerned about me, and I assumed that I was seeing God from behind, not His face; that is, I assumed that God had turned away from me. But now I realize that the back which He showed me is His face. He indeed saw me before; but I, preoccupied as I was with my afflictions, was not able to look closely. Now, however, I know that He loves me and that He cares for me." These words are, therefore, like a universal hymn of all the godly. When there is affliction, we see God from behind; that is, we conclude that God has turned away from us, as He says in Isaiah (54:8): "For a moment I hid My face from you, but with everlasting love I will have compassion on you"; that is, "At first I acted as though I did not know you, as though I had abandoned you." This is the view from behind, when we feel nothing but affliction and doubts; but later, when the trial has passed, it becomes clear that by the very fact that God has showed Himself to us from behind He has showed us His face, that He did not forsake us but turned away His eyes just a little.

April 17

When Abram was ninety-nine years old
the LORD appeared to Abram and said to him,
"I am God Almighty; walk before Me, and be blameless."

GENESIS 17:1

Blameless

If blamelessness is required of Abraham before the law of circumcision is given, who does not see or understand that this covenant of circumcision does not bring about blamelessness but that blamelessness by faith is required of man before the establishment of this covenant? . . . Accordingly, the righteousness of faith is inculcated on Abraham before God commands him to be circumcised. Since he is commanded to remain righteous and blameless, as he had begun to be, he was righteous at that time. That the [Hebrew] noun [translated as "blameless"] in this passage is plural—be a man of perfections or of integrities—one can appropriately relate to the fact that there is a twofold righteousness: (1) the perfect righteousness, through which we are righteous before God through faith; (2) the imperfect righteousness, through which we are righteous before God and men so far as our conduct and reputation is concerned.

"My covenant is with you,
and you shall be the father of a multitude of nations."

GENESIS 17:4

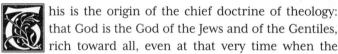

Of the Flesh and of the Promise

his is the origin of the chief doctrine of theology: that God is the God of the Jews and of the Gentiles, rich toward all, even at that very time when the Law and circumcision flourished. For other nations heard Abraham, heard the prophets, saw the worship at Jerusalem, and believed that the God of the Jews was the only true God. Meanwhile the Jews alone had this seal of righteousness because of which they were conspicuous among all the nations. And even though the Gentiles were not circumcised, they nevertheless called upon and worshiped the same God who revealed Himself to the Jewish people through circumcision. Therefore we do not slight St. Paul, the best and most learned interpreter of Moses. For concerning this chapter he teaches us that so far Moses has written about the birth of the son Ishmael and a descendant of Abraham according to the flesh but has said that this descendant was born without the promise. For God did not speak to Abraham about the son who would be born of the maid; it was Sarah's plan that Abraham should consort with the maid. . . . But with regard to Isaac the matter is different. He is born as the result of the promise, and the promise is attached to him. When this difference is recognized, it will shed a bright light on this discussion about circumcision.

April 19

"I will make you exceedingly fruitful."

The People of God

hose who are circumcised are given the promise that they are the people of God and that God wants to be their God. This means that they are in the fellowship of the kingdom of God, since they have been justified by the justifying faith which the Lord grants them through His Spirit. If this was brought about with the Jews in the Old Testament through the medium of circumcision, why would God not do the same thing with the Gentiles through the medium of the new covenant of Baptism? The command (Matthew 28:19) pertains to all: "Go therefore and make disciples of all nations, baptizing them . . ." Hence whereas circumcision was commanded only to the descendants of Abraham, Baptism is commanded to all the nations, with the promise of salvation if they believe. But if, by virtue of the promise, Abraham's descendants had the blessing that those circumcised on the eighth day would receive the gift of faith and become the people of God, why would this be denied the nations now united with God through the covenant of Baptism? For the situation of Baptism will not be worse than that of circumcision.

A Call to Worship

 shall be your God," that is, "In your house I shall set up My worship, and among you and your people I shall be the God who is worshiped, and among your descendants I shall manifest Myself by means of signs and visible marks, by means of miracles and wonders, in order that they may know Me beyond all doubt and may adore and worship Me." . . . To adore God is to go to Him for help when you turn your face toward Him and call upon Him in trouble, when you give thanks for deliverance, when you recall and proclaim His acts of kindness by declaring that He is the Creator, the Benefactor, the Promiser, and the Savior. . . . It is necessary to add that this God, who tells us how to worship Him, is the Giver of eternal life. . . . Therefore He is the God of the godly, the God of Abraham, for example, of Isaac, and of Jacob; these are living and are not dead, even though they are dead so far as we are concerned. Therefore with these words, with which He promises to be the God of Abraham, the Lord calls not only Abraham but also all his descendants, yes, even all the Gentiles who believe as faithful Abraham did, to the hope of eternal life. He promises that they will live as long as God Himself lives, that is, forever. As authority for this conviction we have the Son of God Himself, who says: "God is the God of the living" [Matthew 22:32].

April 21

> *"I will give to you and to your offspring after you*
> *the land of your sojournings . . . and I will be their God."*
>
> GENESIS 17:8

Invisible and Impossible Things

braham has the promise that after his own death the God whom he worshiped and adored in this life will remain in his house and among his descendants. But Abraham's house will remain in the land of Canaan. After his death, however, he himself will live as the true possessor of this land. The Word of God is such a great treasure and brings such marvelous revelations concerning invisible and impossible things that Abraham concludes with certainty that he will live after he has died and that after his death he will possess the land which he was not to possess in this life. Thus he will live with God eternally. Therefore why would he not be glad, and why would he not give thanks to God after he is certain that the Church and the faith which has been sealed by circumcision will remain in his house and among his descendants despite Satan and the world, and that he himself will also remain in eternal life with God? . . . Accordingly, Abraham is a truly remarkable man in his faith. Nor is it surprising if he was calm in dangers and bore misfortunes with the greatest patience. For he knew that the Church would remain in a definite place, among definite persons, and up to a definite time, namely, up to the time of Christ, who was not of the generations of this world. Moreover, he knew that after his death he would live eternally.

"I will be their God."

GENESIS 17:8

Visible Signs

ust as Abraham had circumcision and the glorious words "I shall be God to you and your descendants after you" added to circumcision, so we have several visible signs. In the first place, we have Baptism itself, which is adorned with the most important and pleasing promise that we shall be saved if we believe. But because in this weakness of ours it is very easy for us to fall, there have been added to Baptism the Keys or the ministry of the Word—for these must not be separated—which in itself is also a visible sign of grace bound to the Word of the Gospel in accordance with Christ's institution (Matthew 18:18): "Whatever you loose on earth shall be loosed in heaven." When you take hold of this Word in faith, you will be restored to grace, and the life which was lost through sin is given back. The same thing takes place in the use of the holy Eucharist, for the words (Matthew 26:26–27) "My body given for you, My blood shed for the remission of your sins" are certainly not without meaning; they admirably strengthen the hope of the remission of sins. Thus you see that we have the promise of eternal grace far more richly than Abraham himself had it. Therefore we should also take pride in this gift over against Satan and the world, and we should buoy ourselves up with this comfort in all misfortunes, just as the saintly patriarch did.

The Sign of Circumcision

or what benefit, then, was circumcision given? To make known that the Savior was to be born from this circumcised nation and not from the Gentiles. He who was desired by all the nations did not become incarnate among all the nations; He became incarnate among this one people which had been commanded by God to be circumcised. And the special rite was instituted that it might be an outstanding reminder for the entire world that Christ would come from the Jews; for He had been promised to the Jews alone, even though the Jews would not be the only people to derive benefit from Him. . . . For us this statement remains certain: that we Gentiles are free from the Law and from circumcision, just as before the Law and in the Law many of the Gentiles were converted to God and yet remained free from the Law and from circumcision. . . . But we Christians are free from the Law and from circumcision to a far greater degree. We know that according to the Father's command it is the Son of God who must be heard, not Moses. Even though He was circumcised, He did not command us to be circumcised; He commanded us to be baptized. . . . But just as we no longer have any need of the Sacrament of Baptism when the promise of the New Testament is fulfilled in eternal life, so circumcision is no longer necessary, since the promise given to Abraham has been fulfilled through Christ.

April 24

"He who is eight days old among you shall be circumcised."

Genesis 17:12

The Eighth Day

et the first answer to this question why God wanted the infants to be circumcised on the eighth day be: Because God wanted it this way. In the second place, one can give reasons that are probable and are not fraught with danger, namely, that God had consideration for the weakness of the infant, lest it die. . . . In an allegorical sense the eighth day signifies the future life; for Christ rested in the sepulcher on the Sabbath, that is, during the entire seventh day, but rose again on the day which follows the Sabbath, which is the eighth day and the beginning of a new week, and after it no other day is counted. For through His death Christ brought to a close the weeks of time and on the eighth day entered into a different kind of life, in which days are no longer counted but there is one eternal day without the alternations of night. This has been thought out wisely, learnedly, and piously, namely, that the eighth day is the eternal day. For the rising Christ is no longer subject to days, months, weeks, or any number of days; He is in a new and eternal life. The beginning of this life is perceived and reckoned, but there is no end. In that life the true circumcision will be carried out. At that time not only the foreskin of the heart will be circumcised—which happens in this life through faith—but the entire flesh and all its essence will be cleansed of all depravity, ignorance, lust, sin, and filth. Consequently, the flesh is then immortal.

April 25

"I will give you a son by [Sarah]."

GENESIS 17:16

The Promise of a Son

W hat now follows unfolds the promise concerning Christ, for it gradually began to become clearer and more distinct. First Abraham had doubts concerning an heir, and he came to suspect that if he should die without an heir, his Damascene servant would get possession of the blessing. But later on he is assured by a word of God that an heir shall be born to him from his own body. When he has this explanation and assurance about the promise, there follows another uncertainty—about Sarah, who was advancing in years and was barren. Therefore he acquiesces in her plan and lies with the maid Hagar. From her he begets Ishmael, whom he fully expects to become the heir of the blessing. But now at last the saintly couple is delivered even from this error, for Abraham is promised an offspring from the aged and barren Sarah herself. In the course of time the promise is transmitted to Jacob, not to Esau; and when Jacob had twelve heirs, the promise falls to Judah alone. Eventually David is designated as the heir of the promise. From his house came the blessed Virgin Mary, the mother of Christ, who was the end of the Law and of circumcision.

"I will bless her."

GENESIS 17:16

Temporal and Eternal Promises

he promise made to Sarah here is altogether ines-timable. . . . Paul [in Romans 4:19–24] considers the fact that so far the promise consists of words only but that the reality is not yet at hand. Therefore the godly couple was not lightly disturbed, for what could be expected from a dead womb and one that also because of age was useless for birth? Sarah was like a corpse from which no fruit can be expected. Accordingly, what this story sets forth is analogous to the resurrection of the dead, inasmuch as from a dead womb there is born not only an offspring but a male who is appointed to be the father of many nations and of many kings and peoples. . . . It must be noted especially that these promises include Christ Himself, yes, eternal life, even though they appear to be speaking, not of Christ but of Isaac. For this reason Paul adds (Romans 4:23–24) that this was written, not for Abraham's sake but for the sake of us, who would believe after the example of Abraham; for the promise is temporal, like a nut which covers the kernel, namely, Christ and eternal life. When Christ comes, the shell or hull in which the kernel is enclosed is broken; that is, the temporal blessing comes to an end, and the spiritual blessing takes its place.

April 27

"She shall become nations;
kings of peoples shall come from her."

GENESIS 17:16

Nations and Kings

rom the womb of Sarah there came not only kings—David, Solomon, etc.—but also peoples, the Edomites and others, who are reckoned among the descendants of Esau. This is the physical promise. When Christ was born of the Virgin Mary, the spiritual promise was also fulfilled. That was the real time of blessing. Then there were valiant kings: the apostles and their successors. Next came Gentiles who, because of faith in the blessed Seed, are also descendants of Abraham, not according to the flesh or by nature but "engrafted," as Paul calls them in Romans 11:17. Of course, the promise concerns the spiritual seed, that is, the believers, more than it does the physical descendants. . . . Just as we correctly call Isaac a son of faith and not of the flesh—for if you consider the flesh, Abraham and Sarah are like two corpses which procreate despite this, not by virtue of the corpse but by virtue of faith—so all who believe according to the example of Abraham are descendants of Abraham and partakers of the blessing. . . . Paul calls them fellow citizens of the prophets and apostles (Ephesians 2:19–20).

Then Abraham fell on his face and laughed and said to himself,
"Shall a child be born to a man who is a hundred years old?
Shall Sarah, who is ninety years old, bear a child?"

GENESIS 17:17

Overflowing Joy

hese are words of one who in no wise doubts but is astonished and transported with joy, just as the laughter is also evidence of a heart overflowing with joy. . . . Now he forgets about his own dead body, even about corpselike Sarah, and sees with certainty that an heir is to be born to him from Sarah. . . . Abraham falls to the ground and laughs. This, as Christ explains in John 8, is the gesture of a heart that exults and overflows with joy; for now at last he is sure that he will be the father and Sarah will be the mother of Jesus Christ, the Son of God, through whom salvation and blessing will come to the entire world. Accordingly, Abraham did not fall down from fright, nor did he laugh because he had doubts about the promise; he laughed because he was filled with great gladness and joy. . . . Although we have the Word of God in such richness, our hearts are nevertheless harder than an anvil and, like rocky soil, keep the root of the Word without sap and fruit, while the saintly patriarchs marveled at this inexpressible benevolence of God to the point of being overcome. . . . Therefore we should ask God to give us a joyful heart for such joyful promises, in order that we, too, may exult and be glad with saintly Abraham because we are the people of God.

April 29

Incomprehensible Things

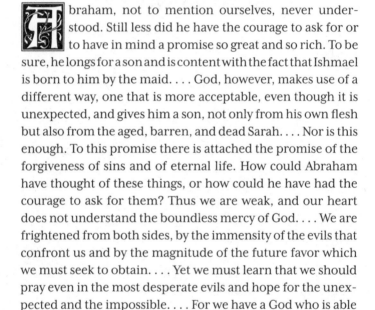

braham, not to mention ourselves, never understood. Still less did he have the courage to ask for or to have in mind a promise so great and so rich. To be sure, he longs for a son and is content with the fact that Ishmael is born to him by the maid. . . . God, however, makes use of a different way, one that is more acceptable, even though it is unexpected, and gives him a son, not only from his own flesh but also from the aged, barren, and dead Sarah. . . . Nor is this enough. To this promise there is attached the promise of the forgiveness of sins and of eternal life. How could Abraham have thought of these things, or how could he have had the courage to ask for them? Thus we are weak, and our heart does not understand the boundless mercy of God. . . . We are frightened from both sides, by the immensity of the evils that confront us and by the magnitude of the future favor which we must seek to obtain. . . . Yet we must learn that we should pray even in the most desperate evils and hope for the unexpected and the impossible. . . . For we have a God who is able to give more than we understand or ask for. Even though we do not know what we should ask for and how, nevertheless the Spirit of God, who dwells in the hearts of the godly, sighs and groans for us within us with inexpressible groanings and also procures inexpressible and incomprehensible things.

*"As for Ishmael, I have heard you; behold, I have blessed him.
. . . But I will establish My covenant with Isaac."*

GENESIS 17:20–21

Two Covenants

his text proves that besides the covenant of circumcision there is another, which pertains to Isaac alone and not, like the covenant of circumcision, to Ishmael also. What, then, shall we say was the nature of this covenant? It was obviously the promise concerning Christ, which Abraham understood well. And this is what I have stated, namely, that God always mixes and includes spiritual and eternal blessings with the physical blessings. The physical blessing is associated with a name, namely, that all the descendants of Abraham should be circumcised; but this second covenant is not associated with a name, nor is it marked by any definite work. Yet it is a spiritual covenant concerning the future Savior. . . . The covenant of circumcision is given for our performance before the Law of Moses and is established for a definite people, in a definite land, and for a definite time, namely, while the generations of Abraham are in existence. The covenant of Isaac, however, is not given for our performance; it is entirely free, without a name, without a time, and yet from the seed of Isaac, lest one look for the blessing from another source. . . . Thus this passage deals with the promise concerning Christ, which goes beyond Abraham's wishes and request.

May 1

When He had finished talking with him,
God went up from Abraham.

GENESIS 17:22

God's Appearance to Us

his closing statement proves that God appeared in some visible form when He had this conversation with Abraham. . . . Nor are we ourselves deprived of this gift. Even though God does not appear to us in an extraordinary form, as He did to Abraham, yet His usual and most friendly and most intimate appearance is this, that He presents Himself to us in the Word, in the use of the Keys, in Baptism, and in the Lord's Supper. . . . Therefore we, too, could glory as the patriarch Abraham did. Indeed, if Abraham himself had seen the kindness God shows by speaking and associating with us daily through the ministry in Baptism and in the Lord's Supper, he would have died from wonderment and joy. . . . Indeed, if I had the matter under my control, I would not want God to speak to me from heaven or to appear to me; but this I would want—and my daily prayers are directed to this end—that I might have the proper respect and true appreciation for the gift of Baptism, that I have been baptized, and that I see and hear brothers who have the grace and gift of the Holy Spirit and are able to comfort and encourage with the Word, to admonish, warn, and teach. For what better and more profitable appearance of God do you want?

Abraham was ninety-nine years old when he was circumcised.

GENESIS 17:24

Evidence of Faith

We do not maintain that Abraham was justified by [his obedience]. For it is not works that justify a person, but a righteous person does righteous works. Yet the works show that faith is being put into practice and that through them it increases and becomes fat, as it were. For while Abraham carries out this act of obedience and is circumcised together with his household, faith thinks of God, who gives us His promises and accepts us. Thus Peter (2 Peter 1:10) tells us to certify our election by doing good works, for they bear witness that grace is effective in us and that we have been called and elected. On the other hand, an inactive faith—a faith that is not put into practice—quickly dies and becomes extinct. . . . But he who progresses in the unremitting exercise of his faith concludes: "I am not in the host that is against Christ; I am for Christ. I do not deny the Word, and I do not persecute the Church. Hence I have been called to the kingdom of God and have been elected." "But if I fall because of weakness, I rise again; I grieve over my sin and pray for forgiveness. Thus through the very works of repentance and love I realize that I am one of those who have been snatched from the conflagration of Babel or from the dregs of the world." Thus even though this obedience does not justify, it nevertheless gives evidence of faith and makes it manifest, as it were, so that it can be seen. Therefore Revelation (22:11) states: "He that is righteous, let him be righteous still."

That very day Abraham and his son Ishmael were circumcised.
And all the men of his house . . . were circumcised with him.

GENESIS 17:26–27

"That Very Day"

et us keep in mind the example of Abraham. It teaches us that before God we must again become children and not argue about how or why God gives us a particular command, but that we must simply hold fast to what God has so commanded and obey. . . . Reason concludes that God could have commanded something far more profitable, more suitable, showier, and better, so that through it Abraham might more properly put into practice both his faith and his obedience than by a work so foolish that the now hundred-year-old Abraham could not carry it out without manifest disgrace. But the saintly man puts up no argument whatever. It is enough for him to know that it pleases God to have him do this. Hence he obeys without delay and without regard for his own opinion and that of others. This is obedience which deserves praise and is set before us as an example—as obedience that has nothing of its own but simply cleaves to God's command. Accordingly, after we have been justified through the mercy of God and have been called into the fellowship of the saints to carry on warfare under God, let us do without any argument what we have been commanded to do.

Refreshment of Spirit and Body

hat extraordinary praise of hospitality which appears in the Letter to the Hebrews (13:2) had its origin in this passage. "Do not neglect to show hospitality to strangers, for thereby some have entertained angels unawares." There is hospitality wherever the Church is. For the Church, if I may say so, always has a common treasury, inasmuch as it has the command (Matthew 5:42): "Give to him who begs from you." And we must all serve the Church and take care of it, not only by teaching but also by showing kindness and giving assistance, so that at the same time both the spirit and the flesh may find refreshment in the Church. But especially the strangers whose lot is rather hard should be received in a kindly manner, for Christ's utterance on the Last Day against the inhospitable is clear (Matthew 25:35): "I was a foreigner or a stranger and you did not receive Me." Also (Matthew 25:40): "Whatever you did to the least of Mine, you did to Me." What greater praise can there be for this virtue than that those who are hospitable are not receiving a human being but are receiving the Son of God Himself? On the other hand, what is more hideous than inhospitality? By it you shut out from your house, not a human being but the Son of God, who suffered and died for you on the cross.

"Let a little water be brought, and wash your feet,
and rest yourselves under the tree, while I bring a morsel
of bread, that you may refresh yourselves."

GENESIS 18:4–5

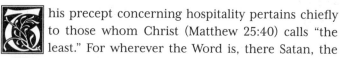

To Comfort Others

his precept concerning hospitality pertains chiefly to those whom Christ (Matthew 25:40) calls "the least." For wherever the Word is, there Satan, the enemy, is stirring up physical and spiritual persecutions. In Paradise itself he was unable to rest until he drove Adam with his Eve into exile. Therefore we must be ready to give comfort to the brethren. Those who are afflicted by spiritual persecution should be comforted and strengthened with the Word; but those who are afflicted by physical persecution should be assisted with bread and water, that is, with love and hospitality, everyone according to his need. This is what Abraham does here. He sees these three strangers. He does not know who they are; but he does know and see that they are poor and that they are tired from the journey. Therefore he quickly fetches water, washes the feet of the guests, orders a calf to be slaughtered, bread to be prepared, and drink to be fetched. But just as he unknowingly receives the Lord Himself in a hospitable manner, so we, too, when we show some kindness to the least in the kingdom of God, receive Christ Himself in a hospitable manner when He comes to us in the persons of His poor.

Abraham went quickly into the tent to Sarah and said, "Quick!
Three seahs of fine flour! Knead it, and make cakes."
And Abraham ran to the herd and took a calf, tender and good,
and gave it to a young man, who prepared it quickly.

GENESIS 18:6–7

Quick to Serve

fter Abraham realizes that these three guests want to stay, he joyfully hastens into the tent and prepares a banquet. For he is sure that in these three guests he is receiving God Himself. It is faith, therefore, that makes him so eager and ready. . . . But that physical appearance is a hindrance to us; and our physical eyes do not see the invisible yet truly present Guest. We must have inner eyes or faith. Since in Abraham this faith is most fervent, he makes haste for great joy and does not walk slowly. He delights in the opportunity given him to deserve well of brethren, and he does not make use of the service of his servants; but he himself starts to run and selects a calf. Furthermore, he orders to make haste and bake cakes. All these details are recorded by Moses for the purpose of stressing that glorious faith of Abraham, whose undoubting conscience persuaded him that he had the God of heaven and earth as a guest. Not indeed that he recognized God as he recognized Him later on, but he is sure that God is coming to him in his brethren. This faith makes him so eager, ready, and zealous, so to speak, to do the good work.

"I will surely return to you about this time next year, and Sarah
your wife shall have a son." . . . *Sarah laughed to herself.*
GENESIS 18:10, 12

Miraculous Works of God

 arah was now eighty-nine years old, and during so
many years she had been hoping for the blessing of
the Lord. When she sees that her hope is futile, she
submits everything to God. Yet she does not utterly despair.
For this reason the Lord puts up with her weakness and is not
offended by her laughter, which has its origin in her thinking about something that is impossible. For what further
hope could there be for a barren and exhausted woman?
Therefore the Lord brings her to faith with a very friendly
reproof. . . . From it Sarah concluded that these were men of
God and prophets, because they are aware of her laughter
and her thoughts even though she is not in their presence.
After Sarah has been so earnestly reminded of God's power,
namely, that nothing is either extraordinary or, as Luke (1:37)
puts it, impossible with Him, she can no longer regard lightly
the prophecy about the son who is to be born. For here her
thoughts are held captive and come to an end when she
hears that the event is miraculous and altogether impossible
before the world yet not miraculous but very easy, yes, even
common, ordinary, and an everyday occurrence for God if
similar works of His are considered.

Impossible Made Possible

our heart is assailed by unbelief, and you doubt that you can be saved; for you know that you are a sinner. In this situation a godly brother . . . will say: "God is truthful; He promises to be gracious to you for His Son's sake. Moreover, the Son of God has absolved you from all your sins by His Word, has baptized you, and has promised you eternal life if you believe, that is, if you conclude that His death is your redemption. Hence either God is truthful in His Word, or you are a liar when you have doubts about the forgiveness of your sins after these promises have been given to you through the Son of God." By means of this axiom doubt is dispelled. Moreover, we must be well fortified against our adversary Satan, for he is a shrewd debater and a good rhetorician. . . . Unless you confront him with the true axiom that the Son of God died for sinners and that those who believe in Him will live the life which He Himself is living, all other reasons that can either be mentioned or thought of are rhetorical, weak, and puny. . . . Therefore call upon God, take hold of His Word, and cling to the sacrificial victim Christ, who has rendered satisfaction for your sin and has transferred your death to Himself and overcome it; and do not let it bother you that you are a sinner. Consider God's command. He wants you to cling to His Son and tells you to believe. . . . These thoughts refresh and strengthen a sick heart.

May 9

Abraham went with [the men]
to set them on their way.
GENESIS 18:16–17

A Guest at the Table

We have heard a most delightful account. Angels were sent to Abraham, and the promise was made to him anew—without any roundabout or indirect talk—that he would have a son from his wife Sarah. Abraham received them generously, and Sarah, too, was brought to faith, with the result that she believed that she would become a mother. To the description of God's inexpressible friendliness toward Abraham there is now added a greater indication of God's kindness, in order that we may learn how pleasing a service and sacrifice to God it is to hear the Word and to receive it with reverence. For, as we see in this passage, God draws near to such people not as a Judge and Lord but as a Friend and Guest at table. But the sad and horrible account which follows shows God's attitude toward those who despise the Word.

The Lord said, "Shall I hide from Abraham
what I am about to do?"

GENESIS 18:17

God's Good Will

he words which the Lord prefixes as a sort of pref-
ace—"Shall I hide from Abraham what I am about
to do?"—carry with them a delightful indication of
His extraordinary good will. Moreover, there was need of
these words in order to strengthen Abraham; otherwise the
announcement of the divine wrath would have overwhelmed
him. The repetition of the promise concerning the Seed and
the blessing of all the nations of the earth pertains to the same
thing. For if Abraham had not heard this promise from God
first, he would have cast away the hope of offspring as well
as of his own salvation in so horrible a display. Therefore it is
an extraordinary proof of God's benevolence when the Lord
declares that He cannot conceal anything from Abraham.

*Then the L*ORD *said, "Because the outcry against*
Sodom and Gomorrah is great and their sin is very grave,
I will go down to see whether they have done altogether
according to the outcry that has come to Me."

GENESIS 18:20

Outcry against Sin

he destruction of the five cities by fire is revealed to Abraham in this passage in order that you may understand that this extraordinary disaster was a punishment inflicted by an angry God because of the sins of the people. . . . God says: "Abraham will command these things to his children"; that is, in the Church of the saints accounts of this kind must be made known and be preserved. . . . Grace and the remission of sins must indeed be preached, but to those whose hearts are blameless and whose consciences are troubled. But to those who are smug and have altogether discarded the fear of God, God's blows and wrath must be presented in order that they may be warned by the example of others and cease to sin. For this is what is meant by saying that everything was written for our instruction [Romans 15:4]. Therefore those who, influenced by I know not what reasons, maintain that the Law should not be preached in the Church are pernicious teachers. . . . Indeed, God wants the destruction of Sodom by fire and that lake of asphalt to be conspicuous to this day and to be spoken of in sermons and made known among all posterity, in order that at least some may be reformed and may learn to fear God.

May 12

Abraham drew near and said,
"Will You indeed sweep away the righteous with the wicked?
Suppose there are fifty righteous within the city."

GENESIS 18:23–24

Bold Prayer

It is a forceful and impulsive prayer, as if Abraham wanted to compel God to forgive. Surely it is well known that because of one righteous man God spares, and shows kindness to, an entire house, city, and region. Thus Syria flourished while Naaman was living. Egypt is blessed because of Joseph, and Laban is blessed because of Jacob. And would God really forget Himself to such an extent that He would have no regard for fifty righteous men? . . . "Far be this from Thee!" he says, as though he wanted to tell God what He should do, just as he adds: "Will not He who judges the entire earth do what is right?" To do what is right means to punish evildoers and to spare the innocent. "And this," says he, "behooves Thee especially. Thou judgest the entire earth. But what sort of right is it to bring even innocent people to trial?" This is surely a bold and impulsive request. Abraham reminds God of His duty to spare the righteous and, because of the righteous, even the wicked. Accordingly, the Lord answers and promises that He will have mercy if there are fifty righteous men. For He is pleased with the fervent prayer in which faith and love are so manifest. But when Abraham hears that fifty are not found, he is somewhat frightened. Nevertheless, he continues to pray.

"Suppose forty . . . thirty . . . ten are found there." He answered, "For the sake of ten I will not destroy it." And the LORD went His way . . . and Abraham returned to his place.

GENESIS 18:29–33

Persistent Prayer

rayer must be bold. Therefore Abraham continues to pray . . . [and] from fifty the number drops to ten, and Abraham is sure that he will get his wish. . . . Consider this example whenever you pray, and learn that persistence is needed in praying. It does not offend God; it pleases Him. But Abraham undoubtedly comforted himself with the account of the flood, when eight souls were preserved. Even though he was unable to ensure the preservation of the others, he was nevertheless sure about his nephew Lot that God would take care of him and that he would be delivered. So he returns home and leaves everything to the just judgment of God. For he realizes that where there is such great malice of human beings, it is necessary for God to reveal His wrath against sin, lest the godly be offended and themselves also begin to turn away. And this is the reason why God commands that this account be committed to Abraham's descendants. God wants to be feared, but the smug He detests and hates. . . . Nevertheless, He does not want fear alone to dominate; He also wants the hope of mercy to be retained in that anxiety of heart.

Sitting in the Gate

 od has put the ministry of the Word into this world, not that the ministers should be silent, but that they should reprove, teach, comfort, terrify, and in this manner save whomever they can. . . . Even the most wicked human beings must be borne with compassion; but when they want to snatch us with them to destruction, compassion must cease. . . . But toward those who are not so obstinate but can be guided God wants us to show compassion, as the parable about the lost sheep teaches (Luke 15:4[–7]). . . . After this it is the work of the Holy Spirit to direct the hearts of men by means of the Word and confession, with the result that the fearful apprehend the comforts but the obstinate are either converted after they have been frightened by the words of the Law or perish utterly. Not all people should be condemned without distinction. Just as the flood and the destruction of the Sodomites are like thunderbolts by which the hearts are frightened, so there is added to these examples of wrath the comforting knowledge that Noah and Lot were preserved. In this way the fearful will be kept from despairing. . . . In these examples the wrath of God is presented in such a way that at the same time the goodness of God, who mercifully preserves the faithful, still shines forth.

"This fellow came to sojourn, and he has become the judge!" . . .
[The men of Sodom] pressed hard against the man Lot,
and drew near to break the door down.

<small>GENESIS 19:9</small>

The Rage of Satan

od does not afflict the godly; He permits the devil to do this, as we see in the case of Job. . . . Therefore when a plague and other misfortunes assail us, we, too, should say that these are the works of Satan, that Satan is raging and is angry, but that God is merciful and is kindly disposed toward us because we believe in His Son. And in this manner the saintly martyrs overcame death and all dangers; for they were sure that God was kind to them. . . . Moreover, these truths should be carefully impressed and taught, lest we yield to the flesh when we are tried or to our reason when we disregard the Word. For it is not God who torments you if you believe in Christ; it is the devil. He hates you and looks for opportunities to trouble you. . . . Hence if any misfortune befalls you, conclude boldly that it is from the devil and does not mean that God is unfriendly toward you, except insofar as He lets this happen as a trial, in order to put your faith to the test for your own good. . . . It is most certainly true that God is not angry with us; otherwise He would not give us the most excellent knowledge of His Son. Nor would He give us the Holy Spirit, whose first fruits we have received.

The men reached out their hands and brought Lot into the
house with them and shut the door. And they struck with
blindness the men who were at the entrance of the house.

GENESIS 19:10–11

Heavenly Protection

he raving people of Sodom were already trying to break open the door. Consequently, it was time for the guests to protect themselves and do a kind deed for so generous and faithful a host who was trying everything that seemed useful for their safety. Lot did not know that they were angels; he thought that they were saintly men who were visiting the churches and were teaching the Word far and wide. Therefore he worshiped God in them and honored them solemnly as guests who had been sent by God. And he and his entire house receive a very rich reward for this godly conduct. In the first place, he is defended against the raving people. . . . The angels do not smite [the men of Sodom] with such blindness that they see nothing at all; but they smite them with confusion, so that even if they did see, they still could not make out what they were seeing. . . . God often employs a miracle like this to rescue His own whom He wants to protect even while enemies are looking on. This is called being deprived of the function, not of the faculty, of sight. The actual seeing is taken away, as is stated in the Gospel (Luke 24:16): "Their eyes were kept from recognizing Him."

May 17

Then the men said to Lot,
"Have you anyone else here? . . . Bring them out of the place.
For we are about to destroy this place."
GENESIS 19:12–13

For the Sake of Believers

ot, having been commanded by the angels to do so, goes out to warn his sons-in-law . . . but they . . . laugh at the pious old man. . . . Lot thought that they were pious and saintly, for he could not look into their hearts. But they were hypocrites; they feigned godliness for a time, but now they revealed their true character when they laughed at the Word. Because they laugh, they perish. . . . No matter how righteous we may be, [the Law] should be proclaimed in the Church frequently, lest we fall into the madness of the antinomians, who remove the Law from the Church, as if everybody in the Church were actually a saint and there were no need for such examples of God's wrath. . . . But St. Paul (Romans 16:18) does not want the Church to be led astray by pleasing speeches; for sins should be denounced, and God's wrath should be exhibited for the sake of the unbelievers who are in the Church, yes, also for the sake of the believers, lest they yield to sin, which still adheres to them, and to their natural weakness. Thus even though Christ Himself most pleasantly invites sinners to come to Him, He nevertheless repeatedly cries out the awful "Woe!" over the impenitent Pharisees.

The Power of Angels

 t is profitable to know these facts; they serve to comfort the godly but to frighten the ungodly. For we who believe must be certain that the princes of heaven are with us, not one or two, but a great multitude of them. . . . But if we were without this protection, and the Lord did not restrain the fury of Satan in this manner, we would not remain alive for a single moment. . . . Accordingly, what Moses states in this passage about the good angels who lay waste and destroy the earth serves, in the first place, to teach us to fear God, since we have such a powerful opponent in Satan. In the second place, it teaches us to trust in the goodness of God, who has appointed such excellent princes and leaders through whom He so mightily defends His people. . . . But this protection of the angels, which God wanted to be more powerful than Satan, gives us comfort. This government of God through His creatures is wonderful, because the angels, who support the godly, defend the entire human race, even though it is exposed to lions, wolves, dragons, and all the horrible leaders of Satan who have been trained to inflict harm not only with the sword, plagues, and countless diseases but also with heresies of every kind.

May 19

*As morning dawned, the angels urged Lot, saying, "Up! Take
your wife and your two daughters who are here,
lest you be swept away in the punishment of the city."*

GENESIS 19:15

The Just Punishment of Sin

od has appointed three social classes to which He
has given the command not to let sins go unpunished. The first is that of the parents, who should
maintain strict discipline in their house. . . . The second is the
government, for the officers of the state bear the sword for
the purpose of coercing the obstinate and remiss by means
of their power of discipline. The third is that of the Church,
which governs by the Word. By this threefold authority God
has protected the human race against the devil, the flesh,
and the world, to the end that offenses may not increase but
may be cut off. Parents are the children's tutors, as it were.
Those who are grown up and are remiss the government
curbs through the executioner. In the Church those who are
obstinate are excommunicated. Thus the divine Majesty, as
It makes use of the service of human beings in accordance
with Its manifold wisdom and unlimited insight, is everywhere discernible. If some are remiss in their calling and
either connive at offenses or do not punish them in earnest,
they take the sin of others upon themselves. . . . Therefore
whether we are officers of the state or private citizens, we
should of one accord oppose sins, lest the wrath of God come
upon us and we all be consumed together.

But [Lot] lingered. So the men seized him and his wife and his two daughters by the hand, the Lord being merciful to him, and they brought him out and set him outside the city.

GENESIS 19:16

Unwise Delay

Lot had God's command to leave the city and abandon it. This command he should have obeyed. For when God speaks, He speaks in earnest and is not jesting or making fun, as we human beings are in the habit of doing. We often say one thing and have something else in mind. But the pious old man is troubled by the trial which plagues all of us too; for just as Satan disturbed Eve in Paradise by injecting the question (Genesis 3:2) why and with what intention God forbade the eating of the fruit, so our reason hampers and deceives us too. Consequently, we are not satisfied with knowing that God has given a command; but in our foolish anxiety we also want to inquire into the reasons for the command. God hates this inquisitiveness and does not want us to make it our business to ask why and wherefore, if I may use this expression; He wants us simply to obey His command and to be satisfied with this one reason, that He Himself has given the command. Hence in this passage Lot suffers from a human failing, inasmuch as he acts slowly and delays too long because of his good intention, as he thought.

"Escape for your life. Do not look back or stop anywhere in the valley. Escape to the hills, lest you be swept away."

GENESIS 19:17

Do Not Look Back

his, too, serves for our instruction; for whenever you see that some, like the people of Sodom, have the Word and despise both its threats and its promises, then keep in mind that you should save your soul, lest you perish together with such people; for such people are like those whom Solomon describes as saying (Proverbs 23:35): "They struck me, but I was not hurt," and their destruction cannot be too far off. Hardened Pharaoh perishes in the sea, and Samuel sheds tears in vain over King Saul. We must be on our guard against those who are thus given over to a wicked disposition, lest we share in their sin and perish together with them. . . . And Paul (2 Corinthians 6:17) enjoins: "Go out from their midst," keeping in mind the angel's command to save your own soul, as though he were saying: "Give thought to your own salvation, for your anxiety about the salvation of others is in vain." The emphasis lies on the pronoun "you." Thus Paul says (Titus 3:10–11): "As for a man who is factious, after admonishing him once or twice, have nothing more to do with him, knowing that such a person is perverted." And in Romans 12:19 Paul says: "Give place to wrath," as though he were saying: "If the unbelievers want to perish, let them perish indeed."

May 22

[Lot said,] "I cannot escape to the hills,
lest disaster overtake me and I die. Behold, this city is near
enough to flee to. . . . Let me escape there."

A Sincere Prayer

his account serves to rouse and spur us on to prayer in all our dangers, since God wants to do what we want, provided that we humbly prostrate ourselves before Him and pray. In this way the Ninevites, to whom the prophet had announced even the day of their destruction, were saved. And in Scripture there are more evidences of this kind; they prove that God allows Himself to be prevailed upon and subordinates His will to ours. Why, then, are we so remiss in regard to prayer? Why are we without faith to such an extent and so fainthearted, as though our prayer amounted to nothing? Let the monks despair of their praying; they have no knowledge of God and are altogether without faith. Their prayer is not a sincere request; it is arduous toil and actually an empty sound. But as for ourselves, who have the knowledge of the Word, when we come together and bend our knees in true humility, we know—because we have been taught not only by the promises but also by examples— that God wants to disregard His own will and do ours. These facts must be earnestly impressed on the people and on us, lest the disposition to pray flag in us. To be sure, God does everything; but we, too, must do what belongs to our calling.

May 23

He said to him, "Behold, I grant you this favor also,
that I will not overthrow the city of which you have spoken."

GENESIS 19:22

The Will of God

It was God's will that the city of Zoar should be destroyed together with the others; but because Lot intercedes for it, God changes His will and does what Lot wants. Similarly, because of Paul alone all who were sailing in the same ship were preserved in the shipwreck (Acts 27:43). . . . These are very strong statements, and they are hard to believe. But we should note them carefully for our learning and comfort, so that we may pray cheerfully and, as Paul teaches, without hesitating and murmuring (cf. Philippians 2:14). It is murmuring, however, when we have been offended by a perplexing situation and ask God why He does this or that in such a manner. . . . We must obey His will; and if anything in His actions offends us, we must pray. Paul calls hesitation doubt. This must be completely excluded from prayer, for it alone is what vitiates prayer. Therefore Bernard admonishes his brothers not to esteem their prayers lightly but to know that their prayers are written in heaven before they themselves have finished them. . . . For who is worthy to speak with the Lord? Therefore let it be enough for us that we have been called to faith through the Word, have been taught by the Word of God, and for this reason are part of the Church, which has the definite command to pray.

The sun had risen on the earth when Lot came to Zoar.
Then the LORD rained on Sodom and Gomorrah
sulfur and fire from the LORD out of heaven.

GENESIS 19:23–24

Salvation and Destruction

et us comfort ourselves, for this account points out both truths: that the enemies of the Church are to be punished and that the righteous are to be eternally saved, provided that we are like Lot and Abraham, that is, provided that we hold fast to the Word and to faith. The Lord knows, says Peter (2 Peter 2:9), both how to rescue the righteous and how to reserve the ungodly for destruction. Yet the ungodly do not believe this, and when they hear such examples applied to themselves, they laugh very pleasantly in a situation that is not at all funny—a situation that cannot be wept over enough and cannot be adequately lamented or expressed in words. Consider what a terrible disaster it was when in a single storm five cities, together with the men, the women, the children, the servants, the maids, the beasts of burden, and the cattle, were swallowed up at the same time, so that not even a straw remained from that entire region. What clearer example can one point out to show that God is sternly angry with the ungodly? Yet Christ and Peter say that this is a small punishment if you compare it with the punishment that awaits [those] who are not only impenitent but are also stubborn.

But Lot's wife, behind him, looked back,
and she became a pillar of salt.

GENESIS 19:26

Departing from God's Command

 ot's wife is held up to us as an example by Christ's teaching, for He refers to her when He says (Luke 9:62): "No one who puts his hand to the plow and looks back is fit for the kingdom of God." And in His earnest address concerning the Last Day He says (Luke 17:32): "Remember Lot's wife." From this we readily understand what it means to look back, namely, to depart from God's command and to be occupied with other matters—matters outside one's calling—like the man who has been commanded to follow Christ and wants to bury his dead first (Matthew 8:21). Hence this is a sign or lesson and a warning not to allow ourselves to be hampered in our calling, as Peter in John 21:20 looked back at John but was rebuked by the Lord. For everyone should stick to his own calling and not concern himself with what others are doing. . . . The Word of God is being preached to us today; we must hear and receive it without any argument. We must not become questioners who ask God why He has brought the sound doctrine to light at this time and not in former times. Thus this account teaches us to remain steadfast, for he who wants to be a Christian must not change his purpose: he must not look for another way or another Gospel. In this one and only way there is salvation; if you enter upon another, you have perished and are like Lot's wife.

May 26

So it was that, when God destroyed the cities of the valley,
God remembered Abraham
and sent Lot out of the midst of the overthrow.

GENESIS 19:29

The Prayer of a Believer

hat Moses has here added about Abraham is intended as a praise of prayer, for he clearly declares that God saved Lot not so much because of his own righteousness as because of the prayer of believing Abraham. (For Lot had already begun to be in danger because of his disobedience and delay. Therefore the angels chide him and say: "Lest you perish in like manner"; but his wife sinned more dangerously and for this reason was punished more severely.) It is as though Moses were saying: "God loved Abraham so much that He saved Lot because of him, for He did not want the heart of saintly Abraham to be saddened endlessly but left him this comfort, lest he have sorrow upon sorrow." Thus in all the accounts of the saints you see trouble alternating with deliverance, suffering with comfort, and tears with joy. Therefore they are the true Atlases who bear heaven on their shoulders, that is, sustain the burden of divine wrath and in such great disasters still keep their trust in mercy, even though they see the opposite. In the end they experience how great the power of believing prayer is.

[Lot's firstborn said to her sister,] "Come, let us make our father
drink wine, and we will lie with him,
that we may preserve offspring from our father."
GENESIS 19:32

No One Is Better

 ou will ask: "But why does God permit His own to fall in this manner?" Although we are not at liberty to inquire too eagerly into God's doings, yet here the answer is easy. God wants us to be well aware of our feebleness, lest we lapse into smugness. Thus Lot and his saintly household had seen the sins of the people of Sodom and had rightfully abominated them, but what happens to them now? The people who are so saintly pollute themselves with abominable incest, something which hardly ever happened among the people of Sodom or at least did not happen commonly. Hence the reason is clear. God wants us all to humble ourselves and to glory solely in His mercy, because, so far as we are concerned, no one is better or saintlier than the other, and no one sins so gravely. If God should withdraw His hand, you will pollute yourself with the same sin. Therefore this awful fall teaches two lessons: (1) that you should humble yourself before God and (2) that you should continually pray to God for the guidance of the Holy Spirit.

From there Abraham journeyed toward the territory
of the Negeb and lived between Kadesh and Shur;
and he sojourned in Gerar.

GENESIS 20:1

A Lodging Place for the Night

he prophets and other saints pondered those wanderings of Abraham more diligently and warned that one must look for another country and fatherland than this physical and transient one; otherwise his physical land would have been given to Abraham himself, to whom it was promised. But not even a footbreadth became his during his entire lifetime. He even bought a burial place for Sarah with his own money (Genesis 23:16). . . . The Letter to the Hebrews (11:8–10) . . . relates these ordinary things to the Spirit Himself and declares that those ordinary deeds were done in faith. In faith he took a wife, and in faith he wandered about; that is, everywhere he sustained himself with the divine promises or the Word and looked for a resting place or abode other than an earthly one. Of this present one he made use of as of food and drink. Hence let us, too, learn to use this life as an inn or a lodging place for the night. If you understand Abraham's wandering in this manner, you will not say that it was something ordinary; for it is a work of faith, and of a very fervent and strong faith at that.

Abimelech had not approached [Sarah]. So he said, "Lord, will You kill an innocent people? Did he not himself say to me, 'She is my sister'? And she herself said, 'He is my brother.' "

The Compassion of God

he prayer with which Abimelech excuses himself before God deserves our careful examination. He does not despair at once because of that awful preaching of the Law which he hears from the Lord: "You will surely die"; but first he asserts his innocence. Furthermore, he has firm hope in God's justice, that is, in His compassion. For God's justice is not, as they have taught in the schools, the severity, sternness, or violent anger with which God condemns; it is the justice through which He has mercy on the humble as He protects them against unjust violence and punishes the guilty. . . . But what Abimelech states in this passage is also required, namely, that he have a pure heart and innocent hands. This means that it is necessary to have a good conscience. But since those who yield to sin and to the flesh cannot have a good conscience, they must, if they are to be converted, first be frightened, and not slightly at that, but in such a way that they do not know where to turn, as we see in Peter and in David. Since they are conscious of their guilt, they do not excuse themselves; but when they acknowledge their sin, they are wretchedly perplexed and humbled. Yet they eventually lay hold of mercy and thus are reconciled through faith, which accepts the Mediator.

Abraham said, "I did it because I thought,
'There is no fear of God at all in this place,
and they will kill me because of my wife.'"

GENESIS 20:11

The Weakness of a Saint

lthough Abraham is full of faith, nevertheless in this
instance he fell through weakness and feared for
himself. . . . In the first place, this fear was a sin; and,
as usually happens, this sin results in the other one. He lies,
and he instructs his wife to lie. . . . Why does God allow such
sins to be committed by His own? Why does He permit His
own to stumble in this way? The most appropriate answer
to this question is given on the basis of the outcome. God
permits it to happen this way in order that He may have the
opportunity to achieve many good results. The saints do not
fall in order to perish; they fall in order that God may bestow
rich blessings on them by heaping greater benefits on them,
as is written (Romans 8:28): "We know that all things work
together for good for the saints," and a gloss to this passage
adds: "Even their very failings." . . .

But, as I have said above, not only the passive evils that are
inflicted on us result in good, but also the active ones, that is,
the evils which we ourselves do. "How can this be?" you say.
Because when a godly person is aware of his fall, he becomes
ashamed and is perturbed. Thus his fall leads first to humility and then also to fervent prayer. It is for this reason that
Solomon says (Proverbs 24:16): "A righteous man falls seven

times in a day and rises again." For they do not persist in their sins; they groan and grieve.

Moreover, the evil which remains in our flesh is like a spur which urges us on, with the result that we are angry with ourselves, condemn ourselves, and cry out with Paul (Romans 7:24): "Wretched man that I am! Who will deliver me from the body of this sin?" Lord, take away and crucify our flesh! Thus faith grows by reason of our failings, the seeds of which remain in our flesh. Therefore God leads His saints in a wonderful manner, as the psalm (4:3) states. "With the pure Thou dost show Thyself pure; and with the crooked Thou dost show Thyself perverse" (Psalm 18:26).

But these statements should not be understood as though we maintained that a failing is something good. For a failing remains something intrinsically evil; but in the case of the saints it becomes the occasion for something good, according to the statement (Psalm 18:25): "With the blameless man Thou dost show Thyself blameless." Whatever the saints do is sanctified; that is, even if those fall who are saintly or justified or believe and fear God, their faith is nevertheless disciplined and increased. To this extent God is wonderful in His saints.

The LORD visited Sarah as He had said. . . .
Abraham called the name of his son who was born to him,
whom Sarah bore him, Isaac.

GENESIS 21:1, 3

The Source of Joy

oses is very wordy in this passage. He repeats nearly all statements twice. Evidently it is his purpose to commend to us that most exuberant joy of the saintly patriarch. After awful misfortunes Abraham has not only found a safe place and a favorably disposed king, but Sarah becomes pregnant and bears him the son who is the heir of the promise. But if the joy of parents is genuine when children are born to them in the usual manner without a promise, how much more Abraham rejoiced over this his son for whom he had now waited so many years after he had been promised! Accordingly, what thus far has been an object of hope, and what he has believed, this is now a reality; and, if I may express it in this way, the promise has now been made flesh. We cannot come close to feeling this joy; for the things which thus far had been invisible and impossible, which Abraham had believed, are now visible and altogether possible—an example for us, that we may learn that there is no real joy in this world except that which the Word brings when it is believed.

Abraham circumcised his son Isaac when he was eight days old,
as God had commanded him.

GENESIS 21:4

As God Commanded

braham assigns the name to his son by divine authority, for the angel of the Lord had stated that this name should be given to him. He also circumcises his son on the eighth day, and Moses adds that this was done in accordance with the Lord's command. Therefore just as Abraham does everything in accordance with the Word and his call, so we, too, should see to it that we undertake nothing without the Word and are not found in a state or work about which we have doubts.

Sarah said, "God has made laughter for me; everyone who hears will laugh over me." And she said, "Who would have said to Abraham that Sarah would nurse children? Yet I have borne him a son in his old age."

<small>GENESIS 21:6–7</small>

Laughter

We shall take the meaning [of the verb] from the subject matter itself and disregard the disputes of the philologians. Accordingly, the proper meaning of the verb is "to laugh." Therefore when Sarah says: "God made laughter for me," this means that she rejoiced in earnest and was glad about the son whom she had borne, not only with a carnal gladness—like that of other mothers of whom Christ says that they do not remember their former anguish after giving birth (John 16:21)—but with a gladness of the Holy Spirit, because she had actually become a mother as a result of God's blessing. On account of her barrenness Sarah had so far been regarded as a woman under a curse, because God was begrudging her the usual blessing. Consequently, she undoubtedly concluded that a great injury was being inflicted on her. But now, after the birth of her son, she, too, boasts of the divine blessing, leaps with joy, and says: "Now God causes me, too, to laugh and be glad of heart because of this His unhoped-for favor."

Abraham made a great feast
on the day that Isaac was weaned.

Genesis 21:8

Celebrating the Lord's Kindness

his was not a feast of frivolous men. No, it was a feast of the saintliest fathers, who thanked God for having confirmed and fulfilled His divine promise; and they not only refreshed their bodies with rather sumptuous food but also refreshed their hearts with sacred discourses, just as Paul states in Acts 14:17 that hearts are satisfied with food and gladness as a result of the Lord's kindness. . . . Here it should also be noted that in this way God gives Abraham a palpable demonstration of His grace. He had promised him a son, but He delays the fulfillment of the promise. Meanwhile Abraham, who is satisfied with the Word alone, believes the promise and simply clings to the invisible things. But it happens in due time that the invisible things become visible. We, too, should imitate this and set it before our eyes. We believe that our flesh will rise again on the Last Day. This should be as sure for us as if it had already happened; for we, too, have the Word and the same spiritual comforts that Abraham had.

[Sarah] said to Abraham, "Cast out this slave woman
with her son, for the son of this slave woman
shall not be heir with my son Isaac."

GENESIS 21:10

Inheritance and Covenant

hat [Sarah] says about the inheritance should not be understood as though she wanted Ishmael to be excluded from the inheritance; she simply says that he should not be made an heir together with Isaac, but that Isaac should keep his portion for himself. . . . She is speaking under the influence of the Holy Spirit, and she relies on the sure promise which she had heard concerning her son. Ishmael, too, had his promise; for the Lord said to Abraham (Genesis 17:20): "I have heard you praying for Ishmael, for of him shall be born twelve princes." But Sarah noted more carefully that an additional statement was made about her son with these words: "But I will establish My covenant with Isaac." . . . Abraham had not given such careful consideration to the promise. Therefore God repeats it and once more expressly states: "Through Isaac shall your descendants be named" [Genesis 21:12]. Accordingly, He does not condemn the saintly will and the just sentiment that Abraham loves his wife and son; but He merely reminds him of the promise which gave to Ishmael the hope of becoming a great nation. The covenant, however, He reserved for Isaac alone. . . . The promises were twofold. The temporal one had concerned Ishmael; the eternal and spiritual one had concerned Isaac.

"Through Isaac shall your offspring be named."

The Power of the Word

he apostle Paul] postulates a threefold progeny of Abraham. The first is physical and without the promise concerning Christ. Ishmael, who was born of the flesh of Abraham, was an offspring of this kind. The second progeny, says Paul, is physical, but with the promise concerning Christ. Thus Isaac, too, was born of the flesh of Abraham; but he had the promise: "I shall establish My covenant with Isaac." The third progeny, says Paul, is not physical but is the offspring only of the promise. Although it certainly does not belong to the flesh of Abraham, still it holds fast to faith and embraces the promise made to Abraham. . . . Therefore Paul is right in stating that those are heirs who are of the promise, that is, who hear the promise and believe the promise, whether they were born of the flesh of Abraham or not. For the promise, which is the Word of God, is so effective and powerful that it calls into existence the things that do not exist (Romans 4:17). Christ says (Matthew 3:9) that children are raised up for Abraham from stones. This power the flesh or physical birth does not have. Only the Word has it, because it is omnipotent.

"I will make a nation of the son of the slave woman also,
because he is your offspring."

GENESIS 21:13

The Prayer of the Church

he Lord commanded that Ishmael should be cast out. Lest He appear to have forgotten His former promise about the twelve princes (Genesis 17:20) and to repent of His plan, He repeats the promise and adds that He will do this for the sake of Abraham, whose descendant Ishmael is. Thus the natural son is indeed cast out. Nevertheless, he is established as a very powerful king of the world. Accordingly, someone will say: "Establishing him king of a very large people is not casting him out, is it?" For Ishmael's descendants occupied the entire southern region, and today the Saracens are still a great people. Thus this account serves to teach us that God allots kingdoms and governments even to reprobate and evil men, not because of their merit—which is nil—but for the sake of Abraham, that is, the Church, which alone in the world prays for kings and governments, in order that it may be able to have a quiet lodging place in this life and to propagate the Word of God in peace.

So Abraham rose early in the morning and took bread and a
skin of water and gave it to Hagar, putting it on her shoulder,
along with the child, and sent her away.

GENESIS 21:14

Loved above All Things

 his is an outstanding example of obedience, faith, and all good conduct, but especially of true obedience toward God; for these events did not happen in as brief a time as the words make it sound. Nevertheless, they had to be described in this manner, in order that we might learn from Abraham's example that God must be loved above all things, and loved so perfectly that you love nothing in the entire world in the same way, neither your wife nor your children nor your own life. . . . It was God's will expressed by a definite word that Ishmael should leave his home and his native country and should wait for God's blessing in another place than in the land of Canaan. . . . [Abraham's] faith, strengthened by a trustworthy assurance, smothers all thoughts of the flesh, though not without difficulty and great grief, and simply clings to this hope: "God will look out for them. God will take care of them, for He loves them more than I do and will be more able to help them." Accordingly, this example is suitable for us to learn to do quickly and without argument whatever we know has been commanded by the Word of God.

[Abraham] sent her away.

GENESIS 21:14

A Father's Love

braham was no ordinary Christian or confessor, if I may express myself in this way. No, he was a martyr of martyrs. For who is there who does not know how intense a father's affection toward his children and wife is? It is easier for a parent to suffer death than to forsake his own or to permit great harm to be done to them. But everything must yield to a command of God; and if you want to be a Christian, this is not a matter of wearing a black or gray garment. No, everything must be risked, not only wife and children but your own life. . . . This account is astonishing; but it is recorded about the saintly patriarch as an example for us, in order that we may learn that we should love and revere God above all things. Similarly, in chapter twelve Abraham is commanded to leave his country; and in Psalm 45:10 the Church which has been gathered from the Jews is told: "O daughter, forget your father's house." And Christ says (Matthew 10:37): "He who loves father and mother more than Me is not worthy of Me."

[Hagar] said, "Let me not look on the death of my child."
And as she sat opposite him, she lifted up her voice and wept.

GENESIS 21:16

A Cry for Solace

 encourage myself with this hope alone, that in the Gospel I see that solace has been promised to the contrite, hope to the despairing, and heaven to those who have been put into hell; and the fact that the Son of God, without our knowledge, offered Himself for us to God the Father, His Father, on the altar of the cross, is sure proof of this hope. If those who have first been humbled in this manner and have been driven to despair begin to be of good cheer because of Christ to the same extent that they despair of themselves, they become children of God and heirs. Yet you may find many who do not want to be humbled but plan vengeance and grumble. These people are doubly obdurate. Therefore when you feel that you are being humbled, cast yourself at the feet of your heavenly Father and say: "O Lord, if Thou dealest with me in this manner, I shall bear it patiently, and I confess that I have deserved something more terrible. Therefore be merciful to me. If Thou dost not want me to be an heir, see to it that I remain a servant (Luke 15:19). Indeed, as the Canaanite woman says, I do not refuse to be a dog in Thy house so that I can at least eat the crumbs which chance to fall to the ground and otherwise are wasted (Matthew 15:27). Thou dost not owe me a thing by any right. Therefore I cling to Thy mercy."

God heard the voice of the boy.

GENESIS 21:17

God of the Humble

his is a very great comfort for all those who feel that they have been cast out, that is, acknowledge their sins and tremble before the judgment of God. For He does not want to cast such people aside, nor can He do so; and if such people were without solace from men, it would sooner be necessary for an angel to descend from heaven to bring them comfort. Accordingly, God is called the God of the humble and afflicted who does not quench a smoldering wick (Matthew 12:20). But after the self-reliance of the flesh has been mortified in Ishmael, he becomes a true son of the promise; and what he first demanded on the basis of right, but did not obtain, he now, in his utmost need and despair, receives by grace. It is a remarkable situation and one most worthy of noting that when Ishmael feels himself utterly cast away, he has God at his side and is very dear to God. And God cannot disregard the voice and the groaning of the afflicted lad. But if God had not heard him here, he would have perished eternally. But to God this is impossible. "For He is merciful and does not want the death of the sinner" (cf. Ezekiel 33:11).

And the angel of God called to Hagar from heaven and said to her, "What troubles you, Hagar? Fear not, for God has heard the voice of the boy where he is."

GENESIS 21:17

Dry Your Tears

ne should not suppose that these words were spoken in a harsh manner, as though he were rebuking her; for they are words of comfort. "Ah," says the angel, "why are you weeping? Why are you sobbing? What do you desire? There is no reason why you should be afraid. Dry your tears. God cares for you and your son. He wanted to crush you. Since this has been achieved, He wants you to be of good hope with regard to His mercy. Before this you, with your son, also prayed in the house of Abraham. But there God was unwilling to hear you, for your prayer was associated with pride and with contempt for your brother. But here He has heard you. Therefore believe that His Church is here. For where God hears prayers, there His sanctuary is, there the Church is, and there the unutterable sighing (Romans 8:26) of those who despair of themselves is." . . . Thus the foremost article of our faith and our highest wisdom are confirmed—that not those born of blood, of the will of man, or of the will of the flesh are children of God, but those born of God (John 1:13), that is, those who believe the promise; for it is through this promise alone that He wants to save those who are not presumptuous because of birth or merit but believe in Christ. This is the angel's message.

"Up! Lift up the boy, and hold him fast with your hand,
for I will make him into a great nation."

GENESIS 21:18

Hold Fast

 hus [the angel] absolves the troubled woman from all excommunication and fear. He receives her again into grace and into participation in the promise of Isaac. . . . God shows the same kindness toward us. He speaks with us through the ministry of men and in this manner conceals His majesty, which is dreadful and unbearable for us. . . . Therefore let us recognize His exceedingly great and incalculable gift: that He emptied Himself in this manner and took on human form. Let us not on this account despise the Word; but let us fall on our knees and honor and prize the holy ministry through which God deigns to speak to us. For we are truly that people. As Moses says about his Jews (Deuteronomy 4:7), we have a God who draws near to us and dwells with us, since through your mouth He speaks with me and through my mouth He speaks with you. Yes, the Son of God Himself came down into the flesh and was made man for the sole purpose of drawing us unto Himself and in order that we might acquire hope in His mercy and not be afraid of Him as we shall be afraid of His majesty, which our nature cannot bear, as is written (Exodus 33:20): "Man shall not see Me and live," and also (Deuteronomy 4:24): "God is a devouring fire." Therefore He assumed a weak form—a form like our own and for this reason completely human.

And God was with the boy, and he grew up.

GENESIS 21:20

God Gives Growth

When the text states that God was with Ishmael, this is rich comfort, which shows that God opens heaven to us when we have been humbled, and that He abundantly pours forth Himself and all things. For Ishmael is not only led back to the right way in order that he may not continue to be presumptuous; but after he has been humbled, he is brought back into the Church from which he had been cast out because of his presumption, and God Himself appoints Himself as his Protector, directs him, blesses him, and now regards with favor everything he does. . . . The verb "he grew up" is to be understood not only of Ishmael's natural growth (for at the time of his excommunication he was twenty years old, more or less) but with regard to the fact that God caused him to become great, in the first place, in the Word and spiritual gifts; for, says Moses, God was with him. In the second place, God also blessed him temporally, so that he begot twelve princes. . . . Thus we learn how powerful a sacrifice a contrite heart is, and how pleasing a smoke or incense humiliation is to God. For the statement of the psalm (145:19) is true, that God fulfills the desire of those who fear Him; for they offer a holy sacrifice to God.

At that time Abimelech and Phicol the commander of his army said to Abraham, "God is with you in all that you do. Now therefore swear to me here by God that you will not deal falsely with me." . . . And Abraham said, "I will swear."

GENESIS 21:22–24

The Godly Oath

braham does not refuse to take the oath, and by his action he teaches that these moral and civil matters should neither be looked down upon nor neglected by the saints under the pretense of their religion. . . . But so far as Christ's command is concerned—"Do not swear at all" (Matthew 5:34)—the reply to this question is very easy if one takes into consideration the causes which Moses points out well in this account. One can truthfully give the simple answer that a righteous man does not sin even when he swears, but that he is rendering a service that is pleasing to God and men. But it is easier to explain the causes. The efficient cause is that Abraham is not swearing thoughtlessly, but because the king ordered him to do so. . . . Therefore an oath which is imposed by the government is in agreement with the command of God, who has commanded us to obey the government. The other, final cause is also indicated here, namely, that in this way peace is established between the domestics of the king and those of Abraham. For Holy Scripture says (Hebrews 6:16): "An oath is the end of all controversies"; that is, it puts an end to controversies and quarrels. Who would deny that this is a holy and good work?

"Take your son, your only son Isaac, whom you love, and go to the land of Moriah, and offer him there as a burnt offering."

GENESIS 22:2

Called to Sacrifice

his trial cannot be overcome and is far too great to be understood by us. For there is a contradiction with which God contradicts Himself. It is impossible for the flesh to understand this; for it inevitably concludes either that God is lying—and this is blasphemy—or that God hates me—and this leads to despair. Accordingly, this passage cannot be explained in a manner commensurate with the importance of the subject matter. We are frequently tempted by thoughts of despair; for what human being is there who could be without this thought: "What if God did not want you to be saved?" But we are taught that in this conflict we must hold fast to the promise given us in Baptism, which is sure and clear. But when this happens, Satan does not cease immediately but keeps crying out in your heart that you are not worthy of this promise. But in this situation there is need of the fervent prayer that God may give us His Spirit, in order that the promise may not be wrested from us. . . . We must hold fast to the promise and maintain that, just as the text states about Abraham, we are tempted by God, not because He really wants this, but because He wants to find out whether we love Him above all things and are able to bear Him when He is angry as we gladly bear Him when He is beneficent and makes promises.

"Offer [Isaac] there as a burnt offering."

GENESIS 22:2

Raised from the Ashes

ven though there is a clear contradiction here—for there is nothing between death and life—Abraham nevertheless does not turn away from the promise. . . . Abraham relies on the promise and attributes to the divine Majesty this power, that He will restore his dead son to life; for just as he saw that Isaac was born of a worn-out womb and of a sterile mother, so he also believed that he was to be raised after being buried and reduced to ashes, in order that he might have descendants, as the Epistle to the Hebrews (11:19) states: "God is able to give life even to the dead." Accordingly, Abraham understood the doctrine of the resurrection of the dead, and through it alone he resolved this contradiction. . . . These were his thoughts: "Today I have a son; tomorrow I shall have nothing but ashes. I do not know how long they will lie scattered; but they will be brought to life again, whether this happens while I am still alive or a thousand years after my death. For the Word declares that I shall have descendants through this Isaac, even though he has been reduced to ashes." . . . Therefore one should hold fast to this comfort, that what God has once declared, this He does not change. You were baptized, and in Baptism the kingdom of God was promised you. You should know that this is His unchangeable Word, and you should not permit yourself to be drawn away from it.

So Abraham rose early in the morning, saddled his donkey, and
took two of his young men with him, and his son Isaac.

GENESIS 22:3

Without Hesitation

his is an extraordinary example and a description of perfect obedience, when so suddenly and at one and the same time Abraham thrusts out of sight and does away with everything he used to hold dearest in his life: his home, his wife, and his son who had been so long expected and upon whom such grand promises had been heaped. . . . Moses states that [Abraham] rose, did not delay, and did not hesitate. When we are sure about God's will and believe that He has commanded what we have under consideration, the matter must be undertaken, not with trepidation or hesitation but with the utmost eagerness, even if one had to expose oneself to a thousand dangers or to death itself. For the Word of God cannot be without effect. But when we obey God's command, the outcome determined in advance surely follows, even though the very gates of hell fight against it. . . . Abraham overcomes his trials by faith. And without a doubt he had very great trials. He knows that God has given him a command. Therefore he hastens to carry it out without regard for a contrary opinion of Sarah or of the domestics or of any other creature. What is stated in the psalm (119:50) is firmly impressed on his heart: "Thy Law is my very great comfort, because it gives me life." In the same way let him who has a sure Word of God, in whatever vocation he may be, only believe and have courage, and God will undoubtedly grant a favorable outcome.

June 18

On the third day Abraham lifted up his eyes and saw
the place from afar. . . . Abraham took the wood
of the burnt offering and laid it on Isaac his son. . . .
So they went both of them together.

GENESIS 22:4, 6

A Bitter Burden

I am truly surprised that the father did not die from that bitter and persistent grief, for he had to make a journey of three days. If that struggle had lasted one or two hours, he would have prevailed rather easily. Therefore this delay makes his obedience greater. Meanwhile he thought: "Behold, I am walking along with my son, who is my greatest hope and a young man; he has to die." During these three days he endured this kind of torture of his flesh and at the same time the darts of Satan. Nevertheless, he had to endure it in silence because of the command, and since he relied on this, he was strengthened and preserved. . . . These two were alone as they walked in the desert. The whole world is ignorant of what is going on here, and there was no one at hand to encourage the sorrowful father. The son, however, does not know that he is to be killed. Nowhere else in Holy Scripture is a walk like this described. There were two. Who were they? The very dear father and the dearly beloved son. In what frame of mind were they? This was their frame of mind: Isaac was unaware of the situation. Nevertheless, he was ready to obey. Abraham was fully determined to immolate his son and reduce him to ashes.

[Isaac] said, "Behold, the fire and the wood, but where is the lamb for a burnt offering?" Abraham said, "God will provide for Himself the lamb for a burnt offering, my son."

GENESIS 22:7–8

God Provides the Lamb

At this point there is surely profound emotion, and there is powerful pathos. Moses did not want to pass this over. Isaac, the victim, addresses his father and stirs up his natural love, as though he were saying: "You are my father." And the father says in turn: "You are my son." These words penetrated into and upset the heart of the father. For the son says: "Behold, the wood; but where is the lamb?" It is evident that he is solicitous about the glory of God, for he knows that his father is about to offer a burnt offering at which he himself wants to be the onlooker. Therefore he gives him a reminder lest perchance he forget the sacrifice because of the very great intentness and devotion of his heart. "Where is the lamb," he says, "for the burnt offering?" Then his father should have answered him: "You will be the lamb." But he does not say this. Then he adds: "God will provide it"; and in this statement he at the same time included God's command.

In the Midst of Death

 oses sums up that remarkable and amazing account in one short sentence. At this very moment the father is about to cut the throat of his son. The son, with his eyes lifted up to heaven, presents his throat and waits to be reduced to ashes. Thus God brings both into extreme danger of their lives. If on that occasion there had been no faith, or if God had slept for a single moment, the life of the son would have been done for, because the knife is ready, the son is bound and placed upon the heap of wood, and the thrust is aimed at his throat. These are works of God by which He shows that He takes care of us in the greatest dangers and in the midst of death. . . . It is an astounding situation that the dearly beloved father moves his knife close to the throat of the dearly beloved son, and I surely admit that I cannot attain to these thoughts and sentiments either by means of words or by reflecting on them. No one else should have expounded this passage than St. Paul. We are not moved by those sentiments, because we do not desire to feel and experience them. The son is obedient, like a sheep for the slaughter, and he does not open his mouth. He thought: "Let the will of the Lord be done," because he was brought up to conduct himself properly and to be obedient to his father. With the exception of Christ we have no similar example of obedience.

But the angel of the Lord called to him from heaven
and said, "Abraham, Abraham!"

GENESIS 22:11

Death Conquered

ere you see with what unconcern the divine Majesty toys with death and all the power of death. Here God is playing with His patriarch and his son, who together experienced the utmost distress and won a very great victory over death. . . . The victory of Abraham, Isaac, and all the saints is faith. He who has faith overcomes the fear of death and conquers and triumphs eternally. About this 2 Corinthians 1:9 says: "We have set our hope on the living God who raises the dead." . . . Christians, who have the Word, should hear it with all eagerness and should meditate on it, in order that their hearts may be stirred up, so that, however much they may be weighed down by the burden of sin and the hindrances of Satan, they nevertheless may attain to that glory and knowledge of God's mind and of immortality and be able to believe that this statement is true and unshakable: "Death is a sport." This is what Abraham believed and felt, and with this confidence he conquered death. "My son Isaac, whom I am killing, is the father of the promise, and this proposition is absolutely true. Consequently, my son will live forever and will be the heir. Therefore even if he has to die now, he will nevertheless not die in reality but will rise again." . . . These things have not been recorded for the sake of Abraham, who is long since dead, but to encourage and stimulate us, in order that we may learn that in the sight of God death is nothing.

June 22

[Abraham] said, "Here am I."

GENESIS 22:11

Here Am I

[A]braham's] obedience gave God extraordinary pleasure. For of all the sacrifices the one most acceptable to God is this: to kill sin, to live in righteousness, holiness, obedience, and mortification of the flesh. This is indeed painful and difficult for us; but one must learn to accustom oneself, as Paul says (Romans 12:2), to "what is the good will of God." We merely talk about these things, but Abraham and Isaac actually did them. And this is the perfect will for God. It has not even begun in us. To God it is well-pleasing and good; to us it is unpleasant and disagreeable. Nothing is more agonizing than the mortification of the flesh and sin. For this reason it seems horrible and impossible, and we shun and hate it. Nevertheless, one must accustom oneself to it and make a beginning, in accordance with the example of Abraham, who does not shun it but waits for it with the utmost readiness. The purpose of his being here is that his son may be killed and that life may follow death. This is a work done in faith—a work in which the angels are wont to rejoice, even in us, when we are engaged in a Christian office and work.

"Do not lay your hand on the boy or do anything to him, for now I know that you fear God, seeing you have not withheld your son, your only son, from Me."

Fear and Reverence

 hen Abraham is praised as one who fears and reveres God, the statement refers not only to his faith but also to his entire worship, to the tree with its fruits, inasmuch as for the Hebrews to fear God is the same as to worship God or to serve God, to love and honor God. . . . God should be feared nowhere except in His Word, in accordance with the command which says: "You shall not worship strange gods, and you shall not make for yourself a graven image, whatever it may be" (cf. Exodus 20:3–4). Where God is revealed in His Word, there worship Him, there exercise your reverence; then you are fearing where you should fear and tremble.

Abraham lifted up his eyes and looked, and behold,
behind him was a ram, caught in a thicket by his horns.
And Abraham went and took the ram and offered it up
as a burnt offering instead of his son.

GENESIS 22:13

The Sacrifice Appears

t does not seem to have been a rash statement on the part of the fathers when they said that the ram was provided from the beginning of the world; for they knew about Christ, the woman's Seed, and understood this ram to be a figure of Him. For Christ existed before the creation, as Paul says (Titus 1:2): "God, who never lies, promised ages ago." Hence before the ages, from eternity, Christ was destined by divine providence to crush the head of the serpent, to become the sacrifice for the human race, to kill sins, and to give us life. But He waited until the predetermined time of His appearance arrived. This is a sufficiently good allegory. I do not disapprove of it. But after they had seen the ram—no matter how he had been brought there by God—Abraham took him and offered him as a burnt offering in his son's place. There Isaac was the acolyte and assisted his father in bringing the sacrifice. Moreover, that ram was a sign by which Abraham was convinced that the ram was to be offered, not Isaac. Thus some sign is always attached to the Word, for Abraham realized at once that the ram had been provided by God for the sacrifice.

So Abraham called the name of that place, The Lord Will See;
as it is said to this day: On the mount the Lord will see.

GENESIS 22:14 (according to Luther's translation)

The Lord Will See

his name, The Lord Will See, has a correlative relation, so to speak, to those who are on the mountain and worship God; for God, in turn, has regard for them and hears them. Therefore this mountain, which long ago was sacred because of the religious practice of the fathers—as was stated above—is now also consecrated by God Himself, since He sanctifies and cares for both the place and those who come there as worshipers. Consequently, the name of the mountain abounds in comfort; for it implies a relation between him who fears—that is, calls upon God and gives thanks—and God, who accepts or hears vows and prayers—between him who adores and Him who is adored. Inasmuch as the place had been appointed previously for the worship of God, Abraham is now fully assured that God is present there and inclines His eyes and ears toward all who worship and adore at this place.

*"By Myself I have sworn, declares the L*ORD*,*
because you have done this and have not withheld your son,
your only son, I will surely bless you."

GENESIS 22:16–17

God's Oath

he fact that God swears by Himself is something great and wonderful. The author of the Epistle to the Hebrews saw this here and weighed it carefully (6:13). For it is an indication of a heart burning with inexpressible love and with a desire for our salvation, as though God were saying: "I desire so greatly to be believed and long so intensely to have My words trusted that I am not only making a promise but am offering Myself as a pledge. I have nothing greater to give as a pledge, because as surely as I am God, there is nothing greater than I. If I do not keep My promises, I shall no longer be He who I am." . . . Accordingly, let us also bear in mind that God enlarges His promise to such an outstanding extent that it surpasses all thinking and faith; for He strengthens and confirms it by His majesty, in order that we may have no reason whatever to mistrust and doubt. . . . God accommodates Himself completely to our weakness. It should be enough if He moved one finger to bear witness of His fatherly goodwill toward us. But now He offers us His Word, and He not only promises but even takes an oath and invokes evil upon and curses Himself—if one were permitted to speak this way—in order to bless us.

June 27

"By Myself I have sworn . . . I will surely bless you."

GENESIS 22:16–17

Christ Is the Pledge

ur trust will be perfect when life and death, glory and shame, adversity and good fortune will be alike to us. But we shall not attain this through speculation; it will have to be learned in trial and prayer. For here there is no argument about the words "God is truth"; but there is an argument about the subject matter, namely, that God does not lie when He swears and when He promises the greatest blessings, life, and deliverance from sin and hell, and when He so firmly assures every one of us: "You, human being, shall surely live, or I Myself shall not live. Hell has been overcome and destroyed for you, or I Myself shall be destroyed and cease to be God. Indeed, in order that you may have no doubt, you have My Son given to you as a gift." To believe these most glorious promises and to expect these blessings from God with firm confidence is true faith. And God wants our hearts to be aroused to this confidence not only by the examples of Abraham and others—and not only by His promises—but also because He has given His own Son for us, to be a gift and a pledge of heavenly blessings.

"By Myself I have sworn . . . I will surely bless you."

GENESIS 22:16–17

God Is for Me

rue faith draws the following conclusion: "God is God for me because He speaks to me. He forgives me my sins. He is not angry with me, just as He promises: 'I am the Lord your God.'" Now search your heart, and ask whether you believe that God is your God, Father, Savior, and Deliverer, who wants to rescue you from sins and from death. If you become aware that you are wavering or uncertain, consider how to correct that doubt through constant use of the Word of God. . . . Besides, this one passage is the only place in which Holy Scripture states that God swore. From it has flowed everything said in Psalm 110:4 and in Psalm 132:11 about the oath sworn to David. For just as the promise of the Seed of Abraham was transferred to the Seed of David, so Holy Scripture transfers the oath sworn to Abraham to the person of David. . . . Thus not only the author of the Epistle to the Hebrews but also the fathers and prophets saw, and marveled at, the abundance of God's grace, which pervades the entire promise and the oath. Therefore they pondered this text with the utmost zeal, and David's most beautiful psalms originated from it. The saints in the New Testament also extol this oath with great joy. Thus Zechariah sings (Luke 1:73): "The oath which He swore to our father Abraham, to grant us." And Mary says (Luke 1:55): "As He spoke to our fathers, to Abraham and to his posterity forever."

June 29

"I will surely bless you, and I will surely multiply your offspring as the stars of heaven and as the sand that is on the seashore."

GENESIS 22:17

Stars and Sand

hese words are the subject matter and the gushing fountain, as it were, of many of the prophecies and addresses of Isaiah, David, and Paul. Moreover, they agree with the preceding promises, which are found in Genesis 12:3: "In you all the families of the earth will be blessed" and in Genesis 15:5: "Look toward heaven, and number the stars, if you are able; so shall your descendants be." But this promise is clearer and more explicit. Above God said: "In you, Abraham, all the families of the earth will be blessed." There his Seed is included, but it is not expressed. But in this passage it is expressly stated: "In your Seed." In opposition to the nonsense of the Jews, however, Paul declares and explains that this Seed is Christ (Galatians 3:16). Then all nations are mentioned. Hence this promise also pertains to us Gentiles and to all who will ever hear and accept it, not only to the Jews.

*"And by your Seed shall all the nations of the earth be blessed,
because you have obeyed My voice."*

GENESIS 22:18 (according to Luther's translation)

The Blessing in the Seed

ll glorying is excluded by the phrase "in your Seed," which is added to the promise. That Seed sets aside all other blessings and the glory of one's own righteousness and bestows His on us, namely, "that which is through faith in Christ, the righteousness from God that depends on faith" (Philippians 3:9). Therefore all nations will bless themselves in no other than "in your Seed." In Him are all the treasures of wisdom, righteousness, and holiness; and whatever there will be anywhere among them that is praiseworthy they will have in its entirety through this Seed. . . . Abraham was endowed with many extraordinary virtues and gifts which he surely should have acknowledged and praised; but he has no glory before God, because all glorying is excluded. . . . Because God blesses solely in this Seed of Abraham, He also wants us to be blessed and to bless ourselves in this Seed; that is, we should glory and maintain with assurance that this Seed is ours and belongs to us with all its good things and heavenly treasures. . . . For from Him and in Him we are the blessed of Christ and the anointed, and every one of us can make this boast: "Christ is my formal blessing, anointing, life, and salvation, because I cling to Him; and by this one who blesses I am designated as blessed, and I call myself blessed."

July 1

"And by your Seed shall all the nations of the earth be blessed,
because you have obeyed My voice."

GENESIS 22:18 (according to Luther's translation)

The Promise Depends on the Seed

he Hebrew way of expressing itself in the case of the verb "to bless" should be carefully noted and pondered: "All nations will bless themselves." For it denotes that full assurance and nature of faith that I must maintain with certainty and without any doubt that I am blessed and declare myself truly alive, saved, righteous, and blessed. Otherwise I do wrong to the Seed of Abraham, namely, to Christ, the Author of life and salvation. For the promise does not depend on my merits or works; it depends on the Seed of Abraham. By Him I am blessed when I apprehend Him in faith; and the blessing clings to me in turn and permeates my entire body and soul, so that even the body itself is made alive and saved through the same Seed. And that begins in this life through faith when the soul, weighed down by death and sin, is buoyed up and receives the comfort of life and salvation. At some later time, in the resurrection of the dead, the body will follow the soul without any hindrance—not instrumentally but effectively and, as it were, formally—to the point that our lowly body will be changed "to be like the glorious body of Christ" (Philippians 3:21).

"By your Seed shall all the nations of the earth be blessed."

GENESIS 22:18 (according to Luther's translation)

We Are Blessed in the Seed

e, too, who believe that this Seed is our blessing, have good reason to glory and act proudly over against all the gates of hell and against Satan himself with all his scales and mobs. To be sure, we are compelled to bear the hate and cruelty of our enemies; but "in all these things we are more than conquerors through Him who loved us" (Romans 8:37). If we are Christians and believe in the Seed who blesses us, what do we care if the devil or the world is angry? For all we care, let them take away what we have, and let them kill the body. They will not for this reason keep us in death, will they? Not at all, for we are blessed and are sure of life over against death and of the grace and favor of God over against the hatred of the world. . . . Thus our doctrine has been clearly proved, and that of our opponents has been refuted. We are blessed in Christ, not in ourselves; that is, we must maintain with assurance that the blessing comes through Christ.

Sarah lived 127 years;
these were the years of the life of Sarah.
GENESIS 23:1

The Kinds of Life

consideration of the years of the lives of Sarah would be more profitable. For Moses is referring to the great and infinite variety of changes, misfortunes, and perils, as well as to the very widely different kinds of life that Sarah saw and bore. She was born in Babylon, and there she married. Soon after this she left with her husband and lived in Haran. Later on she dwelt in the land of Canaan. There Abraham was a sojourner. Finally he came to Egypt and Gerar. These most annoying changes and migrations the very saintly mother endured with great courage, and in regard to every outcome of all her misfortunes she was most patient. . . . Scripture has no comments even on the death of other matriarchs, just as it makes no mention of how many years Eve lived and of where she died. Of Rachel it is recorded that she died in childbirth (Genesis 35:16–19). All the other women it passes over and covers with silence, with the result that we have no knowledge of the death of Mary, the mother of Christ. Sarah alone has this glory, that the definite number of her years, the time of her death, and the place of her burial are described. Therefore this is great praise and very sure proof that she was precious in the eyes of God.

And Abraham went in to mourn for Sarah
and to weep for her.

GENESIS 23:2

Abraham Wept

y this example Holy Scripture shows that mourning or weeping over dead parents, a wife, or friends does not displease God. Indeed, it is wrong not to weep. The world, which is totally leprous, calls the lack of natural affection—which means not being influenced by affection or love for one's wife, children, or relatives—courage; but this is utter madness and is not a virtue. . . . Moreover, it belongs to mourning that you grieve and are sad from the heart, to the extent that a sad face, tears, sighs, and lamenting reveal your grief. It is for this reason that Moses writes clearly and commends Abraham's mourning and lamenting. Observe also how Jacob weeps on account of Joseph (Genesis 37:34–35). Accordingly, the saintly fathers were affected by the misfortunes and disasters of human nature. They wept with those who wept (Romans 12:15). They were not logs and blocks of wood. No, they had most tender emotions and affections. For they had a knowledge of God. He who knows God also knows, understands, and loves the creature, because there are traces of divinity in the creature.

The Honorable Marriage

he canonists [scholars devoted to the study of ecclesiastical law] define wedlock in an exceedingly frigid manner. It is the union of male and female, they say, in accordance with the law of nature. This is a very poor and weak definition. . . . Theology has a different definition. Marriage, it says, is the inseparable union of one man and one woman, not only according to the law of nature but also according to God's will and pleasure, if I may use this expression. For the will and approval and that favor of God cover the wretched depravity of lust and turn away God's wrath, which is in store for such lust and sins. In this way matrimony is treated with reverence. . . . What this passage teaches is that parents should concern themselves about an honorable marriage for their sons and daughters. . . . But I warn again that for entering into marriage it is above all necessary to call upon God that He may choose and bestow the wife or husband. If this is done, God's blessing and all good fortune in marriage follow.

"The LORD, the God of heaven . . .
He will send His angel before you."

GENESIS 24:7

An Angel before You

his very excellent conclusion, by which [Abraham] establishes with certainty that angels will be with his servant, is based on God's promises: "I have a God who has angels; He will send an angel to accompany and help you." This is an altogether marvelous statement and trust which leads him to believe that this work has already been entrusted to the angels in order that they may be present with his servant. He thought: "I shall do my part; I shall give my servant gifts to bring to the bride. God will add an angel to take care of the rest." Thus he commits the matter to God and the angels in complete and perfect faith. He thinks that those heavenly spirits and princes are engaged in this seemingly insignificant, carnal, and foolish work. And so sure is he about their service that he knows and believes not only that he has the angels at home, but that they are also present wherever he sends his servant. Because we have the God of heaven and earth, the angels are our protectors, guardians, yes, our attendants, wherever we are.

"[God] will send His angel before you."

GENESIS 24:7

The Companionship of Angels

 ince we know that we are enjoying the companionship, protection, and friendship of the angels, let us give thanks to God, and let us imitate their virtues and services of love and of mutual goodwill. . . . Let us learn that our best and most steadfast friends are invisible, namely, the angels, who in their faithfulness, goodwill, and friendly services far surpass our visible friends, just as the invisible wicked angels and devils are enemies more dangerous than those who are visible. Whatever mischief is done springs from the former rather than from the latter, whom we see with our eyes. On the other hand, if anything good happens, it is performed entirely by the good angels. Therefore if we believe and are godly, the good angels are our best friends, just as they were the best friends of Isaac and Rebecca, who were sinners and undeserving of such great assistance. But because they believed, they had angels joined to them as their servants. Thus we, too, should maintain that we are enjoying the companionship of the heavenly spirits, no matter how greatly we are marred by sins and how unworthy we are of the service of such excellent creatures.

"O Lord, God of my master Abraham, please grant me success today." . . . Before [the servant] had finished speaking, behold, Rebekah . . . came out with her water jar on her shoulder.

Hearer of Prayer

his passage presents a clear example of God's mercy and kindness in hearing the prayers of the godly. By means of this example we are invited to pray, and our faith is marvelously strengthened against mistrust and doubt. For these events have been recorded, not for the sake of the servant but for your sake and mine. Before he had stopped speaking, behold, his prayer was heard; while he was speaking, God said yes to his prayer. Therefore let us persuade ourselves without any hesitation that God is ever so ready and prompt to hear our prayer and to grant what we ask for, as Psalm 66:20 praises Him: "Blessed be God, because He has not rejected my prayer or removed His steadfast love from me!" And the name of God that is suitable to the highest degree and proper is Hearer of Prayer. Indeed, it is just as proper as the familiar name Creator of Heaven and Earth. And God not only hears a prayer that is offered without specifying particulars; but let us maintain that even at the very moment a prayer is uttered that which is asked for is being done or has been done, just as very many ever so pleasing words of the psalms testify, such as "To Thee they cried, and were saved" (Psalm 22:5), where simply no particular at all is added.

Before the Prayer Is Done

 e should not have any doubt] about being heard; but we should leave the place, the time, and all particulars to the will and counsel of God. Whoever does this will experience through the actual result how wonderful the power and efficacy of prayer is. For "likewise the Spirit also helps us in our weakness . . . and intercedes for us with sighs too deep for words" (Romans 8:26). And Ephesians 3:20 states: "Who is able to do far more abundantly than all that we ask or think." We ask solely for these outward blessings: peace, quiet, good health, and the things necessary for this life. But God's power surpasses all our understanding, hope, and asking. Consequently, God bestows on those who call upon Him more and greater things than the human heart can comprehend or request; for we worship Him whose power and beneficence are boundless. Indeed, He also determines all the particulars, the place, the time, and the person far better and more successfully than we would prescribe with our thinking. Therefore let us habituate and stir up our hearts to prayer, in order that many may pray together; for the greater the number of those who will pray, the more quickly and more abundantly they will get what they ask for.

When [Rebekah] had finished giving him a drink,
she said, "I will draw water for your camels also."

GENESIS 24:19

Kindness to All

t is not hospitable enough to have given him a drink; she also gives a drink to the camels and the rest of the servants. She is so obliging and godly that she does not consider it beneath her dignity to be the maid-servant of the stranger and his camels. For this reason she is later on raised to such a high position of honor that she becomes a matriarch. These were evidently the customs of the most ancient fathers, who accustomed their children to the ordinary duties of kindheartedness and respect toward any people whatever, in order that they might be ready to serve others and to converse with them in a pleasant and friendly manner. These virtues the Holy Spirit commends in this passage. He even describes every particular and motion, in order to indicate that all the works of the godly which proceed from a pure and believing heart are most pleasing to Him.

The man bowed his head and worshiped the LORD.

Thanksgiving for the Smallest Things

 he servant bows and gives thanks for the successful completion of the journey. Even though this is a small and worldly matter, he nevertheless praises God. Thus nothing is so paltry and inconsequential that it cannot be turned into a sacrifice and into worship of God; and in everything that is said and done God should be kept constantly in mind, in order that people may discern the gifts that have been bestowed by God and may be grateful. It is a trifling matter to look at a girl and to give her earrings. Nevertheless, they are all gifts of God, even though they are not great but are small; for the same God dispenses both kinds. Therefore one owes God worship, thanksgiving, and gratitude in very small matters just as in matters that are great. May the reverence and remembrance of God as the Author and Preserver of all things never disappear from the hearts of the godly! "Thus a man will be perfect and equipped for every good work" (2 Timothy 3:17), because he has been so trained that he maintains that God graciously bestows all good things, the smallest and the greatest, and says with this servant: "Blessed be the Lord, the God of heaven and earth." The life of such people is truly holy and is pleasing to God in all their activities, whether they eat, drink, sleep, or are awake.

July 12

*[Laban and Bethuel said], "The thing has come from the L*ORD*;*
we cannot speak to you bad or good. Behold, Rebekah is before
you; take her and go, and let her be the wife of your master's
*son, as the L*ORD *has spoken." When Abraham's servant heard*
*their words, he bowed himself to the earth before the L*ORD*.*

GENESIS 24:50–52

Arranged by the Lord

his marriage was arranged and confirmed by the Lord, who brought Rebecca to Isaac, just as He had brought Eve to Adam. The Holy Spirit has given this description that we may know that the union of a man and a woman is from the Lord, especially if it takes place with the consent of the parents and the girl, as happened here. Therefore the servant adds words of thanks for the bride bestowed by God. To that extent godliness abounds in all his activities, for in small matters as well as in great thanks should be given to God.

Abraham breathed his last and died in a good old age,
an old man and full of years, and was gathered to his people.

GENESIS 25:8

A Precious Death

n all Holy Scripture this is the first passage which declares that the death of the saints is peaceful and precious in the sight of God (Psalm 116:15) and that the saints do not taste death but most pleasantly fall asleep. Isaiah read and carefully expounded this passage, for from it there originated those striking statements he made: "The righteous man is taken away from calamity, he enters into peace; they rest in their beds" (57:1–2) and "Come, my people, enter your chambers, and shut your doors behind you; hide yourselves for a little while until the wrath is past" (26:20). In the eyes of the world the righteous are despised, spurned, and thrust aside. Their death seems exceedingly sad. But they are sleeping a most pleasant sleep. When they lie down in their beds and breathe their last, they die just as if sleep were gradually falling upon their limbs and senses. For previously they have been humbled by various trials, and they have become peaceful and quiet, so that they say: "Lord God, I shall die gladly if this seems best to Thee." They do not dread death as do the ungodly, who tremble and are horribly afraid. This they do to awaken us, in order that we may learn to obey God when He calls us out of this wretched state and may be able to say: "I do not want one hour to be added to my life, Lord Jesus Christ. Come when Thou wilt." In this way Abraham dies full of days, when he was well content.

Abraham breathed his last . . . and was gathered to his people.

GENESIS 25:8

Gathered with the Saints

hese words of the Holy Spirit are by no means useless. Nor are they spoken to beasts, which do not go to their fathers and their people. No, they are spoken to human beings, and they bear witness that after this life another and better life remains, yes, that even before the coming of Christ there was a people of the living which dwelt in the land of the living. To them the godly went away. Therefore from then on the fathers had an understanding of the resurrection and of eternal life, and the words of each passage are used in their proper and clear sense. "You will be gathered to the rest of the saints," they say, "who have died before you. Therefore the fathers are living and are a people." This is not said about the ungodly, but the discussion is about the righteous and the saints. . . . Accordingly this serves to comfort us, lest we, like others, who have no hope (1 Thessalonians 4:13), be frightened by or shudder at death. For in Christ death is not bitter, as it is for the ungodly, but it is a change of this wretched and unhappy life into a life that is quiet and blessed. This statement should convince us fully that we do not pass from a pleasant life into a life that is unhappy, but that we pass from afflictions into tranquility. For since the fathers had this comfort from these few passages long before Christ, how much more reasonable it is for us to guard and preserve the same comfort! We have it in far greater abundance.

July 15

After the death of Abraham, God blessed Isaac his son. . . .
These are the generations of Ishmael . . .

GENESIS 25:11–12

Delayed Blessing

[Moses] says that God blessed Isaac after the death of his father. But he soon breaks off, and in few words he completes what there is still to say about Ishmael. But he does not speak of the blessing [of Isaac] until the proper time for this has come. For it was delayed 20 years, during which Isaac lived with his wife Rebecca without offspring. . . . Reason dreams that God has to be worshiped and appeased with physical sacrifices or other exercises devised by men. But the examples of the fathers show that the foremost and best worship is to wait for God. And this is the real benefit and the most appropriate exercise of faith. For faith first carries us away into things that are invisible when it points out that things that are not apparent to the eye must be accepted. This we can somehow bear and put up with. The heart, however, is not only led into what is invisible; but it is also kept in suspense and is put off for a long time, just as Abraham . . . waited for 25 years before a son was born to him, and Isaac is without offspring for 20 years. But the third and by far the most serious thing is experienced when delay and postponement are followed by a disposition to the opposite effect. It is then that he who is able to endure and wait, to hope for the things that are being delayed, and to be pleased with what is contrary, will eventually learn from experience that God is truthful and keeps His promises.

These are the sons of Ishmael and these are their names, by
their villages and by their encampments,
twelve princes according to their tribes.

GENESIS 25:16

Twelve Princes

 shmael, who is the brother born of a slave woman, is honored by a blessing so great and glorious that in a short time he begets 12 princes. . . . This was surely a severe trial for faith, hope, and love. Would these things not try a heart, no matter how godly and saintly it might be? Above all, however, they try the heart of Isaac, who believed God and heard himself preferred to all nations and to his brother Ishmael. . . . Here, however, everything seems to be changed and turned around. Isaac, who has the true promise, is put after Ishmael; and although the latter has only a carnal promise, he goes very far ahead and becomes a lord of lords. He has 12 princes, while Isaac lives alone and without offspring. . . . When you have a promise of God, it will happen that the more you are loved by God, the more you will have it hidden, delayed, and turned into its opposite. For if God did not love you exceedingly, He would not play with you in this manner; that is, He would not delay His promise and help and turn it into its opposite. . . . Therefore the examples of the fathers teach us what the true forms of worship are, namely, genuine faith, perfect hope, and unwavering love. These virtues lead us to the realization that God is present and beneficent, no matter how He seems to be against us.

July 17

Isaac prayed to the LORD for his wife, because she was barren.

GENESIS 25:21

Call upon God with Persistence

et us seek and let us cast all our care, misfortune, and affliction on God (1 Peter 5:7) and set before Him the examples of every kind of deliverance. Finally let us knock at the door with confidence and with incessant raps. Then we shall experience what James says (5:16): "The prayer of a righteous man has great power"; for it penetrates heaven and earth. God can no longer endure our cries, as is stated in Luke 18:5 about the unjust judge and the widow. But one should not pray only one hour. No, one must cry out and knock. Then you will compel Him to come. Thus I fully believe that if we devote ourselves to prayer earnestly and fervently, we shall prevail upon God to make the Last Day come. In the same way Rebecca took refuge in earnest and persistent prayer and sighed anxiously night and day. Isaac, too, prayed for her and placed before God nothing else than that one trouble, namely, his wife's barrenness. We should learn from this that all our troubles, even those that are physical, should be placed before God, but above all the spiritual needs. . . . Where a promise is lacking, as Rebecca lacked it, prayer should supply this and should come to the rescue. But it is a difficult thing and requires great exertion. It is far more difficult than the preaching of the Word or other duties in the Church. When we teach, we experience more than we do; for God speaks through us, and it is a work of God. But to pray is a most difficult work. Therefore it is also very rare.

July 18

Rebekah his wife conceived. The children struggled together within her. . . . So she went to inquire of the LORD. And the LORD said to her, "Two nations are in your womb, and two peoples from within you shall be divided; the one shall be stronger than the other, the older shall serve the younger."

GENESIS 25:21–23

God Truly Hears

After she has become pregnant, Rebecca has no doubts whatever that she had been heard and helped by God. But that confidence is immediately disturbed by a new and unexpected danger. For the fetuses struggle with each other in her womb, so that she is again driven to despair. But when her trepidation is at its greatest, God buoys her up once more with the Word and indicates that she has been truly heard. . . . An earnest and fervent prayer, which does not cease and does not become tired but keeps on waiting up to the last moment, eventually forces its way through heaven and earth, and it is impossible for it not to be heard. For it is a sacrifice most pleasing to God when we pray in such a way that the prayer surpasses our comprehension and understanding, as is stated in the Epistle to the Ephesians: "Who is able to do far more abundantly than all that we ask or think" (3:20). When the situation is hopeless and all plans and efforts are in vain, then be courageous, and beware of giving up; for God calls all things from the dead and from nothing. When no resource or hope at all is left, then at last God's help begins. And so these are perfect prayers.

She went to inquire of the LORD.

GENESIS 25:22

God Has Promised to Hear

 his is written for our instruction and comfort, in order that we may learn to pray with full confidence and not to despair or have any doubt about being heard. Although prayer is offered contrary to and beyond understanding, yet it is not unavailing; for God does not want us to insult Him by thinking that He is not truthful. And this is why He has told us to pray. He has not only commanded us to do so; but He has also promised that He will hear, in order that we might maintain with assurance that He wants to grant what we are asking for. Therefore it is the highest type of religion and worship to believe that God is truthful. Besides, we have a simple and definite form in which He has prescribed what we should pray for and how this should be done. Therefore if you pray: "Our Father, etc.," think: "Thou, O Lord, hast told me to pray and hast promised that Thou wilt hear him who prays." Nor should you have any doubts about God's truth and promises. Even if the devil were to overturn the entire world in a single moment, the name of God will nevertheless be hallowed. And even if we all had to die, yet we are undoubtedly preserved and watched over for the future resurrection. Indeed, we see the manifest power and efficacy of our prayer; for the government of the world is surely preserved through prayer, our life is preserved, and all the good things we enjoy in this world are preserved.

July 20

Esau was a skillful hunter, a man of the field.

GENESIS 25:27

An Indifferent Life

sau] is completely smug and chooses a kind of life that is not irksome or difficult but pleasant and showy. . . . Such ungodliness and smugness follow when the Word of God is despised and is not made use of. People become atheists, Epicureans [those who are interested in material pleasure and allowing passion free reign], and bereft of reason. The examples of even very excellent people prove this. David was a very saintly man and most ardent in his worship of God. But how quickly he is driven to adultery, murder, and blasphemy! For to be asleep with regard to the Word of God is to open the window to the devil. Therefore we have been commanded to be watchful, as is written in 1 Peter 5:8: "Be sober, be watchful. Your adversary the devil prowls around like a roaring lion, seeking someone to devour." And Ephesians 5:15 says: "Look carefully, then, how you walk, not as unwise men but as wise, making the most of the time." Sluggishness and indifference in sacred matters have often resulted in the greatest lapses and in horrible sins.

Jacob was a quiet man, dwelling in tents.

GENESIS 25:27

The House That Is a Church

he Hebrew word translated as "quiet" here] denotes one who is simple, upright, blameless, and sincere in regard to his will. The same word occurs in Psalm 119:1: "Blessed are the blameless." For, as is evident later on when he buys the birthright from his brother, Jacob is not dull. . . . In the second place, Jacob is not a man of the fields. He has no political and carnal pursuits—although affairs of state can be administered in a godly and proper manner—but he dwelt exclusively in tents; that is, he remained at home with his father and mother, and served them. . . . [The Jewish commentators on this passage] say that tents not only for the households but also for the churches are meant. . . . At that time there was no difference between the sacred tents and those occupied by households. Abraham had in his tent a house of God and a church, just as today any godly and pious head of a household instructs his children and domestics in godliness. Therefore such a house is actually a school and church, and the head of the household is a bishop and priest in his house. Thus the tents in which Jacob dwelt were sacred, and there he sought first the kingdom of God (Matthew 6:33). . . . Yet we, too, shall properly call our houses and churches tents when someone has a church in his home and in it instructs his children and domestics in godliness and virtue. But the more fervent and vigorous the spirit with which the Word is treated, the more fruit it brings.

July 22

Esau said, "I am about to die; of what use is a birthright to me?"

GENESIS 25:32

What Use Is a Birthright?

 his is important evidence of Holy Scripture that Esau has already lost his birthright; for he is judged out of his own mouth. Yet he undoubtedly thought: "I am the lord; I shall indeed sell my birthright, but I shall only fool him. Even if I do sell it, still I can get it back." . . . And today many misuse the doctrine of the Gospel and meanwhile flatter themselves by saying: "Even if I persist in sins and am a godless person, still I shall eventually recover and return to the way." . . . But all these people will finally hear that sad verdict which appears in the Epistle to the Hebrews (12:17) concerning Esau: "For you know that afterward, when he desired to inherit the blessing, he was rejected; for he found no chance to repent though he sought it with tears." . . . Thus when Esau says: "I am about to die; of what use is the birthright to me?" he indicates that he is thinking only of his belly and that he is scorning the promise as worthless and unprofitable for the future life, precisely as the Epicureans [those who are interested in material pleasure and allowing passion free reign] say today: "Why is it necessary to hear the Gospel and to make use of the Keys or the Lord's Supper?" But Jacob thinks differently and knows that these sacred things are preparations for the life to come. Therefore he esteems them highly and burns with desire for them.

Now there was a famine in the land.

GENESIS 26:1

The Purpose of Affliction

he godly, too, are afflicted, just as Isaac endured want and famine in his time. He was a stranger and an exile, and he thought that he should bear the current misfortune calmly. But the purpose of these afflictions should be carefully noted. Although public misfortunes affect the saints and the prophets, this does not happen as a punishment or because of anger, as in the case of the godless and the ungrateful; it happens for their salvation and to test and prove their faith, love, and patience, in order that the godly may learn to bear the hand of God in the management of their households. For God has promised that He wants to support them in the time of famine, as it is written (Psalm 37:25): "I have not seen the righteous forsaken." Likewise (Psalm 37:19): "In the days of famine they have abundance." God confirms these promises with such examples of the saints, and by means of this tribulation in the household He instructs the godly in the Word, in faith, in humility of spirit, in love, and in other virtues.

July 24

And the Lord appeared to [Isaac] and said . . .

GENESIS 26:2

Divine Appearances

 t is surely a great thing for God to appear to a human being and to fit His promises to a particular individual. For this reason many consider the saintly fathers far more blessed in this respect than we are, since they had such definite and individual comforts and appearances from God through the ministry of the angels. Someone will say: "If He were to appear to me, too, in a human form, what great joy this would bring to my heart! Then I would surely not be reluctant to undergo any peril or misfortunes for God's sake. But this has been denied me. I only hear sermons, read Scripture, and make use of the Sacraments. I have no appearances of angels." I answer: You have no reason to complain that you have been visited less than Abraham or Isaac. You, too, have appearances, and in a way they are stronger, clearer, and more numerous than those they had, provided that you open your eyes and heart and take hold of them. You have Baptism. You have the Sacrament of the Eucharist, where bread and wine are the species, figures, and forms in which and under which God in person speaks and works into your ears, eyes, and heart. Besides, you have the ministry of the Word and teachers through whom God speaks with you. You have the ministry of the Keys, through which He absolves and comforts you. "Fear not," He says, "I am with you." . . . What more will you desire? Everything is full of divine appearances and conversations.

"Sojourn in this land, and I will be with you and will bless you, for to you and to your offspring I will give all these lands, and I will establish the oath that I swore to Abraham your father."

GENESIS 26:2–3

Confirmation of the Promises

 od spoke with Abraham rather often. But with Isaac He spoke barely two or three times. And this is also enough, for here, in a kind of summary, He confirms all His promises, lest the very saintly patriarch begin to have doubts about God's will when the devil tempts him. For the devil does not cease to harass even the saintliest and most perfect men with his fiery and poisonous darts (cf. Ephesians 6:16). Furthermore, this promise has two parts. The first is temporal. It deals with the possession of these lands. . . . Yet by means of that earlier connection of Abraham himself and the Seed, eternal life and the resurrection are pointed out to believers, namely, that Abraham, Isaac, and Jacob are the possessors of this land, even though they did not own even a footbreadth. For even though they died, yet they live. Therefore this possession pertains to them, since Abraham is not dead but lives. Furthermore, when God says: "To you and to your descendants," it is also pointed out that the descendants would not have possessed the land if the fathers had not received the promise. And in the faith of the fathers the descendants got possession of the land. The second part of the promise is spiritual, and because of this spiritual promise the physical promise was given.

"And in your offspring all the nations of the earth shall be blessed, because Abraham obeyed My voice and kept My charge, My commandments, My statutes, and My laws."

GENESIS 26:4–5

Abraham's Reward

hese are grand and glorious things, and they cannot be repeated and impressed enough; for they are words of comfort and eternal life. Thus Christ impresses the same things on His disciples often and diligently, as in John 14:1: "Let not your hearts be troubled; believe in God, believe also in Me." Likewise (John 14:19): "Because I live, you will live also." Likewise (John 16:33): "Be of good cheer; I have overcome the world and the devil." How? "Through My victory, which is yours." This passage concerning Abraham's promise and faith is the chief and foremost passage in all Holy Scripture. Thus Christ praises this faith in John 8:56 when He says: "Abraham saw My day and was glad." . . . For this blessing was not given to Abraham in order that he might be made righteous through it; but since he was already righteous through faith, he received this blessing as a very excellent reward. He is righteous, obedient, and saintly. And because he is so obedient, he will be exalted to such an extent that Christ will put on flesh from his seed, as Romans 9:5 says. It it indeed a great honor that He who is the Son of God, the Destroyer of hell, the Victor over death, the Abrogator of the Law, and the Restorer of eternal life comes from the seed of Abraham.

July 27

When the men of the place asked him about his wife, he said,
"She is my sister," for he feared to say, "My wife," thinking, "lest
the men of the place should kill me because of Rebekah."

GENESIS 26:7

No Excuses

 am glad to hear about the failings and the weaknesses of the saints. But I do not praise these failings and weaknesses as good deeds or virtues. Thus I do not excuse the apostles when they flee from Christ, and I do not excuse Peter when he denies Him. Nor do I excuse other weaknesses in them and other foolish and silly things they do. Nor are these things recorded for the sake of the hard, the proud, and the obstinate. No, they are recorded in order that the nature of the kingdom of Christ may be pointed out. In His small flock He has poor and weak consciences that are easily hurt and are not easily comforted. He is a King of the strong and the weak alike; He hates the proud and declares war on the strong. He rebukes the Pharisees and those who are smug. But He does not want to break or confound the fearful, the fainthearted, the sorrowful, and the perplexed. He does not want to quench a dimly burning wick (Isaiah 42:3; Matthew 12:20). This is His way and constant practice. Thus He has acted from the beginning of the world to the end.

How to Overcome Fear

he godly should beware and be intent only on learning to cling to the Child and Son Jesus, who is your God and was made flesh for your sake. Acknowledge and hear Him; take pleasure in Him, and give thanks. If you have Him, then you also have the hidden God together with Him who has been revealed. And that is the only way, the truth, and the life (cf. John 14:6). Apart from it you will find nothing but destruction and death. But He manifested himself in the flesh to snatch us from death, from the power of the devil. From this knowledge must come great joy and delight that God is unchangeable, that He works in accordance with unchangeable necessity, and that He cannot deny Himself (2 Timothy 2:13) but keeps His promises. . . . When the devil assails you with [doubts about salvation], you should only say: "I believe in our Lord Jesus Christ, about whom I have no doubt that He was made flesh, suffered, and died for me. Into His death I have been baptized." This answer will make the trial disappear, and Satan will turn his back.

Abimelech called Isaac and said, "Behold, she is your wife.
How then could you say, 'She is my sister'?" Isaac said to him,
"Because I thought, 'Lest I die because of her.'"

GENESIS 26:9

How to Defeat Doubt

ell-founded fear can be becoming to him and can befit a steadfast man. This is the way Isaac fears and is weak. Yet he is excused, for he is fearful as a steadfast man. But it pleases me to take from this passage the opportunity to discuss doubt, God, and the will of God. . . . You must kill the other thoughts and the ways of reason or of the flesh, for God detests them. The only thing you have to do is to receive the Son, so that Christ is welcome in your heart in His birth, miracles, and cross. For here is the book of life in which you have been written. And this is the only and the most efficacious remedy for that horrible disease because of which human beings in their investigation of God want to proceed in a speculative manner and eventually rush into despair or contempt. If you want to escape despair, hatred, and blasphemy of God, give up your speculation about the hidden God, and cease to strive in vain to see the face of God. Otherwise you will have to remain perpetually in unbelief and damnation, and you will have to perish; for he who doubts does not believe, and he who does not believe is condemned (Mark 16:16).

Abimelech warned all the people, saying, "Whoever touches
this man or his wife shall surely be put to death."

GENESIS 26:11

Peace in the Midst of Enemies

ou see how kind the Lord is to His saints. To be sure, He tests them, sends them into exile, lets them be exposed to danger of their reputation and their life, and permits them to be afflicted with famine and misfortunes of every kind; yet He provides excellent, quiet, and safe hospitality and grants peace in the midst of their enemies. These things are recorded to strengthen our faith—even if perils and misfortunes rush in, just as Isaac is living in the utmost danger—that God nevertheless leads and preserves us. For the Church must have a place and nest on this earth. If one or another prince does not want to protect us, God will give someone else to provide hospitality in a kindly manner. And for the most part He is wont to choose a host without our advice or judgment, yes, even beyond and contrary to our hope and expectation. In this way Isaac obtained safety and quiet in that land, and later on he became exceedingly rich, with the result that the inhabitants begrudged him such great good fortune and he was compelled to move to another place. All this is related in order that we may believe in God, who leads and preserves us; for when we have the Word, we are indeed exercised by sundry perils, but in such a way that we do not perish or despair in the trial but rejoice in peace and give thanks to God.

And Isaac sowed in that land and reaped in the same year a
hundredfold. The LORD blessed him.

GENESIS 26:12

Staying Strong While We Wait

et us learn from this passage to persevere in faith,
lest we doubt or waver if some trial comes upon us.
For note how generously God recompenses Isaac for
the earlier trial, in order that we may know that He is not
angry forever. And since we have the promise, let us hold out
in trials and conclude: "The Lord, who said to me: 'Believe,'
will surely keep His promise. Meanwhile I shall wait in accordance with the words 'Wait for the Lord, be strong, etc.'
(Psalm 27:14), 'Be strong, and let your heart take courage, all
you who wait for the Lord' (Psalm 31:24). The godly should
wait and persevere even in greatest dangers and adversities; for He has promised that He wants to take care of us.
1 Peter 5:7 states: 'Cast all your anxieties on Him, for He
cares about you.'" The exercises of faith are necessary for
the godly; for without them their faith would grow weak and
lukewarm, yes, would eventually be extinguished. But from
this source they assuredly learn what faith is; and when they
have been tried, they grow in the knowledge of the Son of
God and become so strong and firm that they can rejoice and
glory in misfortunes no less than in days of prosperity and
can regard any trial at all as nothing more than a little cloud
or a fog which vanishes forthwith.

So Isaac departed from there and encamped in the Valley of Gerar and settled there. And Isaac dug again the wells of water that had been dug in the days of Abraham his father, which the Philistines had stopped after the death of Abraham.

GENESIS 26:17–18

The Exercise of the Faithful

hese things are presented to us as an example and a comfort; for if we have a promise, then it follows without fail that angels are round about us. This is why Psalm 34:7 states: "The angel of the Lord encamps around those who fear Him." Likewise Psalm 91:11: "He will give His angels charge of you." This they believed firmly and without any doubt. Therefore we, too, if we are godly, should believe in the promise of Him who cannot lie. Then we are surely under His protection, and it is also certain that angels are with us. But if any evil befalls us beyond, or contrary to, this trust and protection, this happens because of a special purpose that is hidden from us and especially from our adversaries. . . . But without a trial we learn nothing and make no progress. For this is the warfare and the exercise of Christians through which we learn that we are under the protection of the angels, and that although we are plagued by severe and difficult trials, yet they do us no harm. This is our theology. It is not learned easily or suddenly; but we must meditate constantly on the Law and stand in battle array against the devil, who tries to draw us away from the study of the Word and to make our faith weak.

August 2

And the LORD appeared to [Isaac] the same night and said,
"I am the God of Abraham your father. Fear not, for I am with
you and will bless you and multiply your offspring
for My servant Abraham's sake."

GENESIS 26:24

I Am Your God

We should sustain ourselves with this comfort, and we should look for it with firm confidence. The voice from heaven sets it before us: "I am your God; I am the Gods of Abraham; you are My servants." As Isaiah 26:19 says: "Arise, O dwellers in the dust; because My dead bodies shall arise. Thy dew is like the dew of the meadows." There God speaks with the dead just as if they were living; and this very Word is the most powerful proof that we are not mortal, but that we are immortal even in death. For God speaks with us even in our own speech and in human language. God knows that this life is short. But why would He speak with us, and indeed in such a manner that He employs our own language, if we did not live forever? For otherwise He would be uttering His Word in vain for the sake of only a moment of time. But He does not speak in vain. . . . The person of God, who speaks, and the Word point out that we are the kind of creatures with whom God would want to speak eternally and in an immortal manner. Such a God or Gods, as He is called here, Abraham has; and he who clings to Abraham's promise has the same God and is a servant of God. Eventually he will live while he sleeps, even though he is dead.

Look for Eternal Blessings

s for you, if God tries and scourges you, believe, and be satisfied with the Word you have in Psalm 91:15: "I am with you in trouble. I will deliver you, not only from trouble but from death, sickness, and shame. I will care for you." To be sure, the eyes do not see this, nor do the hands touch it; but to the believer all things are possible. And what has been said in this passage to the patriarch Isaac, the same thing is said to us: "I am with you, and I will keep what I have promised. From Me you must look not only for physical blessings but also for eternal blessings." "But assuredly the opposite is apparent," says Isaac. "It seems that Thou art cursing me. I must perish of thirst together with my wife, my children, and my whole household. This is not a divine blessing, is it?" God's answer is: "Fear not. You will not perish of thirst." And He adds: "I will multiply your seed for My servant Abraham's sake. I will multiply you not only now but also your seed and descendants in the future." This is a repetition of the blessing together with an amplification by which He reassures him about eternal life and immortality.

Rebekah said to her son Jacob, "I heard your father speak to your brother Esau, 'Bring me game and prepare for me delicious food, that I may eat it and bless you before the LORD before I die.' Now therefore, my son, obey my voice as I command you."

GENESIS 27:6–8

The Foolishness of the Saints

At the beginning of this chapter the following facts should be carefully noted: in the first place, that the First Table [Exodus 20:3–8] must be given precedence over the Second [Exodus 20:12–17]; in the second place, that God pardons the foolishness and rashness of His saints, yes, even causes it to turn out successfully. Consequently, if you do anything wrong in any walk of life, you should not despair; but you should acknowledge your mistake with humility and think as follows: "God, who was able to lead Rebecca and Jacob out of such great danger, is all-powerful. Therefore I, too, shall not despair but shall be confident that He will bring me out of this misfortune." Although Rebecca's plan was rash, it had a fortunate outcome, because God brings the plans of the ungodly to nothing but honors and helps His saints.

"Now therefore, my son, obey my voice as I command you."

GENESIS 27:8

God's Instruments

et everyone diligently and faithfully do his duty which has been committed to him by God. But let him beware of relying on his own strength or his own wisdom and of considering himself such a great man that everything should be directed in accordance with what he counsels. For it is incurable and damnable rashness and arrogance on my part when I claim to be such a person and such an extraordinary man that I can manage the state, the home, and the church wisely and properly. But if you are a judge, a bishop, or a prince, you should not feel ashamed to fall on your knees and say: "Lord God, Thou hast appointed me as prince, judge, head of the household, and pastor of the church. Therefore guide and teach me, give me counsel, wisdom, and strength to attend successfully to the office committed to me." . . . Hence everyone should learn to acknowledge his weakness humbly and to ask *God* for wisdom and counsel. For men are not summoned to govern because they should arrogate to themselves perfect knowledge of everything, but because they should be taught and learn what God is and what He does through the government and the rulers, who are the instruments of God's works through which God rules the people. Then they become truly wise and successful in governing.

August 6

Jacob went near to Isaac his father, who felt him and said, "The voice is Jacob's voice, but the hands are the hands of Esau."

GENESIS 27:22

Blessing Versus Curse

od brings it about that Isaac is intent on his duty of blessing and removes [the doubt] from his mind. . . . Thus Holy Scripture presents the accounts of the saints in such a way that it gives praise to the power of faith. . . . Rebecca proves this power and might of faith with her exceedingly dangerous deed, where it was a matter of an eternal curse or an eternal blessing. For the blessing is eternal life; the curse is death. There is a debate about whether or not Jacob, and his mother with him, would be eternally cursed. In a conflict so great and arduous Rebecca sets the kingdom of heaven before her eyes as open and appoints herself the mother of the blessing. On what basis? On the basis of the Word. For nobody does anything successfully or believes without the Word. This text, "The elder shall serve the younger" [Genesis 25:23] gave her courage. From it she concluded that the blessing belonged to the younger, not to the older. To be sure, Isaac did not understand it; but the mother pondered it carefully, and the Holy Spirit collaborated. He gives no one faith through mere speculations. No, He gives it through the Word. . . . For since the things that are of the Holy Spirit are not apparent, everything seems hostile and dead. But when the heart takes hold of the Word, then the enlightenment of the Holy Spirit follows, and the power and might to do amazing things.

August 7

[Isaac said,] "May God give you of the dew of heaven and of the fatness of the earth and plenty of grain and wine."

GENESIS 27:28

Daily Bread Comes from God

his is the form of the blessing, and its first part pertains to the sustenance of the body; for without this we cannot live even in the kingdom of God so far as this life is concerned. For the body must be nourished if we must teach and govern the Church. Accordingly, the first part pertains to the management of the household and to household supplies, in order that wife, children, and domestics may have the necessities of daily life. In the Lord's Prayer this is called "daily bread," that is, everything that is needed in the house for the sustenance of the body. . . . Accordingly, Jacob is sure of sustenance in the household for himself and his descendants. And that sustenance will not be meager. No, it will be sumptuous and luxurious. And one can surely see in the Books of the Kings how this promise was fulfilled. Therefore the godly should acknowledge that they have their earthly things because God gives and blesses. Nor should they dream, as the heathen and the unbelievers do, that either the good or the evil things in this life come about by chance. On the contrary, they should acknowledge that these great gifts come from God. Therefore they should be grateful to God for these benefits, as the apostles declare in Acts 14:17: "He did good and gave us from heaven rains and fruitful seasons, satisfying our hearts with food and gladness."

August 8

"Let peoples serve you, and nations bow down to you."

GENESIS 27:29

Earthly Authority

 he second part of the blessing has to do with the state and pertains to authority; for Jacob is appointed lord over peoples and nations. His descendants will be princes and kings, not only heads of households. For peoples will serve him when they will be subjected, not to heads of households but to princes and kings. Not only one people but many peoples and many tribes will be subject. This was also fulfilled at the time of the judges and the kings, when the children of Israel occupied the land of Canaan, when they not only subjected the Idumaeans but also exterminated all the peoples and kings of that land.

"Cursed be everyone who curses you,
and blessed be everyone who blesses you!"

GENESIS 27:29

Victory in the Cross

 n the last part, the holy cross follows. Yet at the same time it is victory through and in the cross. . . The fact that Isaac pronounces this verdict shows that he has great power—power at which hell, together with its demons, and the whole world, with all its might, are compelled to tremble. For this is what he wants to say: "I know that these blessings will be odious to the devil, the world, and the flesh. I know that this is bound to happen, O Jacob. To be sure, I am heaping great gifts on you; I am exalting and glorifying you. For you will be a father without poverty, a king without hindrance, a priest and a saver of souls against the will of the gates of hell (cf. Matthew 16:18). But remember that all these things are a matter of promise, that they have not come to fulfillment in the complete victory which is still hoped for and in prospect. Therefore you will have these things in such a way that it will seem to you that you have nothing at all. For you will be assailed in the household, in the state, and in the church. The ungodly will envy you all these things, and you will be cursed by them in such a way that the curse has been made ready alongside the blessing. Although I am blessing you, the devil and the world will come, your brothers will come, and will curse you; they will persecute you and attempt to defeat and destroy your blessings."

August 10

Be Strong in the Face of Curses

ow many even very pious people . . . feel the curses and anguish of hell more than they feel the divine and heavenly blessings. . . . However, nothing departs from the blessing. No, the blessing remains unalterable, firm, exceedingly rich, and greater than we understand. Paul has the same complaint when he says (2 Corinthians 12:7) that a thorn was given him in the flesh and also (Acts 14:22) that we must enter the kingdom of heaven through many tribulations. Accordingly, curses will not be lacking. But go forth to face them more boldly, be strong, and cling steadfastly to the blessing, no matter how much everything seems to be full of a curse. For this is what we should conclude: It is sure that I have been baptized. I have heard the Word from the mouth of the minister. I have made use of the Sacrament of the Altar. This is the divine and unchangeable truth. Even though I am weak, it is sure and unalterable. . . . And if we are unable to confess with a loud shout, let us at least make ourselves heard in a low murmur as best we can. . . . For this reason Christ so assiduously exhorts us to persevere. "By your endurance you will gain your lives" (Luke 21:19). You are children of the kingdom, your sins are forgiven, the devil has been overcome and laid low under your feet, sin and death will do you no harm; but you are blameless. Therefore bear the hostile curses with equanimity.

Blessing through Trials

fter Isaac has mentioned the curses, that is, the cross and the trials which accompany those outstanding and rich blessings, he goes on to add: *"Blessed be everyone who blesses you!"* It is as though he were saying: "They will not all curse or assail you, but many will come who will bless you and share in your blessings. This will be the fruit of your trials if you continue steadfastly in the faith." Thus Christ says (John 12:24): "Truly, truly, I say to you, unless a grain of wheat falls into the earth and dies, it remains alone; but if it dies, it bears much fruit." One Christian who has been tried does more good than a hundred who have not been tried. For in trials the blessing grows, so that with its counsels it can teach, comfort, and help many in physical and spiritual matters. Thus in the world you are cursed, but at the same time you are filled with a heavenly blessing.

And Isaac . . . blessed [Jacob] . . .

GENESIS 27:27–29

Blessing Assailed but Not Overcome

ventually the outcome was in accord with the prophecy. For how much Jacob suffered immediately after the beginning of the blessing! . . . But this must be accepted and waited for with faith. Thus Jacob concluded in faith that nothing would ever be lacking in his household. And eventually the outcome was in very beautiful accord with this; when the blessing followed, he became richer than his father-in-law, Laban, but through trials. He was tried but not forsaken. For the blessing is assailed but not overcome. It is battered and jostled but not felled. Thus the psalm states (Psalm 118:13–14): "I was pushed hard, so that I was falling, but the Lord helped me. The Lord is my strength and my song; He has become my salvation." The Lord bestows a blessing mixed with patience and adorned with reminders of the holy cross, in order that we may be instructed in our trials and learn that our life depends not on bread alone but on every word of God. In the end, however, God surely and without fail supplies us with bread after we have been disturbed in faith about whether we are willing to believe God in His promises. For He makes a promise; but He tests us and withdraws His blessing, as though no blessing should be expected. But He really reflects on and is aware of the blessing when we feel the curse. Consequently, the blessing can be assailed and repressed; but, as is said about truth, it cannot be overwhelmed and subdued.

August 13

An Unchangeable Work

t this point the question is raised why Isaac did not revoke the blessing, since Jacob took it away with guile. . . . One should not imagine that Isaac, even though he was violently terrified, gave thought to a revocation; for he knew that the blessing was an utterly permanent and unchangeable work and gift of God. Thus when I give Baptism to someone, then my heart and will are completely certain that I really want to baptize. But if he who is being baptized acts deceitfully, I have still administered a true Baptism which is not my own but is truly a divine work. In this way Isaac also said: "I have blessed him, and he shall be blessed" [Genesis 27:33]. And this he previously decided earnestly in his own mind, and it was not without special deliberation that he put it off to the end of his life. Therefore he was certain that when he blessed, he was uttering a definitive statement pronounced and confirmed by divine authority. And it was the same blessing that he had received by hereditary right from the fathers: from Adam, Noah, Abraham, and the others. Such statements cannot and must not be changed, for God does not change His gifts. He does not revoke Baptism, absolution, and the other gifts He bestows through His Word. If He forgives me my sins, then they have truly been forgiven.

Esau said, "Is he not rightly named Jacob? For he has cheated
me these two times. He took away my birthright, and behold,
now he has taken away my blessing."

GENESIS 27:36

The Beginning of Hatred

With these words [Esau] lies most shamefully by saying that he is the firstborn when he is not and by saying that the birthright which he previously had given up voluntarily belongs to him. . . . He does not say: "I have sinned. Until now I did not realize and did not understand that I sinned. Now I am being taught by the punishment itself and by God's judgment. Now it is time to acknowledge my sin; for I realize that God has been horribly offended by my sale, by my contempt. But I do not begrudge my brother this blessing. No, I am sincerely fond of him, and I am glad that he got this blessing. I have sinned, and I am heartily sorry, not so much because the blessing has been lost as because God's wrath has been stirred up against me." He does not say or think this at all. Indeed, he glories in his wickedness. "I am righteous; my brother is wicked. He has fraudulently taken away what belongs to me, and he has possession of what does not belong to him. May this turn out badly for him!" In this manner he condemns the righteousness of another and defends his own sin. Finally he conceives horrible hatred for his brother, begrudges him the grace which God has bestowed on him and which he himself has lost in a lawful way and by his own fault. Over and above this, he threatens him with death. Truly a fine repentance!

August 15

"Have you but one blessing, my father? Bless me, even me also,
O my father." And Esau lifted up his voice and wept.

Treasure the Blessing

 et us enjoy the blessing we now have and the grace
that is offered after the light of the Gospel has reap-
peared, and let us not be indifferent or ungrateful.
For once the blessing has been taken away, it is not in our
power to recover it; it can be recovered only by reason of a
free gift of God, and in such a way that He is influenced by no
one's tears, cries, and exertions. First I saw this well, namely,
that the free gift is absolutely necessary for obtaining the light
and the heavenly life, and I worked anxiously and diligently
to understand the well-known statement in Romans 1:17:
"The righteousness of God is revealed in the Gospel." Then
I sought and knocked for a long time (cf. Matthew 7:7), for
that expression "the righteousness of God" stood in the way.
It was commonly explained by saying that the righteousness
of God is the power of God by which God Himself is formally
righteous and condemns sinners. This is the way all teachers
except Augustine had interpreted this passage: the righteousness of God, that is, the wrath of God. But every time I read
this passage, I always wished that God had never revealed
the Gospel—for who could love a God who is angry, judges,
and condemns?—until finally, enlightened by the Holy Spirit,
I weighed more carefully the passage in Habakkuk (2:4),
where I read: "The righteous shall live by his faith." From

this I concluded that life must come from faith. In this way I related the abstract to the concrete, and all Holy Scripture and heaven itself were opened to me. At this time, however we see that great light very clearly, and we may enjoy it richly. But we despise and disdain this jewel and heavenly treasure. Accordingly, if one day it should be taken away again, we shall cry and knock once more, as Christ says about the foolish virgins in the parable (cf. Matthew 25:11). But we shall cry and knock in vain. Therefore let us fear God and be grateful. Above all, however, my own example and the example of others should move you. We lived in death and hell and did not have the blessing so abundantly as you have it. Therefore occupy yourselves diligently with the doctrine of the blessing, and think about it, in order that you may be able to keep it yourselves and also to make it known to others.

Now Esau hated Jacob.

GENESIS 27:41

The Raging of the Devil

ou see how the devil rages in the home life and the household of even the saintliest people. It is not without cause that we warn so often and exhort and cry out so often that you should pray diligently and without ceasing. For the devil is not far away. No, he is in our midst. Observe what a disturbance he caused in the very holy Church of the fathers, in the house of Isaac, where Esau is plotting the destruction of his brother, the murder of his parents, and the overthrow and devastation of the entire Church. On the other hand, this grief is justifiable, and Esau has good reason to be so greatly disturbed. But it is his own fault; for he himself sinned, since he esteemed lightly and despised what he now desires so much. And now, when he feels God's wrath, he is driven to madness because of grief and impatience. Let us recognize this great malice of the *devil*.

[Rebecca said to Jacob,] "Arise, flee."

GENESIS 27:43

Live by Faith

his, then, is one of the wonderful examples of the divine government by which God shows that He requires confidence in His Word and promises, even if the opposite of what is contained in the promise happens. He does so in order that we may accustom ourselves to trust in God in things that are absent and are placed far out of our sight. For Jacob has the promised blessing, but he has it in accordance with faith, which is a matter of things that are hoped for, not of things that are visible (cf. Hebrews 11:1). Thus I believe that God, who promises, loves me, has regard for me, cares for me, and will hear me; and this I regard as something present and at hand, although it is not visible. Therefore Jacob lives in faith alone. He is wretchedly cast out, is lonely and destitute, and has nothing in his hand but a staff and a morsel of bread in a little sack. This is the beginning of the blessing, for what is begun through faith is not yet in one's possession but is hoped for. Thus God has promised us eternal life and has given absolution and Baptism. This grace I have at hand through Christ; but I await eternal life, which is promised in the Word. Those who live by this Word are saintly and blessed; but the godless live only by bread, not by the Word. Therefore they do not believe and do not wait for eternal life.

[Rebecca said,] "Arise, flee."

GENESIS 27:43

The Promised Glory Will Follow

ne learns by experience how difficult and full of trials it is to leave parents, a blessing, and an inheritance, and to flee to a place of wretchedness and poverty. . . . Thus we who believe the Word of God are the Church. We have a most certain promise, into which we have been called and baptized, and by which we are nourished and sustained; we have the Sacrament of the Altar and the power of the Keys. But we are not Christians and have not been baptized in order that we may get possession of this land. Nor have we been baptized and born again into this life; we have been baptized and born again into eternal life. But what happens in regard to us too? Surely this, that when the Church must be glorified and brought to those eternal joys which it awaits in the Word and in hope, then it is subjected to countless persecutions of tyrants and devils; it is harassed and torn by false brethren in many most pitiable ways. This is not what being led to eternal life means, is it? Indeed, it means being exposed to eternal misery. Yet hearts must be buoyed up and strengthened against this way of the cross. For we have the Word and the promise. Therefore the glory that has been promised is sure to follow. And meanwhile the Church lives and is preserved by faith, which concludes firmly that *God* does not lie. . . . We must depend simply on the invisible God and give thanks to God with joy that we have the Word of God, which makes the promise.

August 19

Isaac called Jacob and blessed him and directed him, . . .
"Take as your wife . . . one of the daughters of Laban your
mother's brother."

GENESIS 28:1–2

The Twofold Purpose of Marriage

hristians should so prepare themselves and so arrange their life that they do not consider marriage a rash or fortuitous matter depending on our judgment and a fortuitous outcome but regard it as a lawful and divine union. Clear proof of this is the fact that God created man and woman, and that neither a man alone nor a woman alone is born, but that both man and woman are born. Therefore this union has its origin in the first birth, and for this reason it is truly lawful and divine. Furthermore, God did not institute marriage for the sake of lust and the pleasures of the flesh. This is not the final cause, but marriage serves a twofold purpose: in the first place, to be a remedy against lust; in the second place—and this is more important—to be a source and origin of the human race, in order that offspring may be born and the human race may be propagated, or, as the jurists say, to replenish the city. But from the Holy Scriptures one should add the purpose of bringing up children in the discipline and fear of the Lord, in order that they may be equipped to govern the church and the state.

"God Almighty bless you and make you fruitful and multiply you, that you may become a company of peoples."

GENESIS 28:3

The Immediacy of the Blessing

bove Isaac gave blessings to his son Jacob. These he repeats in this passage with a wish. But the blessing, as we have also pointed out above, is the very thing that has been handed over and given forthwith. Thus Baptism is handed over to me now, and forgiveness of sins is handed over; for I do not hope for the remission of sins, but I have it forthwith in faith. I do not believe that Christ is going to suffer for me. No, through faith I am sure that He has suffered for my sins and risen for the sake of my righteousness (cf. Romans 4:25). Therefore it is not a mere prayer or wish; it is that by which through the power of the Keys I hand over to you now the remission of sins, the grace and favor of God, in order that you may be able to conclude with certainty that you have God, who is well pleased with you. This I hand over to you as a sure possession. Thus the Church has the favor and goodwill of the divine Majesty, of the Father, the Son, and the Holy Spirit, forthwith, of Christ and the angels, who give their congratulations, and of all creatures, who applaud and wait for its redemption, as is stated in Romans 8:19.

[Jacob] came to a certain place and stayed there that night,
because the sun had set. Taking one of the stones of the place,
he put it under his head and lay down in that place to sleep.

GENESIS 28:11

A Stone Pillow

 his is the constant course of the Church at all times, namely, that promises are made and that then those who believe the promises are treated in such a way that they are compelled to wait for things that are invisible, to believe what they do not see, and to hope for what does not appear. He who does not do this is not a Christian. For Christ Himself entered into His glory only by first descending into hell. When He is about to reign, He is crucified. When He is to be glorified, He is spit on. For He must suffer first and then at length be glorified. Moreover, God does this in order to test our hearts, whether we are willing to do without the promised blessings for a time. We shall not do without them forever. This is certain. And if God did not test us and postpone His promises, we would not be able to love Him wholeheartedly. For if He immediately gave everything He promises, we would not believe but would immerse ourselves in the blessings that are at hand and forget God. Accordingly, He allows the Church to be afflicted and to suffer want in order that it may learn that it must live not only by bread but also by the Word (cf. Matthew 4:4), and in order that faith, hope, and the expectation of God's help may be increased in the godly. For the Word is our life and salvation.

August 22

A Ladder to Heaven

hen Philip brings Nathanael to Christ, Christ says, John 1:51]: "Truly, truly, I say to you: 'You will see heaven opened, and the angels of God ascending and descending upon the Son of Man.'" We should believe and be content with this explanation of our Savior; for He has a better understanding than all other interpreters, even though they agree properly in this point, that this dream signified that infinite, inexpressible, and wondrous mystery of the incarnation of Christ, who was to descend from the patriarch Jacob, as God says: "In your seed, etc." Therefore He revealed to Jacob himself that he would be the father of Christ and that the Son of Man would be born from his seed. God did not speak this in vain. Indeed, He painted that picture of the ladder to comfort and console Jacob in faith in the future blessing, just as above (Genesis 22:18) He gave the same promise to Abraham and Isaac in order that they might teach and transmit it to their descendants as certain and infallible, and expect a Savior from their own flesh. In this way God strengthens Jacob, who, like the useless trunk of a tree, is wretched and afflicted in a foreign land; and by means of this new picture He transfers to him all the blessings, to assure him that he is this patriarch from whom the Seed promised to Adam will come.

And behold,
the angels of God were ascending and descending on it!
GENESIS 28:12

Angels Ascending and Descending

hat is this ascent and descent? I reply that it is this very mystery that in one and the same person there is true *God* and man. . . . For we believe in the one Lord, His only-begotten Son, born of the Virgin Mary, true God and man. This mystery is so great, so grand, so inexpressible, that the angels themselves cannot marvel at it enough, much less comprehend it. But, as is stated in 1 Peter 1:12, these are "things into which angels long to look." . . . We carnal and ignorant human beings do not understand or value the magnitude of these things. We have barely tasted a drink of milk—not solid food—from that inexpressible union and association of the divine and the human nature, which is of such a kind that not only the humanity has been assumed, but that such humanity has been made liable and subject to death and hell yet in that humiliation has devoured the devil, hell, and all things in itself. This is the communion of properties. *God*, who created all things and is above all things, is the highest and the lowest, so that we must say: "That man, who was scourged, who is the lowest under death, under the wrath of God, under sin and every kind of evil, and finally under hell, is the highest God." Why? Because it is the same person. Although the nature is twofold, the person is not divided.

The Angels of God

[C]hrist] did all this for us. He descended into hell and ascended into heaven. This sight the angels enjoy forever in heaven, and this is what Christ means when He says (Matthew 18:10): "Their angels always behold the face of My Father who is in heaven." They look constantly at the divinity. And now they descend from heaven after He has been made man. Now they look upon Christ and wonder at the work of the incarnation. They see that He has been made man, humiliated, and placed on His mother's lap. They adore the man who was crucified and rejected, and they acknowledge Him as the Son of God. . . . Later there is another union—a union between us and Christ. . . . [Christ] says: "You in Me, and I in you" (John 14:20). This is the allegorical meaning of the ladder. But the allegory should nourish faith and not teach about our affairs or our works. Therefore we are carried along by faith and become one flesh with Him, as Christ says in John 17:21: "That they may all be one; even as Thou, Father, art in Me, and I in Thee, that they also may be one in Us." In this way we ascend into Him and are carried along through the Word and the Holy Spirit. And through faith we cling to Him, since we become one body with Him and He with us. He is the Head; we are the members. On the other hand, He descends to us through the Word and the Sacraments by teaching and by exercising us in the knowledge of Him.

August 25

"I am the Lᴏʀᴅ, the God of Abraham your father
and the God of Isaac. . . . In you and your offspring
shall all the families of the earth be blessed."

Gᴇɴᴇsɪs 28:13–14

Our Lord, True Man

 he Gospel concerning Christ the Savior cannot be preached without adding that He was born from Abraham, from Jacob. For we must have sure proof that He was in all truth the Son of Man, a natural man, and not a specter, not an apparition. . . . Therefore we have His ancestors, who were true men. Nor can He be named without these fathers, without Abraham, Isaac, Jacob, and Adam, in order that He may have a definite lineage, a true father, a true mother, and that it may be certain that He is from a human seed and that He took upon Himself human nature, not the angels, not any other creature. Accordingly, a definite place was assigned to the nativity of Christ for the fathers and the prophets, and definite persons from whom He had to descend were named. Consequently, we cannot doubt that He is in very truth our flesh and blood, bone of our bones. Accordingly, when He is preached and praised, His parents, from whom He assumed flesh, are named at the same time. And at the same time we, too, are included—we for whose sakes He became the Seed of Abraham, Isaac, and Jacob, not the seed of angels. Therefore He so carefully inculcates and so often repeats the words "in your seed, etc."

"In you and your offspring
shall all the families of the earth be blessed."

GENESIS 28:14

Certainty of the Blessing

od] means to say: "Not only will you possess the land in which you are sleeping, but you will break out in such a way that the blessed Seed will proceed without any resistance and will be spread out with might into the whole world." . . . This is how God consoles Jacob, and in him the whole Church, in order that he may be certain about his descendants. For although Esau exercises dominion after Jacob has been cast off and driven into exile, and even though he is really king and priest in the meantime, so that everything is full of despair and nothing is less likely than that Jacob will be the future heir and ruler in the house or the Church, yet this is of little importance. "Be stouthearted, and endure. For not only will you be the heir in the house, and not only will the blessing of Abraham and the possession of this land be bestowed on you; but I also assure you that you will be a patriarch over the whole earth and the father of the blessed Seed, through whom all the nations will be blessed. And I will accomplish this when I rage against him who rages." . . . God shows His strength, according to the saying (2 Corinthians 12:9): "My power is made perfect in weakness." . . . Thus Christ was strongest when He was dead and weakest. For in that weakness He condemned the world and the ruler of this world together with all their power and wisdom.

August 27

"Behold, I am with you and will keep you wherever you go."

GENESIS 28:15

Shield and Protection

his is a twofold promise concerning the Seed of Jacob, in whom all the nations of the earth are to be blessed, that is, a promise concerning Christ which he includes in the temporal promise as in the one that is less significant, just as a child is wrapped in rags, a gem is inserted in gold, or a precious treasure is kept in an earthen container. The temporal blessing is great and rich enough, but the one about raging into the world is greater. But He repeats the temporal blessing and binds it up into a little bundle with this temporal promise concerning the descendants. For He says: "And behold, I am with you, etc. You have the eternal promise and the temporal one concerning your descendants. Now I shall add this third point: I will be with you on this journey and during this exile so far as your person is concerned, and I will even protect you yourself; for in order that the things I have promised may be fulfilled, you must live and be protected. Your brother Esau is plotting against you. The devil hates you when you sleep and when you are awake; but I want to walk with you, and I will be your companion." Oh, what a desirable and stout companion! "I will not only go with you to escort you; but I will be your wall, your protector. I will fight for you—I, who am to be your Son from your seed, through whom all the families of the earth will be blessed. I will be with you, I will shield you and protect you."

August 28

"Behold, I am with you and will keep you wherever you go."

GENESIS 28:15

Safe and Sound

This should be applied to our use, in order that we may acknowledge the magnitude of God's grace, which has been revealed and given to us through the Gospel. For we are absolved through the Word, and on the authority of Christ we are told: "I baptize you; I extend to you the body and blood of Christ; I tear your soul by force from the power of the devil; I set you free from eternal death and damnation; and I make you a child of God and an heir of eternal life." . . . But how few there are who believe these things as they should! Much less do we comprehend them, but we only take hold of them in one way or another. Yet they are completely true. And surely we must die in this faith. Otherwise we shall fall from our salvation and not remain safe and sound against the devil for even one moment. For he rages horribly when he hears that this is taught in this way, and he persecutes those who preach it or who listen to this doctrine and embrace it. But we should listen with grateful hearts and with joy, and we should believe at least weakly. Only let us not fight against it, blaspheme, persecute, reject, and deny. . . . But how? Believe in the Seed of Abraham, the Son of God. This faith is our victory which overcomes the world (1 John 5:4), vanquishes the devil, and destroys the gates of hell (cf. Matthew 16:18).

"For I will not leave you until I have done what I have promised you." Then Jacob awoke from his sleep.

GENESIS 28:15–16

Promise and Command

t is clear and manifest enough that there is a difference between the Word, which promises, and the commandment, which orders to do something. Therefore the legends of the saints and all life should be divided into these two parts: the Word of God and our work. The former belongs to God alone; the latter is ours, namely, love, patience, and the castigating and crucifying of the flesh. This is a life; but it is a life of works, and it does not take hold of the sanctity of the Word, which is the soul of life. Therefore the Word has to precede; for it is the Word and promise of God, who blesses, promises, receives us into grace, and forgives sins. This surely must precede: "Your sins are forgiven you; I am your God; do not fear the devil; I am with you; I will protect you; I will not forsake you." But after the forgiveness of sins this follows: "Take up your bed and go home" (Matthew 9:6). This precedes: "Take heart, My son"; that is, "First acknowledge Me as propitious, as placated, as being favorable, and as absolving you. First receive My blessing, in order that you may be freed from sin and death. Afterward, when you have been healed, take up your bed and walk; teach, and do works." Thus after Jacob has first been strengthened in faith because of grace and the blessing, he walks, works, and suffers, as is stated in what follows: "He awoke from his sleep, etc."

August 30

"How awesome is this place! This is none other than the house of God, and this is the gate of heaven."

GENESIS 28:17

Where God Dwells

his is a very wonderful speech. All Holy Scripture has nothing like it either in the Old or in the New Testament. For this place is called the house of God and the gate of heaven, and this is stated only in this one passage and nowhere else. This is nothing else than calling it the kingdom of heaven and heaven itself, for the place where God dwells is the house of God. But where does God dwell? Does He not dwell in heaven? Therefore he joins the earth with heaven and heaven with the earth. He sets up a heavenly habitation and the kingdom of God at that place on the earth and says: "The kingdom of heaven, the gate to heaven, is where the approach to heaven is open and also where the exit from the house of God is open." For [Jacob] distinguishes between heaven and earth, that is, between the present and the future life; for after this life he promises himself eternal life and the kingdom of heaven, which begins in the present life. Indeed, Jacob already feels that he is and lives in that kingdom. . . . For here nothing else is meant than the Church and the teachers and hearers in it. Then the Church is defined here, what it is and where it is. For where God dwells, there the Church is, and nowhere else; for the Church is God's house and the gate of heaven, where the entrance to eternal life and the departure from the earthly to the heavenly life are open.

August 31

*"This is none other than the house of God,
and this is the gate of heaven."*

GENESIS 28:17

The Gate of Heaven

God governs us in such a way that wherever He speaks with us here on earth, the approach to the kingdom of heaven is open. This is truly extraordinary consolation. Wherever we hear the Word and are baptized, there we enter into eternal life. But where is that place found? On earth, where the ladder which touches heaven stands, where the angels descend and ascend, where Jacob sleeps. It is a physical place, but here there is an ascent into heaven without physical ladders, without wings and feathers. This is how faith speaks: "I am going to the place where the Word is taught, where the Sacrament is offered and Baptism is administered." . . . Direct your step to the place where the Word resounds and the Sacraments are administered, and there write the title *The Gate of God*. Let this be done either in the Church and in the public assemblies or in bedchambers, when we console and buoy up the sick or when we absolve him who sits with us at table. There the gate of heaven is, as Christ says (Matthew 18:20): "Where two or three are gathered in My name, there am I in the midst of them." Throughout the world the house of God and the gate of heaven is wherever there is the pure teaching of the Word together with the Sacraments.

Now as soon as Jacob saw Rachel
the daughter of Laban his mother's brother . . .

GENESIS 29:10

Love at First Sight

 hen in his exile [Jacob] found Rachel, his blood relation, he took courage and gained great hope that at last he would obtain what he had in mind and what his father had commanded him with respect to taking a wife. Therefore he is immediately inflamed with love at first sight, and natural desire toward his kinswoman comes to the fore, so that the twofold impulse of faith and love made his body and heart more animated. For he wanted to show himself as a man of strength and agility—in order that he might capture the maiden's heart and entice her to fall in love with him. And these things, too, are only natural. But they are recorded by the Holy Spirit in order that no one may think that they are disgraceful or forbidden. For it is a Christian and godly thing to love a girl to join her to you in marriage, since there is a natural desire and inclination of sex to sex. Although this is not completely without sin, yet God does not want it to be despised as dishonorable. For it is a work of God created in man's nature, and it should not only not be despised or vilified but should even be honored. For God wants to be glorified in all works, both small and great.

September 2

When the LORD saw that Leah was hated,
He opened her womb, but Rachel was barren.

GENESIS 29:31

The Sight of God

od] is the Creator and Governor of everything. But who would believe that God cares for Leah? Surely all men should conclude firmly that God has regard for and cares for them, no matter how small, abject, and lowly they are. For this is why Moses so carefully depicts the condition of Jacob's household affairs and sets it before our eyes. . . . This is wonderful and great consolation for the afflicted and wretched, who should rouse themselves to faith and hope, since they hear God described and defined as He who is always pleased with the prayer of *The Humble and the Meek*, as Judith 9:11 says. The sobbing, yes, the death, of those who are downcast is precious in the Lord's sight. He who can believe this is undoubtedly pleasing and acceptable to God. For it is certain that He neither wants nor is able to bear contempt for His creature, whether it is small or great. He does not want the great ones to boast or to be proud that they have the means with which to protect and defend themselves. But He does not want those who are downcast to despair, for they have one who has regard for them and receives them. Therefore God, who has regard for the lowly things in heaven and on earth, should be blessed. . . . Poor Leah was harassed by these sorrows and this grief; she was sad and pained that she was despised by her lord. But listen to Moses, who says: "*The Lord saw*, etc."

September 3

And [Leah] conceived again and bore a son, and said,
"This time I will praise the Lord."
Therefore she called his name Judah.

GENESIS 29:35

Praise the Lord

yra [a 13th-century Bible commentator] . . . distinguishes the trials of Leah piously enough according to four points: she was despised by Rachel, neglected by her husband, regarded as a foreigner and an outsider by the neighbors and the household, and finally cast off by God. . . . But against these four evidences of sorrow and despair God gives Leah four other evidences of consolation, namely, four sons. In the first place, against Rachel's contempt He has regard for her humility. Second, because she was being neglected so far by her husband, He hears her prayer. Third, lest she seem to be a stranger and completely excluded, God grants that her husband is joined to her and clings to her. Fourth, she triumphs victoriously over all trials. She is no longer looked down on and despised, but she praises God and gives thanks. We, too, should follow this example and learn that after a trial God is wont to grant liberation and consolation in rich abundance. In this way all sorrow and disturbance is overcome. But it is hard for the flesh to wait for consolation from God. Therefore such examples of faith are set forth in order that we may see how Leah cried out, believed, waited, and bore every wrong and vexation from her sister in faith and hope. And finally God had regard for her as she hoped in Him, and He comforted her richly.

September 4

Then God remembered Rachel,
and God listened to her and opened her womb.

GENESIS 30:22

God Searches the Heart

 oses has employed a significant word: "The Lord remembered." It is as though he were saying: "She had almost despaired within herself, and she was convinced in her heart that God would never remember her, yes, that He had forgotten her forever." "I shall not be a mother," she thought, "but I am the most wretched of all women. I should have been the mother of the house, but God has forgotten me." In this way she was led down into hell, where no hope of help seems to be left. In despair she takes hold of her maidservant and hands her over to her husband, which she would not have done if she had not given up all hope. Yet she despairs in such a way that she retains a spark of faith. In her despair she retains that sobbing which Paul calls ineffable (cf. Romans 8:26), but this is so deeply buried and covered with impossibility and contrary emotions of the heart that she is barely conscious of that sobbing or sighing. Thus Hannah, the mother of Samuel, also despaired of off-spring and could not be conscious of her sobbing and of that desire for offspring in the inmost depths of her heart. But God, who searches the heart, understands the inef-fable sobbing, which can neither be felt nor expressed with any words.

September 5

Then God remembered Rachel,
and God listened to her and opened her womb.

GENESIS 30:22

Below the Surface

[G]od] does not give what His saints seek on the surface of their hearts and with that foam of words, but He is an almighty and exceedingly rich Bestower who gives in accordance with the depth of that sighing. Therefore He lets prayer be directed, grow, and be increased; and He does not hear immediately. For if He were to answer at the first outcry or petition, prayer would not increase but would become cold. Therefore He defers help. As a result, prayer grows from day to day and becomes more efficacious. The sobbing of the heart also becomes deeper and more ardent until it comes to the point of despair, as it were. Then prayer becomes most ardent and passionate, when it seems that now the sobbing is nearly at a standstill. But if He heard immediately, prayer would not be so strong, so alive, and so ardent; but it would be only a superficial and pedagogical sobbing which is still learning to pray, to sob, and to desire, and is not yet a master of prayer. But when the point of despair has been reached and the afflicted heart thinks: "Alas, nothing will come of it; all is lost!" yet a spark and a dimly burning wick remain (cf. Isaiah 42:3), then be strong and hold out. For this is the struggle of the saints who think that the rope will now be torn yet who continue to sob. Then, therefore, prayer is perfect and strongest.

September 6

God remembered Rachel, and God listened to her.

GENESIS 30:22

Ask, Seek, Knock without Ceasing

This is how we, too, should learn to ask and hope for help whenever there is misfortune and faith totters. For we have the promise of the Gospel; we have Baptism, absolution, etc., by which we have been instructed and strengthened. We have the command by which we are ordered to pray; we have the spirit of grace and of prayer. But as soon as we have begun to pray, our heart is troubled and complains that it is accomplishing nothing. Therefore one must learn that if you accomplish nothing by asking, you should add searching, that is, you should seek; if that, too, seems to be useless, and God conceals and hides Himself even more, add knocking, and do not cease until you storm the door by which He has been confined (cf. Matthew 7:7-8). For there is no doubt that our prayer is heard immediately after the first syllable has been uttered. . . . But the fact that God does not immediately give what we pray for—this happens because He wants to be sought and to be taken by storm by insisting beyond measure, as the parable of the unrighteous judge teaches in Luke 18:2[-8]. For then He comes and liberates the elect and gives more abundantly than we have prayed, sought, and knocked. But He defers in order that our praying may increase and that our sobbing may become stronger.

Then the Lord said to Jacob, "Return to the land of your fathers
and to your kindred, and I will be with you."

For Those in Need

It is manifest what great troubles and annoyances Jacob endured, if, indeed, it is necessary for the Lord to have regard for him and to rescue him from these straits. For the Lord does not speak in vain, nor does He offer His Word to the lazy and smug, but to those who are in need, who toil, who are afflicted and are undergoing a very difficult conflict against the flesh and all external appearances, that is, against those things which according to human sense and reason fight against faith, as Hebrews 11 says, so that the afflicted can rely on the sole protection of the Word of God and be sustained by it. Wisdom does not live "in the land of those who live pleasantly," says Job (cf. 28:13), because it is a word of the cross and despair. It pertains only to the troubled and mortified, the despised, those driven into despair, and the oppressed. Such was Jacob in his exile in the house of his unjust and greedy father-in-law. . . . In these straits the Lord speaks to him when he would have nothing else but faith and prayer left, embraces him when he is kept at arm's length and hated by all men, and supports his plan to depart: He orders him to leave a family group that is so hostile to himself and to his wives, and to take thought for his own house. By this word God testifies that the whole life of the patriarch Jacob and all its activities are pleasing to Him.

September 8

God Cares for Us

M en should be individually certain about this, that they are the people of God, or members of the Church. Above all things this faith is necessary which firmly apprehends the following syllogism. The whole people of God is blessed, holy, pleasing, and acceptable to God in such a way that it cannot be torn from the hands of God. We are the people of God. Therefore God exercises care for us. The major premise is eminently true, because even the death and blood of the saints are precious in the sight of the Lord (cf. Psalm 116:15); all they do and suffer is pleasing to God. On the contrary, their errors and lapses have been covered and forgiven, as Psalm 32:1 testifies. But about the minor premise there is some question. For also the Turk, the pope, and the Jews boast that they are such a people, pleasing and acceptable to God. And so we must see to it that we are certain about the minor premise, namely, that we are the sons of God, members of the flock and people of God, under the one Shepherd, Christ. If you can firmly and surely determine this, then you are blessed. Therefore be of good courage and do not be disturbed or fearful even if the whole world should crash into ruin, for, indeed, you are sure that you are under that Shepherd who is Lord of heaven and earth.

[Jacob said,] "The God of my father has been with me."

GENESIS 31:5

The Fight against Doubt

ow am I to know for certain that I belong to the people of God? Before the incarnation of Christ the fathers had the promise, the Word, and the voice of God. They also had the sign of circumcision. We today have the Keys, Baptism, the Eucharist, and the promises of the Gospel. From this source you are to gather arguments and demonstrations by which you may become certain that you are a Christian, that you have been baptized and are walking in a godly and holy calling. See that you do not blaspheme but love the Word and serve God in some honorable employment. If this remains fixed in your heart, even though there will have to be a fight against doubt, you may nevertheless conclude and infer that you are a person whose deeds are all the object of God's care and please Him. You should think as follows: "I shall follow my calling and perform a servant's, master's, child's duties with Jacob. For I know that all these things are held in honor and are precious before the Lord our God." It is necessary for these matters to be repeated because of the continuous struggle against doubt. For the opposite of the Word and divine comfort is thrown up to our senses. The flesh has a different experience, so that all things seem to be inflicted on the godly in an adverse manner, since, indeed, the ungodly are fortunate and the godly are afflicted. Therefore faith is a matter of invisible things until the final outcome proves the truth of the promises.

September 10

So Jacob arose and set his sons and wives on camels. . . .
Laban had gone to shear his sheep.

GENESIS 31:17, 19

The Proper Use of Reason

t is to be observed carefully that Jacob does not tempt God but seizes an advantageous occasion to avoid the offenses which he could escape. For dangers are not to be invited but avoided. Although we have the Word of God on which we can and should safely rely, nevertheless, of itself it loads us with many great dangers, and so other unnecessary dangers are not to be invited. Nor should we snore in ease and smugness, but natural wisdom and industry should be used, and likewise human counsels and help, so that we do not seem to tempt God. . . . If, therefore, you have the Word, you do well when you obey it. But prepare yourself to use those things which are at hand, according to the Word. Thus Jacob has the command about leaving this land and returning to his fatherland. He also has the promise concerning God's protection, that he should not fear, however great the dangers would be and however varied the difficulties that would be thrown in his way. . . . Nevertheless, he waits for an opportunity and a time when Laban is a three days' journey from home to shear his sheep. . . . So Jacob seized a very fine opportunity with singular prudence and wisdom. For so God has given us reason and all creatures and all our temporal blessings to serve our uses.

September 11

God came to Laban the Aramean in a dream by night
and said to him, "Be careful not to say anything to Jacob,
either good or bad."

GENESIS 31:24

God Restrains Satan

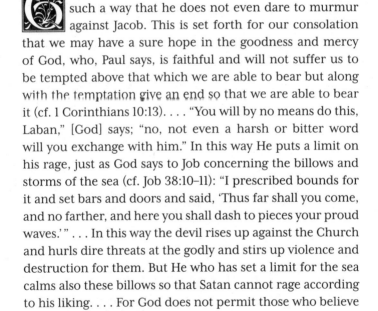

od breaks and restrains the angry mood of Laban in such a way that he does not even dare to murmur against Jacob. This is set forth for our consolation that we may have a sure hope in the goodness and mercy of God, who, Paul says, is faithful and will not suffer us to be tempted above that which we are able to bear but along with the temptation give an end so that we are able to bear it (cf. 1 Corinthians 10:13). . . . "You will by no means do this, Laban," [God] says; "no, not even a harsh or bitter word will you exchange with him." In this way He puts a limit on his rage, just as God says to Job concerning the billows and storms of the sea (cf. Job 38:10–11): "I prescribed bounds for it and set bars and doors and said, 'Thus far shall you come, and no farther, and here you shall dash to pieces your proud waves.'" . . . In this way the devil rises up against the Church and hurls dire threats at the godly and stirs up violence and destruction for them. But He who has set a limit for the sea calms also these billows so that Satan cannot rage according to his liking. . . . For God does not permit those who believe and have His Word to be afflicted and tempted beyond their strength. He is the faithful Guardian of those who guard and keep His Word.

September 12

*God came to Laban the Aramean in a dream by night
and said to him, "Be careful not to say anything to Jacob,
either good or bad."*

GENESIS 31:24

God Does Not Forsake Us

hus God does not forsake believers, especially when they cry to Him in true faith. . . . For where the Word is, there faith is also; and where faith is, there is also a cry because of temptation. It is impossible for this cry not to be heard. Once heard, this cry breaks all the might of heaven and earth as well as that of all the gates of hell (cf. Matthew 16:18). . . . But let us apply the example before us for our doctrine and use . . . that we may see that God is present with His own although they are wretched and weak. Laban is far more powerful than Jacob, who finds himself in the greatest of danger unarmed and poor. But Jacob has the Word. Accordingly, *God* and His host of angels are present with believing Jacob as he prays. For just as God led the patriarch out of his father's house, so He leads him back, employing the protection of the angels. In the same manner, if we believe the Word and adhere to it in firm and steadfast faith, He will also help us and set us free, even in the very midst of plague, death, and war. For it is impossible for the man who believes God's Word to be forsaken and not defended.

September 13

Laban said to Jacob, "What have you done,
that you have tricked me?"

GENESIS 31:26

Bearing Reproach

 aban's accusations against Jacob are] certainly offen-
sive and undeserving, but they are written in this way
so that we by steadfastness and by the encouragement of the Scriptures might have hope (cf. Romans 15:4). No
one sins in this world except the only-begotten Son of God.
On the other hand, no one is righteous but the devil. . . . But
since it thus seems good to God and it cannot be otherwise
but that there should be a flock which for God's sake is . . . a
reproach of men and rejected by the people (cf. Psalm 22:6),
we are certainly not reluctant to be regarded as such in the
world. For we have His richest consolation, which has said
(cf. Matthew 5:11–12): "Blessed will you be when men hate
you and when they cast you out, insult you, and utter your
name like an evil omen on account of the Son of Man. Be
glad on that day and rejoice, for behold, your reward is great
in heaven." It is a matter of a short time. Life is brief and
wretched, but the joy and glory we await is eternal. Since,
therefore, it pleases God that we should be a little flock,
insignificant and despised, let us bear the troubles of this
life with a calm and joyful heart, just as Jacob bore reproach,
abuse, and contempt from the proud Labanites and hypocrites. . . . We will conquer because of our Leader and Lord,
the Son of God, who Himself bore the same reproaches and
conquers in all His saints.

September 14

[Jacob answered,] "Anyone with whom you find
your gods shall not live."

GENESIS 31:31–32

The Failings of the Saints

ere the Holy Spirit describes the human side in the saints. For however sublime they are in faith and spirit, they nevertheless not only err and are ignorant of many things, but they even take a fall according to the flesh. Jacob thinks that he is beyond all blame, suspicion, and danger, and that in this respect satisfaction had already been rendered to Laban. . . . But in this manner a very dear wife is handed over to death by her husband. For if God had not intervened and prevented it, Jacob would thoughtlessly have offered his dear wife Rachel to be slaughtered. . . . So the Holy Spirit is at hand and finds a remedy against the permission which Jacob had given. . . . This is the work and skill of God, to correct and emend what had been ruined by Jacob's error. He can make evil matters good when we have spoiled and harmed matters. And so, in the great infirmity characteristic of human affairs, not even the saints can be without many great lapses. . . . God so governs His saints that even though they err and stray, the outcomes are nevertheless salutary or without great loss. For all things work together for good to the elect and those who believe (cf. Romans 8:28), even errors and sins, and this is absolutely certain. For God is accustomed to make all things out of nothing, and so He can call forth and produce good from evil.

"If the God of my father, the God of Abraham and the Fear of Isaac, had not been on my side, surely now you would have sent me away empty-handed."

GENESIS 31:42

The Fear of Isaac

hat, then, does the Holy Spirit mean in making mention of the "Fear of Isaac"? . . . I shall follow the simple and common meaning, that he calls God by this name because of the outstanding and singular worship of his father Isaac, who feared and worshiped God with singular piety. . . . Others interpret it to mean that Isaac was afraid, since he was to be sacrificed. But this is a foreign and wicked meaning, for Isaac was neither afraid nor terrified but of his own accord obeyed his father and God. . . . For fear signifies that sin is ruling, and sin was not ruling in Isaac, but an obedient spirit. . . . But besides this meaning, I think that Christ is also pointed to. . . . "In Isaac shall your seed be named," which is nothing else but Christ Himself. He is the true Seed. For the fathers looked beyond the bodily blessing which Ishmael and Esau had, chiefly to the spiritual blessing, which is Christ Himself. Therefore I see the Trinity here, and elsewhere too, wherever I can dig out that mystery from passages of the Old Testament. Therefore "Fear" here signifies the Son of God incarnate, whom the patriarchs and prophets beheld in the promises and whom they taught.

September 16

God Is on My Side

 hese things the Holy Spirit wanted set before the churches and the believers as an example and for their strengthening, that they may know for certain that God has regard for all the works of the saints and the godly, yes, that He even numbers their hairs one by one (cf. Matthew 10:30). . . . This consolation, moreover, is especially necessary for the Church because the devil, together with the whole world and our flesh, in wretched fashion afflicts and harasses those who have the Word. Consolation or protection must not be expected from the world and the princes of this world, nor should carnal counsels be sought from ourselves, for they are vain. Indeed, those who seek or await help of this kind experience what is said in the psalm (116:11), "All men are liars," and again (Psalm 146:3), "Put not your trust in princes, in a son of man, in whom there is no help." . . . Hence, God must have regard and care for His own, who, destitute of all help and counsel, have their eyes fixed on His Word. For they bear the cross and their troubles. . . . God numbers all our actions and thoughts, however trifling and abject they may be, if only we believe in Him. For if we care for His Word, He in turn cares for us in all adversities which are thrown in our way by the world and Satan.

September 17

Jacob swore by the Fear of his father Isaac.

GENESIS 31:53

Fear and Worship of God

acob does not swear by the God of Nahor or Terah, but he swears by a God who is closer, that is, by the God whom his father fears and worships, by Christ, according to the commandments and promises of God. For hypocrites also serve God but by the commandments and tradition of men. It is as Isaiah and Christ say (Isaiah 29:13; Matthew 15:8): "This people honors Me with their lips, but their heart is far from Me." No one comes closer to God with the lips, no one employs the name of God more frequently, than hypocrites. But God proclaims that their worship is idolatrous. . . . If Christ, then, is to be our fear, that is, when He should be worshiped by us, it is necessary that we have the Word and promise of God. Such fear or dread is true worship, which brings it to pass in us that we despise all other dread and terrors, as Isaiah says (8:12–13): "Do not fear what they fear, nor be in dread. But the Lord you shall regard as holy." He will protect you well, and you must consider that He is to be feared, revered, and worshiped, who speaks with you. "If you do this, then I the Lord will be your fear," He says. For you have a certain and firm Word, and when you retain it, you will not err in your divine worship.

Jacob went on his way, and the angels of God met him. And when Jacob saw them he said, "This is God's camp!"

GENESIS 32:1–2

The Troops of God

hese are words of joy and triumph for the patriarch with great confidence and a feeling of security because of the peace given to him by God, just as though he meant to say: "Now the angels are appearing, heaven is laughing, the stormy winter has passed, and now the clear and serene light of day is shining forth." . . . But it is a matter of great and wonderful wisdom that Jacob can recognize the angels who meet him and that he can call them God's hosts, our Lord God's troops. Surely God does not have armies and hosts on earth? Yes, this is what Jacob calls all the angels. . . . The Epistle to the Hebrews (1:14) describes them in the words: "Are they not all ministering spirits sent forth to serve, for the sake of those who are to obtain salvation?" They are not gods or goddesses but ministers who serve the world, and who do so on account of those who will inherit eternal salvation. . . . In short, all things in heaven and earth are ordained to this end, that the righteous should be gathered together and the number of those who are to be saved should be filled up. Accordingly, this is a truly heavenly doctrine and not a matter of human reason and wisdom that in this life empires, states, and households, and, in short, whatever this world has are all governed by the ministry of the holy angels.

September 19

Wait, Endure, Hold Out!

f God were not to govern the world through His angels even for one day, the devil would certainly strike down the whole human race all of a sudden, plunder it, and drive it off, destroying it with famine, plague, wars, and fires. These things would have to be endured not only by the evil but also by the good. But that we can be secure and safe from such great perils under the protection of the armies and hosts of heaven, this we should determine for certain. At times the angels even permit some evils to happen. But they do this so that we may be tried and that our faith may be proved and exercised and that in this way we may learn to recognize God in His wonderful counsels and works and give thanks to Him for His wonderful government, as this example of the patriarch Jacob teaches us. . . . When all things already seem to be at the point of crashing into ruin, all hope and confidence is still not to be completely cast off. Wait, endure, and hold out! God is still living; the angels are ruling and defending. . . . This, then, is the doctrine which is taught in this passage, that the angels are ministering spirits and servants of creation. They fight for the safety and welfare of the world and the godly, and this is their lower office. Their higher office, however, is to sing "Glory to God in the highest" and "We praise Thee, O God, etc." In heaven likewise they see the Father's face (cf. Matthew 18:10).

Unmerited Promises

 he promise of grace is this, when God says: "You have done nothing; you have merited nothing. But I shall do this for you and present it to you by mercy alone." Such promises are unmerited, and the promises of the patriarchs Abraham, Isaac, and Jacob were like them. They have been recounted above: "May your mother's sons bow down to you" and "I have established you with oil and wine." Here no condition is attached: "If you do this, you will be blessed," but "You have this promise and blessing gratis." Moses, to be sure, is full of legal promises, but the patriarchs have simple, unmerited promises. Thus Jacob is confident and joyful in accordance with these; he congratulates himself on the very rich consolation and very strong protection of the angels. . . . God is laughing, the angels leap in joy and exultation, the spirit rejoices in the Lord, and therefore Jacob does not fear. He is persuaded that his brother's wrath has cooled off after such a long time, especially since none of his power and wealth had departed in the meantime and he had remained at home in his homeland, whereas Jacob himself had endured wretched slavery in banishment and exile and was still wandering without a definite abode. For Esau held the whole property and land of his father. Therefore Jacob feels secure and is certain that his brother has been placated. So he lovingly and kindly greets him by means of messengers, not in alarm or suspecting any evil.

September 21

Steadfastness amid Tribulation

oses is very obliging and generous in his description of this trial. For it is a memorable example of how God exercises the saints by various trials and consolations. . . . Such is this life, full of griefs and troubles! The life to come has been promised so that by steadfastness and by the encouragement of the Scriptures we might have hope (cf. Romans 15:4). In the meantime, these two are mingled, steadfastness, or encouragement, and tribulation. For if encouragement is present, all is prosperity and joy; again, when darkness and tribulation break in, the devil reigns and Christ is crucified. Therefore we are instructed by these examples not to despair but to expect the best and hope for a certain and rich redemption from evils and the end thereof, even though in these evils we can see neither their end nor God's presence, which is hidden to the understanding of the flesh. Accordingly, the Word must be learned, and a person must exercise himself in it and get to know these continuous alternations which are customary in the life of the saints and of all believers who wish to please God. . . . Thus Paul says of himself in 2 Corinthians 1:8: "We were so utterly, unbearably crushed that we despaired of life itself," but there is no need for you to fear that you will be burdened by God beyond measure, because the statement stands firm: "God is faithful, etc."

September 22

"[Esau] is coming to meet you,
and there are four hundred men with him."

GENESIS 32:6

Despair Turned to Joy

 hese matters should instruct and confirm the Church in all adversities. For they are set forth in this way that the Church may believe and trust when all things seem impossible and lost and no place is left anymore for counsel and help. It is stated in Psalm 107:27: "All their wisdom has been devoured." In such a case you should learn to come to this conclusion: "Although all things are done in great weakness and already seem lost, nevertheless, for God nothing is impossible." . . . For He once created all things out of nothing; He still retains this ability and in the same manner still preserves and governs all things. What is nothing for us is everything for God; and what is impossible for us is very easy for Him. By the same power, on the Last Day He will raise the dead who from the foundation of the earth have lain in the dust of the earth. So much about the alarm of the patriarch Jacob in very great peril. This is a proof that the flesh is alive and flourishing even in the saints. For this reason the saintliest man, even after such great promises and consolations, very nearly slips into despair. . . . Let us remember that we should do and learn this most of all, to trust in God in all temptations. For it is His special work to make the dead alive, to render those who are completely confused peaceful and tranquil, and to make those who are wretched happy and those who are in despair joyful.

September 23

Jacob was greatly afraid and distressed.

Weakness Turned to Strength

 e have often said that when faith is weakest, it is strongest. So wonderful are the works of God. Isaiah says (60:22): "The least one shall become a clan, and the smallest one a mighty nation." Paul says likewise in 2 Corinthians 12:9–10: "I will all the more gladly boast of my weaknesses . . . for when I am weak, then I am strong." Jacob here is very weak in his terrors and troubles, amazed, and dejected above measure. Yet his faith was never stronger, because faith which struggles against unbelief draws, as it were, the last and deepest sighs. But this sighing no one understands, neither Jacob nor anyone else. It is the ineffable groaning of which Romans 8:26 says: "The Spirit Himself intercedes for us with sighs too deep for words." It is not the voice of triumph, but in reality it is a groaning by which the afflicted heart only sighs and seems to draw breath with difficulty. Isaiah calls it a smoking flax and a reed which is not whole but crushed and shattered (Isaiah 42:3). But although there is nothing weaker and more feeble than this groaning (for it is, as it were, the last breath), it is nevertheless ineffable.

"I am not worthy of all the mercies and all the truth which Thou hast shown to Thy servant."

GENESIS 32:10 (according to Luther's translation)

Mercy and Truth

his phrase, however, is well-known: "Mercy and truth." For these are always joined in Holy Scripture, in Micah 7:20, for example, and elsewhere in the Psalms. "Mercy" signifies the specific act of kindness or the quality of kindness, as Christ, quoting Hosea 6:6, says in Matthew 9:13: "I desire mercy and not sacrifice." ["Merciful"] refers to him who loves his neighbor and does good to him, and it also refers to the one to whom good is done, to the one who is blessed with many mercies and kindnesses by God. . . . Truth is promise, as Paul says in Romans 15:8–9: "For I tell you that Christ became a servant to the circumcised to show God's truthfulness, in order to confirm the promises given to the patriarchs, and in order that the Gentiles might glorify God for His mercy." Christ was promised to the Jews, and so truth was kept with them. He was not promised to the Gentiles but was given to them by mercy. None of our fathers had the promise. God, indeed, promised that He is determined to be God to all men, and this knowledge has been implanted in the hearts of men, as Paul testifies in Romans 1:19. The works and worship of all the nations testify that to be God is nothing else than to do good to men. . . . God is one who promises, and He is truthful.

September 25

"I am not worthy of the least of all the deeds of steadfast love and all the faithfulness that You have shown to Your servant."

GENESIS 32:10

Three Conditions of Prayer

ne must not pray . . . like the Pharisee in the Gospel with his: "I fast twice a week, I give tithes of all that I get" (Luke 18:12). . . . We should follow the example of Jacob, who says: "I am not worthy of all Your mercies. I am not worthy, no, not even of one act of mercy or truth which You have ever shown me, are even now showing me, or will show me hereafter without any merit on my part. For it is impossible that I should merit anything. Therefore I do not rely on my worthiness but on Your promises and mercies." This is a truthful heart and a true prayer. . . . Therefore, there are those three conditions of a good prayer, which make it very pleasing and a sweet-smelling odor before God which cannot fail to be heard. The first is that you should take hold of the promise. The second is that you should be mortified in your distress. The third is that you should give thanks and acknowledge that you are not worthy of one act of mercy but are seeking and hoping for help through mercy alone. . . . Our confidence should not rely on the Law and its works, although they should be present, but on the mercy and truth of God. Then prayer and groaning is a golden sacrifice.

September 26

"Please deliver me from the hand of my brother."

GENESIS 32:11

All Is Not Lost

uch prayers, which are poured out in extreme despair and the greatest dangers, are very pleasing to God. These are the ineffable and vehement groanings by which the godly rouse themselves against despair. . . . This is the struggle of the godly, in which they awaken faith powerfully by the remembrance of the promise and the divine command and by trust in it. I must and will preach, but the devil offers resistance. Very well, preaching there must be, even if the world should be torn apart! . . . Here the devil urges that all is lost. "Why do you cry out?" he suggestively asks the afflicted man. "It is all over with you and time to give up." But the Spirit says in opposition: "All is not lost; quite the contrary! It is by no means all over! I know that God has determined and promised something else in regard to me." This is the great fervency and power of the Spirit in weakness. It is a very pleasing sacrifice to God according to Psalm 51:17, for it is the sacrifice of mortification: "The sacrifice acceptable to God is a broken spirit, a broken and a contrite heart, O God, Thou wilt not despise." . . . Therefore we should learn to be strong and unbroken in courage, whatever evils and dangers confront us and however much despair catches the attention of our hearts. . . . In this manner God wants our faith to be exercised and aroused that we may grow from day to day and become stronger.

September 27

And Jacob was left alone.
And a man wrestled with him until the breaking of the day.

GENESIS 32:24

Wrestling with God

ur opinion is this, that the wrestler is the Lord of glory, God Himself, or God's Son, who was to become incarnate and who appeared and spoke to the fathers. For God in His boundless goodness dealt very familiarly with His chosen patriarch Jacob and disciplined him as though playing with him in a kindly manner. But this playing means infinite grief and the greatest anguish of heart. In reality, however, it is a game, as the outcome shows when Jacob comes to Peniel. Then it will be manifest that they were pure signs of most familiar love. So God plays with him to discipline and strengthen his faith just as a godly parent takes from his son an apple with which the boy was delighted, not that he should flee from his father or turn away from him but that he should rather be incited to embrace his father all the more and beseech him, saying: "My father, give back what you have taken away!" . . . These games are very common on the domestic scene, but in the affairs and contests of the saints they are very serious and difficult. For Jacob has no idea who it is who is wrestling with him; he does not know that it is God, because he later asks what His name is. But after he receives the blessing, he says: "I have seen the Lord face to face." Then new joy and life arises from the sad temptation and death itself.

September 28

A man wrestled with [Jacob] until the breaking of the day.

GENESIS 32:24

God in Hostile Form

he chief significance of this story, then, is the example of perfect saints and of temptations in high degree, not against flesh, blood, the devil, and a good angel but against God appearing in hostile form. For although Jacob does not know who this man is, he nevertheless feels that he has been forsaken by God or that God is opposed to him and angry with him. . . . For Moses wrote the story as Jacob recounted it, like this, no doubt: "Suddenly he attacked, and a man fell upon me." This was a shape, or an appearance. But he does not discuss who that man was, because he does not know. But later, when he sees his back, he recognizes him and says: "I have seen the Lord face to face." That attack, accordingly, was the same as if a great strong man had fallen upon him and attacked him. Who it was, he did not know. Jacob himself was a man of regular strength with powers intact such as are usually found in a sound and strong body. Although he fought without sword and arms, he offered stout resistance. He still had a degree of faith in the promise. Although he was alarmed, his thoughts had not yet reached finality and become conclusions. His faith was, indeed, assailed and tried, but he still held to this conclusion firmly: "I have the promise."

September 29

Jacob said, "I will not let You go unless You bless me."

GENESIS 32:26

Do Not Yield, but Press On

hy do you not let him go? Your thigh is hurt and you are already lame; what will you do? "I feel no weakness," says Jacob. Who is strengthening you? "Faith, the promise, and indeed, this weakness of faith." In this manner God is conquered when faith does not leave off, is not wearied, and does not cease but presses and urges on. So it makes its appearance in the Canaanite woman, with whom Jesus was wrestling when He said: "You are a dog, the bread of the sons does not belong to you" (cf. Matthew 15:26). The woman did not yield here but offered opposition, saying: "Even the dogs eat the crumbs that fall from their master's table." And so she was victorious and heard the excellent word of praise: "O woman, great is your faith!" Such examples teach us that faith should not yield or cease urging or pressing on even when it is already feeling God's wrath and not only death and sin. This is the power and strength of the Spirit.

September 30

God Can Be Conquered?

od] is not conquered in such a way that He is subjected to us, but His judgment, or His wrath and fury and whatever opposes us, is conquered by us by praying, seeking, and knocking, so that from an angry judge, as He seemed to be previously, He becomes a most loving Father and says (Matthew 15:28; Luke 7:50; cf. Matthew 8:13): "O woman, great is your faith. Your faith has saved you. As you have believed, so be it unto you. Oh, how you hurt Me with your cry!" It is the fullness of consolation that God exercises us in such a way and exhorts us to fight and shows that it is to Him a most pleasing sacrifice to be conquered by us. . . . God is conquered in this way as soon as He has surrendered Himself to us, so to say, and revealed Himself in His Word, promise, and Baptism. It remains that you should conquer those things which want to take this God away from you, namely, through the truth of the promises and faith. Or, if He pretends that He is unfriendly and angry with you inasmuch as He does not want to hear you and help you, then say: "Lord God, You have promised this in Your Word. Therefore You will not change Your promise. I have been baptized: I have been absolved." If you persistently urge and press on in this way, He will be conquered and say: "Let it be done unto you as you have petitioned, for you have the promise and the blessing. I have to give in to you. For a constant and persistent seeker and petitioner is the sweetest sacrifice."

October 1

Jacob said, "I will not let You go unless You bless me." . . . Then
He said, "Your name shall no longer be called Jacob, but Israel."

GENESIS 32:26, 28

In the Arena with God

 ven if [God] hides Himself in a room in the house and does not want access to be given to anyone, do not draw back but follow. If He does not want to listen, knock at the door of the room; raise a shout! For this is the highest sacrifice, not to cease praying and seeking until we conquer Him. He has already surrendered Himself to us so that we may be certain of victory, for He has bound Himself to *His* promises and pledged His faithfulness with an oath, saying (John 16:23): "Truly, truly, I say to you, if you ask anything of the Father, He will give it to you in My name." Likewise (Mark 16:16): "He who believes and is baptized will be saved." These promises will never disappoint you, unless you refuse to follow and seek. In this case, through your fault, by snoring and sleeping, you lose the most certain promises and Christ Himself, because you refuse to enter this arena and take up the contest with God where the possession of these promises is seen and flourishes. This Man exercises Jacob until true strength and firmness of faith shows itself. For this reason, He changes his name. He says: "Your name shall no more be called Jacob. You were previously called a trampler because of your brother, but they have not yet imposed your true name on you. Your name will be *Israel*. For your fortitude and the invincible strength of heart by which you have conquered God and men have merited this."

Pressed to God's Heart

 et us compose a proverb from this history: when you think that our Lord God has rejected a person, you should think that our Lord God has him in His arms and is pressing him to His heart. When we suppose that someone has been deserted and rejected by God, then we should conclude that he is in the embrace and the lap of God. So Jacob feels and thinks nothing else but that he will be destroyed. But when he takes stock of matters, he is held fast in the embrace of the Son of God. The example of Job in his humiliation and affliction teaches the same. For in this wonderful manner the Lord treats His saint (Psalm 4:3), namely, when we think that it is all over with us, He embraces and kisses us as His dearest sons. This is what Paul means when he says: "When I am weak, I am strong; when I die, I live" (cf. 2 Timothy 2:11; 2 Corinthians 12:10).

October 3

"I have seen God face to face,
and yet my life has been delivered."

GENESIS 32:30

Face to Face with Our Lord

 his is the joyful climax of this contest. For now Jacob returns from hell to heaven, from death to life. It was certainly a very fierce and difficult ["contest"] which he had hitherto sustained. So he gives thanks to God and confesses his distress. Now he no longer wants this place to retain its former name but calls it Peniel, as though he meant to say: "It should not be called a struggle or vision of hell but a vision of God." Therefore he says: *"I have seen the Lord face to face."* "And now I see clearly," he says, "that the wrestler who tested me was God Himself. Why was I so terrified? Why was I so alarmed? I did not know that this was the Lord my God." . . . He Himself, our Lord Jesus Christ, tested Jacob not to destroy him but to confirm and strengthen him and that in this fight he might more correctly learn the might of the promise. Indeed, He added this strength and power to Jacob that he might conquer and joyfully praise the vision of the Lord.

October 4

Jacob lifted up his eyes and looked, and behold, Esau was coming, and four hundred men with him.

GENESIS 33:1

God Changes the Heart

 he matters recounted in this chapter are clear and easy because they deal with moral issues, civil life, and human affairs. . . . For as an example for our faith and to strengthen it, Moses describes how God hears the groaning of a weak and struggling faith. These groans are, indeed, ineffable but not without great fruit. Thus Jacob belongs to the number of those of whom Christ says (Mark 9:23): "All things are possible to him who believes." For by faith he has come forth as the conqueror of God and men so that neither God nor man wishes to harm him or is able to do so. God has blessed him, but his brother Esau has experienced such a change that he not only does not want to harm him but even wants to help, love, and be good to him. His anger has been changed into brotherly kindness. . . . This victory, that he was about to overcome his brother, was promised to Jacob by God gratis and out of pure goodness. Esau is not conquered by strength, diligence, plans, evil tricks, or pretense but solely by the goodness of God, for his will is changed. This is the most illustrious victory of all, when men are brought to such a point that their hearts and wills are changed. . . This is the work of the power and majesty of God alone, to change an angry and offended heart and mind into a quiet and kind one.

[Jacob] himself went on before them, bowing himself to the ground seven times, until he came near to his brother.

Honor and Respect

Although Esau had previously been reconciled by the power of God through the victory and struggle of prayer and faith, nevertheless, Jacob does not omit the external indication of his goodwill, lest it might seem that he is tempting God or disturbing the peace and concord which has been initiated and offending his brother's heart anew by a kind of pride. Accordingly, Jacob bows down with his wives, maids, and children before Esau, although he himself is the son and heir of a better blessing. For he had the spiritual blessing on account of the promised Christ joined with the bodily blessing. Esau did not have the promise that Christ was to be born from his flesh, and yet he who is greater subjects himself and conducts himself as if he were the lesser one. In this manner we also should be subject to every divine ordinance for God's sake because it is God's creature (cf. 1 Peter 2:13). Superiors should therefore be honored by us with whatever respect we can, but in such a way that we do not reject or deny the Word of Christ and the promise of grace on their account and lose the spiritual blessing. For all respect, honor, and services of every kind are to be paid to magistrates with a good conscience and joyful heart if they remain within the prescribed limits, that is, provided that obedience to God and confession of the Word remain intact.

October 6

"Please accept my blessing that is brought to you, because God has dealt graciously with me, and because I have enough."

GENESIS 33:11

I Have Enough

 acob] wants to say: "I have not brought a magnificent and imposing gift which is worthy of admiration, but it is the blessing of God. I beg you to accept it on this account, that it may be a pledge and reminder of my gratitude and the blessing of God, by whose gift and grace I offer this to you, such as it is." . . . Previously Esau said: "I have . . . plenty" [Genesis 33:9]. [Jacob] amplifies his blessing: "I not only have abundance, but I have everything." These are words of a person in exultation and transport over the joy occasioned by the face of God and brother shown to him in grace, mercy, and goodwill. "If only I have God's grace and yours," he means to say, "it is enough and more than enough for me, nor would I suffer any loss if I gave everything to you. I am losing nothing, and I shall never be in need since you have become reconciled to me. I am a rich lord because I have God and you as my friends." All this shows how faith revived and was aroused in Jacob and how he now reigns and triumphs again. For Jacob has now come to the conclusion that his blessing is equal to all the wealth of the whole world.

Jacob journeyed to Succoth,
and built himself a house and made booths for his livestock.

GENESIS 33:17

Good Fruits of Domesticity

he Holy Spirit set forth these matters, namely, to testify that all the works of the saints, however lowly and childish they may be, are pleasing and acceptable as good fruits in the sight of God. Included are not only those sublime theological virtues like contests with death, sins, and other temptations and the victories over the same fraught with great perils, but even those lowly, domestic, and humble services, so that we may learn to regulate our life in this manner that we may be certain that we are pleasing to God in all our acts of duty. I do not always pray, nor do I always meditate on the Law of the Lord and struggle continually with sin, death, and the devil; but I put on my clothes, I sleep, I play with the children, eat, drink, etc. If all these things are done in faith, they are approved by God's judgment as having been done rightly.

October 8

Jacob came safely to the city of Shechem. . . . He bought for a
hundred pieces of money the piece of land on which he had
pitched his tent. There he erected an altar.

GENESIS 33:18–20

An Altar Is Raised

 acob, accordingly, on receiving consolation is safe and sound and freed from the terrors of death, and after the pain from his dislocated thigh has subsided, he raises an altar that he may give thanks to God for this restitution of his health. For he sets up the altar that the Word might be taught, that invocation, giving of thanks, and other acts of divine worship might be made there. For when Holy Scripture says that altars were raised, it is just as if it were saying that schools or churches were established where sacred things which belong to the worship of God might be administered. The altars were not erected in the interest of showing spectacles and processions, nor for the sacrifices of Masses, but for the preaching of the Word. In this way, then, Jacob is described as of a tranquil and joyful heart after his liberation. However, in his happiness, he does not forget God, his Liberator, but he erects an altar, he teaches his children, he rules his household and church, and exhorts them to invocation and thanksgiving.

Jacob said to Simeon and Levi, "You have brought trouble on
me by making me stink to the inhabitants of the land."

GENESIS 34:30

Do Not Rely on Yourself

here is faith here and the remembrance of the
promises? Why does [Jacob] not induce his heart
to say: "You have prevailed against God. How much
more, then, will you prevail against neighboring nations?"
All this has slipped away from him. Trial devours the splendid promises and most glorious victories of faith. But he
does not yet despair, although he is very similar to one in
despair. He does not fall into misbelief and is not an unbe-
liever, although it appears so. This is trial, just as Paul says
of himself: "So that we might not rely on ourselves, we had
the sentence of death in ourselves" (cf. 2 Corinthians 1:8–9).
It is necessary for the saints to be disciplined in this way,
to descend into hell and the abyss, and to be recalled from
there into heaven. For so far Jacob retains a smoking flax in
his heart. When it was announced that Simeon and Levi had
smitten and plundered the whole city, it was impossible for
him not to be deeply moved on account of so many murders.
So there was undoubtedly very great weakness here, com-
plaining, wailing, and crying out to God. . . . This prayer was
heard according to the promise, for he had the spirit of faith
or of grace and prayers.

God said to Jacob, "Arise, go up to Bethel and dwell there."

GENESIS 35:1

From Grief to Joy

n extreme necessity and despair, as it were, God comes to the help of His patriarch, as is stated in Psalm 9:9–10, and He is really a helper in need. . . . Therefore after God sees that Jacob is forsaken and despised and ridiculed by his own sons and that they are not very much distressed for having brought their father into a very critical situation and for having made him very sad, He is present in season and comforts him. For his groaning filled heaven and earth. "Your prayer and tears," He wants to say, "compel Me to come to your aid. The things which seemed to threaten you with destruction will not harm you at all. I am the Lord your God! The Shechemites were killed by My permission, and this whole tragedy was enacted that I might prove you, discipline you, and make you approved and chosen. But be of good courage! I will restrain and check all the fury and raging of the people and change your grief and lamentation into joy. You will be a lord in Shechem, for so it has been ordained by Me." . . . God permits all these things to be done that He may teach us to pray, cry out, and groan. For this is the column of smoke ascending from the desert. In this manner a very great storm is calmed here, and Jacob receives very welcome consolation and peace of heart.

Recall the Promises

he Lord orders the patriarch to build an altar at Bethel, and He reminds him of his former tribulation and comforts him with the examples of preceding temptations and rescues, as though He meant to say: "Recall the promises made to you before this time and reflect what happened to you previously when you fled from your brother Esau and what you suffered and in what a kindly manner I rescued and defended you." . . . "Remember, therefore," the Lord went on to say, "that you also had a promise of protection previously in Bethel and how I rescued you like a father from many great temptations and kept My promises faithfully." At this statement Jacob breathed again and recovered his courage. The wound inflicted by his sons was suddenly healed, because the Word of God makes alive and gives comfort. . . . This, therefore, is a glorious consolation which God shows to Jacob. For it is just as if He were saying: "I have death and life and all times in My hand. Only believe, and you will be saved."

"Let us arise and go up to Bethel, so that I may make there an altar to the God who answers me in the day of my distress and has been with me wherever I have gone."

GENESIS 35:3

The Lord Has Been with Me

ecause of [our ingratitude] we do not acknowledge God or give Him thanks that the Son of God has changed eternal death into temporal punishment. For we want to live agreeably and in ease in this life, and we shudder at and avoid even a small cross. But there is need of the mortification of the flesh, and this obedience must be shown under the cross with a calm mind so that we are grateful because we know that Christ died for our sins. . . . Since Jacob praises God with such great joy as his Liberator from bodily temptations, how much more appropriate will it be for us to confess and give thanks for eternal and temporal blessings! To the fact of being heard he adds that God "has been with me wherever I have gone." He was truly with Jacob and attested it by His actual work of liberation. But this was quite hidden and not apparent. It was as Jeremiah says (Lamentations 3:22): "It is of the Lord's mercies that we are not consumed." For as far as appearances and outward sight was concerned, the devil, Laban, and despair were with him, but Jacob says: "During all of these 30 years the Lord has been with me."

October 13

As they journeyed, a terror from God fell upon the cities
that were around them, so that they did not pursue
the sons of Jacob.

GENESIS 35:5

Terror from God

he neighbors [of Jacob] were so overwhelmed by terror that no one dared even to make a sound, to say nothing of drawing a sword. For [God] shattered the power of their bows, as well as shields, swords, and warfare so that they were not ready and brave enough to fight, although they were otherwise very powerful and warlike. Nor did this happen through the services or stratagems of Simeon or Levi but by the power of the promise and the faith of the patriarch and his own, however weak it may have been. The Holy Spirit reminds us by this example that we should learn the doctrine of creation correctly, namely, that all things are in God's hand, and that we should accustom and encourage ourselves to confident trust in our Creator, which, to be sure, is still very small and weak in us. For if we firmly concluded that God is our Creator, we would certainly believe that He has heaven and earth in His hands and all things which are contained by these.

October 14

*God said to him, "Your name is Jacob; no longer shall your
name be called Jacob, but Israel shall be your name."*

GENESIS 35:10

A Name of Great Importance

 hat he might have a sure pledge and testimony of the divine will, [God] changes Jacob's name and calls him Israel. This change of name shows that God is dealing with him not concerning common matters but concerning special matters of the greatest importance. . . . We are born into this life as sons and daughters of carnal parents and, as Paul says (Ephesians 2:3), as "children of wrath," bringing with us the name of sinful and corrupt nature because of original sin. But when we are baptized, we receive a new name . . . namely, he is called a Christian. This name reminds us of Baptism, which should be practiced in daily tribulations and produce its effects so that we grow into a new and perfect man (cf. Ephesians 4:13–15) and in this way the name of Christian be perfected until our name and old Adam are abolished. Therefore it should be noted that *God* Himself gives a name to the patriarch Jacob, and by this new name a difference is made between the flesh and the spirit. For Israel is a divine name, and God has a different reason for giving a name from that which is customary with parents, relatives, neighbors, the fatherland, and the condition in life. But the name by which God calls and recognizes us is a special one, as He says to Moses in Exodus 33:12: "I know you by name."

October 15

Rachel died, and she was buried on the way to Ephrath
(that is, Bethlehem).

GENESIS 35:19

God Is Present at All Times

he circumstances of this story increase and emphasize [Jacob's] grief, nor is it yet the end of his troubles. For after the loss of the mother, soon and almost in the same year, he loses the firstborn of this mother, Joseph. In a third calamity, Bilhah, Rachel's maid, is defiled by Reuben, the firstborn of the other wife. Surely that is not the meaning of blessing, is it? . . . Such temptations, moreover, become more severe when terror of conscience becomes an additional factor in them and Satan adds oil to the fire. For when the devil sees hearts tried and terrified, he is not slow to hurl his fiery and poisonous darts (cf. Ephesians 6:16) against them so that they think God is angry with them and opposed to them. Therefore in all temptations it affords great comfort to be able to conclude that God is present and favoring us. But the human heart finds it difficult to embrace this comfort when our Lord presses a person to His bosom in such a way that his soul wants to depart. . . . In this manner the troubles of the holy fathers are set before us for an example, that we may see how they were disciplined and note their illustrious faith in the midst of disasters and learn not to lose the sight of God smiling, blessing, and promising if ever He takes from us those things which are sweetest and have been established by His promise. . . . Faith should come to this conclusion: "Although this disaster is very bitter for me, nevertheless, I believe that God is true."

October 16

Isaac breathed his last, and he died and was gathered
to his people, old and full of days.

Genesis 35:29

Pleasant Rest

 he Holy Spirit does not say: "He disappeared after he ceased living" but "he was gathered." He was not scattered, tossed this way and that, or afflicted as he was in a wretched and disastrous life but freed from all evils and gathered to his people like the other fathers who sleep in peace and whom God gathers into His bosom, where they enjoy pleasant rest. This is the force of these words which are used quite significantly. There is a people of the dead, among whom are Adam, Seth, Abraham, Deborah, etc. These people have been gathered into the bosom and arms of God. There they enjoy pleasant rest and they will be resurrected in their time. By this figure, then, Holy Scripture shows that the fathers died not as the heathen die, but that they have been gathered together and are preserved under the hands of God. In Isaiah 57:2, for example, we read: "Let peace come; may he rest in his bed who has walked in his uprightness." And the hour will come in which they will appear again and come forth from their graves more beautiful than the sun and the stars, namely, those who walked uprightly. . . . Such passages should therefore be carefully noted together with the words which the Holy Spirit employs. God does not cast off or scatter the saints but gathers them, and in such a way that not even one of their bones or hairs perishes.

October 17

These are the generations of Esau (that is, Edom).

GENESIS 36:1

Generations

he genealogy of Esau, then, is fittingly added to the history of the two patriarchs Isaac and Jacob. For in this we see the glory and flourishing of the flesh and of ungodly men in this life. . . . On the other hand, Jacob, who has the promise and is the highest patriarch in the whole world and the governor of the true Church, is oppressed in a wretched manner and afflicted by domestic and other troubles, so that it seems that he has been deprived of the spiritual blessing and grace. Yet in the end finally follows what is stated in Mary's song: "He puts down the mighty and exalts the lowly" (cf. Luke 1:52). This is the conclusion, this is the end of the ungodly and the godly, as Christ says (Luke 6:24–25): "Woe to you that are rich, for you have received your consolation. Woe to you that are full now, for you shall hunger," and again (Matthew 5:4): "Blessed are those who mourn, for they shall be comforted." . . . The godly, who are oppressed for a time, have certain protection and consolation in *God*, who is present and sustains the afflicted, mitigates their troubles, and gives eternal life and glory to the little flock when it again emerges from troubles. Nor should we be shattered in spirit . . . but we should conclude that God's Son, our Lord Jesus Christ, the guardian and leader of all who labor and are oppressed in the world, is at our side even as He has promised (Matthew 28:20): "I am with you always, to the close of the age."

October 18

Jacob lived in the land of his father's sojournings,
in the land of Canaan. . . . Joseph, being seventeen years old,
was pasturing the flock with his brothers.

GENESIS 37:1–2

Sustained through Troubles

 his story, then, is the last trouble of the saintly man and by far the most serious one of all, and it is a very horrible one. The very beginning and the whole exposition contains a sharp and very vehement struggle. For it is full of shameful and wretched grief which all but kills the saintly old man, who is exhausted by so many troubles and hardships. There is also the additional crime of his son Judah perpetrating incest with his daughter-in-law Tamar, which also increased the grief and sorrow of the father. But he nevertheless retains hope and confidence with wonderful constancy, and by reason of the numerous examples of illustrious rescues which he experienced throughout his whole life he encourages and sustains himself until new light and consolation shine forth. For there follows the wonderful and peaceful outcome by which his great and unexpected grief is changed into the greatest unexpected joy. For Joseph, whose destruction the father had mourned, is recalled from darkness to light, from death to life, after being preserved by God and rewarded with great honor and dignity by the king of Egypt after he himself had also emerged from many difficulties.

October 19

[Joseph shared his dreams with his brothers]: "My sheaf arose and stood upright. And behold, your sheaves gathered around it and bowed down to my sheaf. . . . Behold, the sun, the moon, and eleven stars were bowing down to me."

GENESIS 37:7, 9

Joseph's Dreams

oses has related the two dreams of Joseph with which the Holy Spirit plays a prelude to the illustrious history about Joseph's future dominion in Egypt, or, as Scripture explains it elsewhere, concerning the man sent ahead of Israel that it might be preserved in a time of famine (cf. Psalm 105:17). From this we should learn to know God's providence and solicitude for us, inasmuch as He indicates and foretells a long time before what the future will be and He regulates and controls it by His goodness in such a way that it may have a tolerable outcome. This is how Joseph himself will interpret it below [Genesis 45:7; 50:20]. Therefore it is certain that God exercises faithful and diligent care for us before we even think about our successes. To be sure, the folly of men is also reproved by such examples. . . . These brothers, for example, are insanely intent on their brother's destruction when he was about to be their own salvation and that of the whole land of Canaan, and if he had been destroyed, they themselves would have been compelled to die of hunger. But God in a wonderful manner turns all the evils they are meditating into good even contrary to their deliberations and before they had formed them.

Joseph went after his brothers and found them at Dothan.

The Wisdom of God

In such danger we see the deepest silence of God and the angels. They allow Joseph to rush headlong into the most sorrowful disaster and death itself; they see that the father will be very wretched and afflicted on account of the death of his son, yet they do not hinder the endeavors of the brothers. Let us therefore mutually exhort one another to endurance by the examples of these men, who were like us in the bearing of the cross. . . . For by means of this trial and vexation God will take care that Jacob does not perish of hunger together with his sons, and He will bring it to pass that Egypt is converted to the true knowledge of God and many are gained and won over. . . . Christ says of His saints in the New Testament: "Will not God vindicate His elect, who cry to Him day and night? I tell you, He will vindicate them speedily" (Luke 18:7–8). Oh, that we could believe this! If we could firmly assent to this voice of God's Son and have this spirit which could say with joy, "Let life, body, and goods be taken away and all things be lost, I am sure that God does and permits this by His excellent wisdom," then we would be true Christians and conquerors of the whole world, and that would truly be giving oneself over to the obedience of God and His will.

October 21

They saw [Joseph] from afar, and before he came near to them
they conspired against him to kill him.

GENESIS 37:18

The Purpose of Temptation

et us consider these matters carefully so that, after we have begun to believe and have hope in the future life that has been granted us through the Word and Baptism, we may learn to endure patiently whatever evils ensue and come to the conclusion that all things take place for our salvation not haphazardly but according to the Father's plan. This is the understanding which we eventually have when the trial is ended. When one is in the very throes of trial, this is not understood, for the feeling of the flesh tears us away from the promise. When a man is involved in tribulation and anxiety, it does not enter his mind to say: "I have been baptized; I have God's promise," but his heart is quite overwhelmed by complaints, grief, and tears according to the flesh. However, the flesh should be crucified and mortified, for it hinders the understanding of the promise and the truth of God's Word, which is perceived in temptation if one clings to it in firm faith. What is stated in the psalm (34:8) follows: "Oh, taste and see that the Lord is good!" God allows us to be tempted that He may have an opportunity for satisfying, comforting, and filling those who have been emptied of all strength and stripped of all help. Otherwise we are sluggish and hear the Word with loathing and become quite torpid.

"Here comes this dreamer.
Come now, let us kill him and throw him into one of the pits."

GENESIS 37:19–20

Where Is God?

Jacob and Joseph are submitted to a very hard trial in a manner plainly different from and contrary to the promise. Nothing at all can be seen of God's care and concern. He does not send an angel and, to be sure, not even the leaf of a tree by which the devil is checked, but He even opens the window for him that he may rage against the father and the son. Jacob indeed has a very ample promise and also its fulfillment in living experience in the blessing implemented through 12 sons. But he comes into conflict with difficulties which are put in his way as if he had neither God nor any promise. However, we should not conclude that he is wholly forsaken. For the promise of Isaiah 49:[16] remains immovable: . . . . "Behold, I have graven you on the palms of My hands, etc." Why, then, are such awful experiences thrown in our path at the hands of our flesh, sons, and offspring? My reply is that this is the manner of God's government, and such is the life of the saints in this world. Therefore there is need of wisdom and doctrine exceeding the whole grasp of human reason, by which I am able to say: "I have been baptized; I have been absolved from my sins; I have eaten the body and drunk the blood of Christ; I have the most certain Word of God; He will not lie and not deceive me, however much all things seem to be carried in a contrary direction."

October 23

Judah said to his brothers, "What profit is it if we kill our brother and conceal his blood? Come, let us sell him to the Ishmaelites, and let not our hand be upon him, for he is our brother, our own flesh."

GENESIS 37:26–27

How Great Is the Father's Love

nto these troubles the holy patriarchs Jacob and his son Joseph are now hurled. This cross was fabricated for them by the artifices and stratagems of the brothers. They are very poor carpenters who fabricate and forge this hard cross for their father and their brother Joseph. The only ones who can endure such a cross are excellent and saintly parents. God keeps quiet and makes out that He does not see, as though He were helping these carpenters, and yet He sees that they are setting these doings into motion. But why does He allow this? Why does He not hurl His thunderbolts at them and prove Himself the undoing of these wicked attempts with their authors? Or why does He not rather allow robbers, adulterers, and tyrants to be tormented and afflicted and spare such saintly men? My reply is that God wants us to consider and learn how great the love of parents toward children is, that we estimate from this the magnitude of God's love by which He embraced us when He was willing to let His only-begotten Son suffer and be crucified for us. For Joseph is the image of God's Son.

Rescue Will Come, but Not Yet

od wanted His saints and Church to endure such horrible trials that their hearts might be aroused to reflect what a great thing it was that the Son of God was on our account also torn away for a time, so to say, and sent into exile and cast into hell that He might rescue us from the exile of the most obstinate sin and eternal damnation. . . . This is the picture of the Church of all times, which God has set forth in His Son and His saints. If you want to be Christians, adapt yourselves to it! Therefore let us learn to obey God in such troubles and adversities and to keep our eyes fixed on heaven. . . . This, then, was God's purpose in what befell Joseph and Jacob. "My dear Jacob and Joseph, I see what evils are bearing down on you; I am not sleeping, but I do not want to remove them and comfort you at present. For the time of rescue is not yet at hand, but you must first experience and learn what the devil, the world, sons, brothers, and death are, so that My grace may become even sweeter and that you may see that you were under My care in tribulation and death. For not even a hair of your head will fall without My nod and will, provided you are not broken in spirit but learn to endure and to bear the cross. I will certainly keep what I have promised. I have promised that I will bless you; I will keep that promise and I will not lie. The flesh indeed murmurs, but resist it and rule over it by faith and the expectation of rescue!"

October 25

They drew Joseph up and lifted him out of the pit,
and sold him to the Ishmaelites for twenty shekels of silver.

GENESIS 37:28

Cut off and Removed

 oseph was sold for a smaller price than Christ was, and I think that the price was about 20 thalers. I am not inclined to engage in rather minute discussions on silver coins. But from this passage Zechariah undoubtedly derived his prophecy concerning Christ (Zechariah 11:12): "They weighed out as my wages thirty shekels of silver." For facts and circumstances agree excellently, and there cannot be a greater similarity than that between Christ crucified and Joseph; the selling and death of both are in agreement. For as Isaiah (53:8) says of Christ, "He was cut off out of the land of the living," so also Joseph is removed from the land and sight of his father, just as if he would never return to his father or see him again.

They took Joseph's robe and slaughtered a goat
and dipped the robe in the blood. And they sent the robe
of many colors and brought it to their father.

GENESIS 37:31–32

Hope for Life amid Death

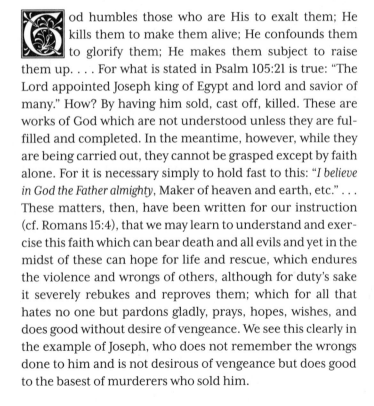

od humbles those who are His to exalt them; He kills them to make them alive; He confounds them to glorify them; He makes them subject to raise them up. . . . For what is stated in Psalm 105:21 is true: "The Lord appointed Joseph king of Egypt and lord and savior of many." How? By having him sold, cast off, killed. These are works of God which are not understood unless they are fulfilled and completed. In the meantime, however, while they are being carried out, they cannot be grasped except by faith alone. For it is necessary simply to hold fast to this: "*I believe in God the Father almighty*, Maker of heaven and earth, etc." . . . These matters, then, have been written for our instruction (cf. Romans 15:4), that we may learn to understand and exercise this faith which can bear death and all evils and yet in the midst of these can hope for life and rescue, which endures the violence and wrongs of others, although for duty's sake it severely rebukes and reproves them; which for all that hates no one but pardons gladly, prays, hopes, wishes, and does good without desire of vengeance. We see this clearly in the example of Joseph, who does not remember the wrongs done to him and is not desirous of vengeance but does good to the basest of murderers who sold him.

They took Joseph to Egypt. . . . Thus his father wept for him.

GENESIS 37:28, 35

Exile and Weeping

nhappy Joseph is carried off by those who bought him and compelled to pass by Hebron; and then, to be sure, the thought enters his mind: "Behold, my father is living here, and he does not know what is happening to me, nor am I permitted to speak to him, to look upon him, and to leave him my last farewell." This was assuredly a great and wretched misfortune! I forbear making mention of the father, who, after he had discovered the deed cried out: "I shall go down to Sheol; I shall be buried with my son. After losing him, this life will never be pleasant and welcome to me." . . . Meanwhile, during this horrible cross of the father and the son, God is deaf and dumb, taking no thought of the things that are done and not knowing them. But faith is present, and God is still speaking to his heart, saying: "O Joseph, wait; be patient; believe! Do not despair! Cling to the promise which you heard from your father!" In this way God speaks to him through the word of his father. "God promised seed to your great-grandfather, your grandfather, and father. Persevere in that promise with firm faith!" But He speaks with him in a wonderful silence. . . . Later, He will really speak with him in a wonderful manner when He appoints him king and savior of Egypt. But now Joseph is buried and dead, and he has his Preparation and Sabbath; his father is also dying, but they will both rise again by the power of God, which makes the dead alive.

October 28

Proof of Grace

hese examples, therefore, are set before us that we may accustom ourselves to endurance in afflictions so that we may not be impatient and murmur, no matter by how many great disasters we are overwhelmed. It certainly hurts, as it undoubtedly also must have hurt the tender heart of Joseph. Certainly, the human heart cannot endure and overcome these hardships without great grief and pain. Thus Joseph was no doubt deeply stricken and disturbed and thought that he was being torn from his father in an unworthy manner, thrown to strangers, and consigned to perpetual slavery, where he could never obtain anything that was his own or hope for liberty but would be compelled to be a slave of slaves. For slavery, even of itself, is burdensome and wretched enough even when other difficulties are not added to it. But it is more troublesome for the excellent youth because he is deprived of parents and all the advantages of this life in the flower of his youth. Therefore if our Lord God lets such experiences come upon His children, we should not murmur when things do not always turn out for us just as we want them to. If God lets His saints, whom He loves dearly, be so afflicted, then let us, too, bear it patiently if at some time sad and adverse experiences fall to our lot. For these matters are not signs of wrath and of being forsaken but rather proofs of grace for the testing of our faith.

October 29

"Tamar your daughter-in-law has been immoral.
Moreover, she is pregnant by immorality."

GENESIS 38:24

Tamar and Christ

hy did the completely clean mouth of the Holy Spirit lower itself to the basest and most ignoble matters, yes, to matters that are even repulsive, filthy, and subject to damnation, as though these things were particularly profitable for the instruction of the Church of God? What has the Church to do with this? I reply as before. These things are mentioned for the sake of Christ, who is described throughout all Holy Scripture as our blood relative, our brother, and more closely joined to us than any other relation of ours. For according to the line of Abraham, He is the brother and cousin of all the sons of Israel. According to His mother, He is a brother and also a cousin, on the fathers' as well as the mothers' side, of all Egyptians, Canaanites, and Amorites; for He was born from Tamar, from Ruth, from Rachel, and from Bathsheba, the wife of Uriah. . . . Here therefore the blessed Seed is described. It is descended from the accursed, lost, and condemned seed and flesh. Nevertheless, It Itself is without sin and corruption. According to nature, Christ has the same flesh that we have; but in His conception the Holy Spirit came and overshadowed and purified the mass which He received from the Virgin that He might be united with the divine nature. In Christ, therefore, there is the holiest, purest, and cleanest flesh; but in us and in all human beings it is altogether corrupt, except insofar as it is restored in Christ.

October 30

Judah identified [the belt, staff, and signet] and said,
"She is more righteous than I, since I did not give her to my son
Shelah." And he did not know [Tamar] again.

GENESIS 38:26

Humiliation and Confession

hese matters are set forth for our consolation. Great saints must make great mistakes in order that God may testify that He wants all men to be humiliated and contained in the catalog of sinners, and that when they have acknowledged and confessed this, they may find grace and mercy. If one falls, how is he to get help? Nevertheless, those who crucify Christ hear this prayer: "Father, forgive them; for they know not what they do" (Luke 23:34). To be sure, one must beware of sins; but if anyone has fallen, he should not become despondent on that account. For God has forbidden both despair and presumption, turning aside to the left hand and to the right. There should be no presumption on the right and no despair on the left. One must stay on the royal road. The sinner should not abandon his confidence in mercy. A righteous man should not be proud. For "the Lord takes pleasure in those who fear Him and in those who hope in His mercy" (Psalm 147:11). He hates those who are proud and presumptuous, and He loves those in whom fear still retains some hope and confidence, not in ourselves but in the mercy of God.

The LORD was with Joseph, and he became a successful man,
and he was in the house of his Egyptian master.

GENESIS 39:2

The Word Planted in the Heart

he Word spoken by his father reigns in [Joseph's] heart. This he retains with the utmost firmness. "My father has taught me. No matter how long God wants to forsake me, I will hold out. My father has taught me to believe and to wait patiently for God's help, no matter how long He postpones or delays. 'Wait for the Lord; be strong, and let your heart take courage'" (Psalm 27:14). For Joseph had the entire Psalter in his heart, since in actuality and in effect he does everything taught in the Psalms about faith, patience, and waiting. He waits, and he sustains himself with the divine promises which he heard from his father. He does not despair; nor does he murmur against God. . . . These are truly miracles. The Holy Spirit was present there in Joseph, and the Word planted in his heart is kept impressed and rooted in such a way that it becomes an immovable rock against the devil on the right and on the left. This is a miracle of miracles set before the whole world.

November 1

Joseph found favor in his [master's] sight and attended him,
and he made him overseer of his house
and put him in charge of all that he had.

GENESIS 39:4

Favor in His Master's Sight

his managerial position that Joseph holds is both honorable to the highest degree and exceedingly hard. For who could bear this as easily as he did? For 11 years he has endured the most wretched slavery without any wages, unless perhaps some profit came his way later, when he gained his freedom. But while he is a slave, all his labors redound to the advantage of his master. Therefore besides food and clothing, and in very meager supply at that, he had nothing; and the fact that he bears the direst poverty with equanimity is also praiseworthy. For at that age he should have contracted matrimony, begotten children, and supported a household of his own. All these things he has to do without, and still he foresees no end of his slavery. Nevertheless, he endures it and depends on God's help with firm hope and faith. For he thinks: "Even if this burden has to be borne longer, I will not be broken in spirit; nor will I despair. I have learned from my father to endure, to wait, and to call upon the Lord. This teaching I will retain and practice till the end of my life."

November 2

Blessing for the Sake of the Godly

od is accustomed to bless even unworthy and ungodly men for the sake of one godly and good man. . . . Therefore just as Jacob was a blessing in the house of Laban, so Joseph was a blessing in the house of his Egyptian master. This is the way our Lord God does things. He so loves those who call upon Him and wait for His help and gifts that for the sake of one man He blesses a whole land. . . . Accordingly, one must note carefully that God blesses the ungodly for the sake of the Church. For if the world were without the Church and the Gospel were not taught and learned, the world would have perished long since. Thus God is with us today, for we have the Word and the Sacraments. He speaks and works through us; He frees many from death and eternal damnation. We are the saviors of the world; and whatever good Germany has is not the result of her own power, virtue, or wisdom, but has been received from those rejected, despised, and accursed people who are called Christians.

November 3

He left all that he had in Joseph's charge, and because of him
he had no concern about anything but the food he ate.

Let Us Do Our Duty

 hatever we do in this world, all this we refer to the glory of God, in order that many may be converted and saved. Therefore we eat, drink, engage in household as well as political matters, and also gather a church by teaching—all this for the purpose of seeking the life to come, as did Joseph, who had no hope of freedom or of royal authority in Egypt but nevertheless looked forward to eternal glory and happiness in heaven. We shall have the same hope, even though in this life too God heaps many good things upon the godly. But this is not the chief reward. Eternal life and everlasting joy, these at last are the true reward of the godly in heaven—the reward which Christ and all the saints have received. Farewell to the world, then, with its harpies! Let us do our duty, as we still teach by the favor of God and endure great troubles with the utmost patience; for in all ways we desire to be mindful of those who are godless and ungrateful, and we are satisfied with the knowledge that our pursuits and labors are pleasing to God. What we cannot take away we can leave behind. If we have the assent and the favor of God, who says: "Behold, your service is pleasing to Me; I will be your reward, and I will render abundant satisfaction for your service to ungrateful men," this promise and consolation is far richer than all the treasures of the whole world.

Now Joseph was handsome in form and appearance.
And after a time his master's wife cast her eyes on Joseph
and said, "Lie with me." But he refused.

GENESIS 39:6–8

Persevere in True Godliness

 oseph spurns and rejects an opportunity so convenient and so full of safety, power, favor and pleasure. Surely this is clear proof of the greatest probity and continence. And these virtues flowed from the fact that in his heart the Word of God and reverence for and fear of God were established, because faith reigned there through the Holy Spirit. . . . What a great thing and how pleasing it is to the Lord to keep the faith, to fear and revere His commandments, and not to withdraw from Him but to persevere in true godliness of heart. Christ admonishes us to conduct ourselves in this way when He says: "By your endurance you will gain your lives" (Luke 21:19). Likewise: "He who endures to the end will be saved" (Matthew 24:13). For the devil is not exhausted, and he does not cease. No, he is insistent, and he forces opportunities. Nor do the toil and exertion of one day or of one year suffice, but there is need of patience and persistence in fighting until he either conquers or is conquered and has his head crushed (cf. Genesis 3:15).

As soon as she saw that [Joseph] had left his garment
in her hand and had fled out of the house,
she called to the men of her household.

GENESIS 39:13–14

A Hypocrite's Conduct

ll [Joseph's] most excellent virtues disappear, and as a reward for them he is accused of adultery, hypocrisy, and crimes of every kind, as if with singular cunning he had made a pretense of this innocence and faithfulness in office in order that he might be able to have intercourse with the lady of the house whenever the opportunity was favorable. Thus he bears the disgraceful conduct of the harlot. It deforms his best works most horribly and defiles them with the poison of the devil. . . . The same thing actually happened to Christ. For why does He raise the dead, heal the sick, and perform other miracles? "With no other end in view," reply Annas and Caiaphas "than to be made king and to destroy the place and us all. Away with Him! Away with Him! Crucify Him! He wanted to deceive and destroy us with His hypocrisy, with which He has deluded the stupid mob up to this day." Indeed, even the people themselves cried out later: "We thought that He wanted to benefit us, but with those benefits He would almost have destroyed us." Such a hypocrite is the devil. Sometimes he does good in order that he may do more harm. But this mark he later fastens on the works of the godly, as though the things they do piously and usefully were done to harm and overthrow the whole world.

November 6

As soon as his master heard the words that his wife spoke
to him . . . his anger was kindled.

GENESIS 39:19

The Devil's Attacks

hese things are set before us in the Church by the Holy Spirit for our instruction, that we may learn to believe in God and to fear Him, but later to fight and stand against the devil when he assails our faith and chastity as he attacks the faith of Joseph here by means of lust. For after chastity has been violated by adultery or promiscuous lusts, faith, too, is immediately violated. Therefore let us make a stand for the Word and for faith and a good conscience, on the right and on the left, when the report is good and when it is evil (2 Corinthians 6:7–8). So far indeed Joseph has been in the best repute because of his most respectable morals, by which the heart of the lady of the house was inflamed so strangely to lust. In this respect, of course, he has been a happy and fortunate man who was most pleasing to all the members of the household. But now that his good reputation has been lost, he must contend with the most evil infamy. He goes through this too. But these things were not written for the sake of Joseph himself, who did not know that they were ever to be put down in writing by Moses. No, they are set before us in order that we may imitate the examples of godliness and chastity; and to this end they must be retained, dealt with, and learned in the Church.

Joseph's master took him and put him into the prison.

GENESIS 39:20

An Unjust Reward

his is assuredly the greatest and heaviest cross, and truly shameful pay is given to Joseph for the services he has performed most faithfully for 18 years. Not only his labors but also his virtues are paid for with punishment and a most disgraceful death. . . . In great part we serve, teach, admonish, suffer, give consolation, and do the things commanded by God for unworthy men. Here we gain nothing for our services but hatred, envy, and exile; and our whole life is nothing else than the loss of kindnesses. Therefore you must never hope that the world will acknowledge and remunerate your faithfulness and diligence; for it does the opposite, as this example attests. . . . Let us not bear this ingratitude with impatience, since we have been born and placed into this life and station by God to serve the world and to gather the elect for eternal salvation. If there are any good men who acknowledge our services, there is reason for self-congratulation on our part. But if the greater part curses, condemns, and slays us, we should know that this is our reward. And in this we should become like the Son of God and all the saints, who, in return for the greatest services, experienced the utmost ingratitude of men.

November 8

Joseph's master took him and put him into the prison.

GENESIS 39:20

Falsely Imprisoned

Where is Joseph's God now, to liberate and rescue him? Why does He desert him? I reply: He is not deserting him but is plaguing him as an example and for the comfort of all the saints, in order that we may learn to persevere, hope, and trust in the Lord—no matter what happens—in much patience, in afflictions, in times of necessity, in honor and dishonor, in ill repute and good repute, as Paul admonishes in 2 Corinthians 6:8. For it is certain the Church and the angels of God are honoring us. Let this suffice for us, and let us not be broken in spirit. If the devil and the world revile us with lies and slanders or kill us outright and destroy us, nevertheless God looks upon our affliction with open eyes; He smiles at us and takes delight in the virtue and victory in our afflictions. Accordingly, we should know for certain and determine that God is not angry with us when we are afflicted. For thus Joseph, too, thought: "To be sure, this prison, confusion, and dishonor are very troublesome to my flesh; but I will look back upon the promises I have heard and the examples I have seen, and in reliance on them I will await help from the Lord."

November 9

The LORD was with Joseph and showed him steadfast love.

GENESIS 39:21

The Lord Begins to Help

hrist, the Bishop of souls (1 Peter 2:25) who is mindful of hell and death, is the *only one* who sees Joseph, the *only one* who cares about Him. He rejoices that such a beautiful sacrifice is being offered to Him. Therefore when all things seem hopeless, and no help or comfort is left, then the help of the Lord begins. He says: "Behold, I am present, Joseph; let it be enough for you that I am mindful of you." Accordingly, this text—"The Lord was with Joseph"—is full of consolation and joy. For although he is not yet liberated, God is nevertheless already thinking about raising him up from death and hell after his blood has cried long enough to heaven (Genesis 4:10) and has brought it about that the Lord became the Bishop of his soul and inclined His mercy to him. . . . Christ gave Joseph the Holy Spirit in prison, the Spirit of truth, who sustained him in death, disgrace, and confusion, and inspired in him this feeling: "Do not fear; let your heart be strengthened; wait for the Lord!" This is complete and very great comfort, namely, that God has regard for him and inclines His gift to him, that is, breathes into him the spirit of fortitude and wisdom, and makes of him a firm, strong, and living saint. For He quickens him in the midst of death and mortifies him in damnation itself. Therefore his heart can conclude: "No matter how much the master rages against me, I will nevertheless not die; my virtue and good name will not perish."

November 10

The Lord . . . gave [Joseph] favor
in the sight of the keeper of the prison.
GENESIS 39:21

External Comfort

[Joseph's] conscience is again uplifted and glad-dened; for God speaks to his heart, that is, win-ningly and pleasantly: "My grace is sufficient for you (2 Corinthians 12:9); I give you My Spirit, that you may not perish. I will give you a cheerful heart, that you may be able to endure." And this was the first consolation, when his conscience within him was gladdened, made peaceful, and healed, and his life and his well-being itself were restored. The other comfort is external. The Lord gave him grace or favor, and it is favor that is felt; that is, it made him popular in the eyes of the keeper of the prison, who observed outstanding natural ability in this youth. For when the gift of the Holy Spirit is given to men, it shines forth on the outside, with the result that this grace is seen in the demeanor, the words, the face, and the gestures. Accordingly, while the others who were being kept in the same prison were groaning, wailing, and raging, Joseph alone was resolute in heart. He taught and comforted the rest, although he was in the same danger. Yet he did not conduct himself otherwise than as if he were completely free and altogether certain of his liberation.

November 11

Whatever [Joseph] did, the Lᴏᴢᴌ made it succeed.

GENESIS 39:23

Faith in the Unseen

hese examples are set before us to instruct and strengthen us, in order that we may learn faith and hope in the Lord. But it is not a faith in things that are seen. No, it is a faith in things that are invisible (Hebrews 11:1). Thus Joseph believes in the Lord, whom he does not see; and he hopes to have His grace, which he does not perceive. He feels that everything unfavorable is being put in his way. Nevertheless, he receives what he has believed and hoped for. Up to now, therefore, he has walked like a blind man in the thickest darkness. He has seen neither God nor his father nor anything else than death and destruction. But he has clung to the Word which he had heard from his father: "I am the Lord your God, and the God of your fathers." This Word has been his life, and from this life he will later be raised to immeasurable glory and honor. This is surely an example of the works of God. It shows how God exalts His saints, so that in trials they learn patience in faith and hope, even though hope is truly patience itself, because our life must be hidden. One must say: "Close your eyes, and sustain yourself with the Word," not only in perils and conflicts but also in the chief articles of the Christian doctrine.

"Remember me, when it is well with you."

GENESIS 40:14

Faith, Hope, and Patience

oseph] continues in faith, hope, and patience, is content, does not murmur, is not angry, and does not curse God or men. For among the very saintly patriarchs there was most certain faith in and knowledge of the heavenly doctrine which we have by the kindness of God; that is, they believed in Christ and because of Him looked forward to eternal life. The doctrine of the resurrection was implanted in their hearts, because they endure not only in death but also beyond and after death. Joseph is threatened so often with death and killed so often that it can be said in all truth that he endured beyond death. . . . Therefore all the fathers who hoped in God undoubtedly also believed in the resurrection of the dead. This can be clearly demonstrated from the argument of Christ: Abraham, Isaac, and the other patriarchs endure even unto death with the firmest faith; therefore they believed in the resurrection of the dead. For if no other and better life remains after this one, what need is there of faith or of God Himself or of hope in God beyond death? If the resurrection is not to be expected, there is also no faith and no God. On the contrary, if there is faith and any hope in God, it is necessary that there be a God who is the God of all who trust and hope in Him and for His sake retain the hope of immortality. For since all must face death and the godly trust in God despite this, they confess of necessity that after this life another, eternal life remains.

November 13

The chief cupbearer did not remember Joseph, but forgot him.

GENESIS 40:23

Let Prayer Sustain Us

Again Joseph, who is very good and very pious, is tried. He feels that his hope and the confidence he has gained that the hour of his liberation was drawing near have been frustrated. He had asked the butler to remember him when it was well with him. But what happens? Joseph is forgotten, and God lets him be tried and vexed again in that hope and consolation for two whole years. . . . At the same time a teaching concerning the ingratitude of the world is presented, namely, what recompense it is wont to make for the greatest benefits. It is truly a horrible picture of this height of ingratitude. Joseph had served the lady of the house, Potiphar's wife, not only according to her good pleasure but even to the point that she desired him with an insane love. What does she give him in return? Death and misfortunes of every kind. . . . Accordingly, Joseph is kept in bonds and in hell, and although he had conceived the hope that he was to be liberated at an early date, he nevertheless sees that this hope is futile. But he has the Spirit of prophecy, who consoles him, so that he sustains himself with the doctrine of the fathers. "Now God will help, but He is tarrying too long." But it is decidedly irksome to hope and always to be mistaken and frustrated, and this heaps up grief for those who are afflicted. . . . But let prayer be constant and importunate, let it not cease, let it not grow weary, and let it resist mistrust and despair.

November 14

After two whole years, Pharaoh dreamed . . .

GENESIS 41:1

Wait for the Lord

t is a very great and an incomparable example because of the countless sufferings which concurred in one man and continued for so long a time and offered no hope. . . . From such examples, however, have flowed those remarkable exhortations in the psalms and in the prophets. "Wait for the Lord; be strong" (Psalm 27:14). Likewise: "If it seem slow, wait for it; it will surely come; it will not delay" (Habakkuk 2:3). Likewise: "Then you will know that I am the Lord; those who wait for Me shall not be put to shame" (Isaiah 49:23). The weak flesh says: "It is lasting too long. Help is delayed for five, 10, or 20 years; and no end of the trial is in sight." But remember that you have the promise and have God as your Friend and Father. . . . Thus today we are tormented and afflicted by Satan and the world in various ways. . . . But what else should you do than wait for the Lord? You have the promise that God is your Father. Add faith and love to this, have no doubt about the promise, and wait, since what is promised is not shown immediately. . . . Let us rather conclude: "I know that I have been baptized, that I have eaten the body and drunk the blood of the Son of God, that I have been absolved by divine authority, that all my sins have certainly been forgiven me, and that victory over the devil, death, and hell has been promised me. What more should I ask for?"

November 15

Joseph answered Pharaoh, "It is not in me;
God will give Pharaoh a favorable answer."

GENESIS 41:16

God Will Give an Answer

Those who enter upon civil authority or any other position of government, who are summoned to give advice at court, should prepare themselves for humility and the fear of the Lord. Thus Pharaoh, a heathen king, does not rely on his own prudence but respectfully consults others, who have sound judgment in affairs of state and in religion. But Joseph respects and fears God much more and replies in all modesty to the petition of the king: "Ah, who am I? God can surely do it through someone else." These examples should be carefully observed, and there should be no doubt that political power is a divine arrangement ordained for the benefit of this life and also of the Church, which it serves when it fosters and preserves peace, even though the Church has another office, which pertains to the future life. Then, since it is certain that political power is an ordinance of God and is not in our hands and counsels, we should bend our knees and call upon God with reverence and fear, saying: "Lord God, I am a prince, a magistrate, a counselor, an overseer, a preacher, a teacher; but the government is Thine. Thine is the kingdom, the judgment, and all counsel. Grant me this grace and competence, that my counsels and actions may be successful."

Fixed by God

[oseph] gives a reason why the dream is twofold and yet signifies the same thing. For what God speaks is certain and will have a speedy outcome. Accordingly, there are, as it were, two witnesses for one thing. It is to be certain and will come soon. "God will not leave you in doubt and uncertainty." . . . This certitude is necessary in every kind of teaching, especially in sacred teaching. For I must be certain what I am to think about God, or rather what He thinks about me. . . . Therefore one must learn that God is not uncertain, ambiguous, equivocal, and slippery like a wavering reed, but that He is unequivocal and certain. He says: "I baptize you in the name of the Father and of the Son and of the Holy Spirit; I absolve you of your sins, etc." Here the Father, the Son, and the Holy Spirit make no mistake; they are not tossed about by the wind but are rocks and Selah, as God is often named in the Psalms because He is absolutely firm. You may rely solidly on Him and say: "I am holy and saved; I am God's son and heir, because I have been baptized."

This proposal pleased Pharaoh and all his servants.

GENESIS 41:37

The Blessing of Listening

 t is also a gift of God that the words spoken by this prophet Joseph pleased the king and all the princes, counselors, inspectors, and subjects: for he calls all these the king's servants and ministers. Accordingly, it is a special blessing of God to be able not only to teach but also to listen when taught; for here the devil is excluded. He has the power to make false accusations and to set up hindrances or to alienate the hearts of the listeners, especially as soon as the Word of God and prophecy, not only in spiritual matters but also as it pertains to the church and state, appears. Therefore it is a most excellent gift that the king, together with his counselors, soon admits and approves of this Word of God, as Solomon says in Proverbs 20:12: "The hearing ear and the seeing eye, the Lord has made them both." . . . When God is propitious and visits us in His mercy, He gives a seeing eye and a hearing ear. Thus Joseph is a seeing eye in the kingdom of Egypt. Pharaoh, together with his princes and ministers, is a hearing ear. . . . This indeed is exaltation after tribulation, provided that we are able to endure in trials, just as Joseph stood firm with great courage in the greatest difficulties. Therefore ineffable fruit follows, both in respect to the Church as well as in respect to the state and domestic economy.

November 18

"You shall be over my house, and all my people shall order themselves as you command."

Far More Abundantly

How splendidly God honors and exalts those who wait for the Lord and are able to bear a father's hand and rod. Therefore this example should be carefully inculcated and set before all men in the state and in the church, in order that they may learn to wait and to endure in trial. Hold fast! Hold fast! "If you believe," says Christ to Martha, "you will see the glory of God" (cf. John 11:40). Faith must precede, and then the waiting must follow, just as Joseph, in fetters and imprisonment, waited for the Lord. . . . How truly, therefore, Paul says: "God is able to do far more abundantly than all that we ask or think" (Ephesians 3:20)! Our petitions are too weak and feeble. Joseph did not have the courage to pray for what he obtained; but he held in his heart a dimly burning wick and a bruised reed, yes, that ineffable groaning (Romans 8:26) which was a sweet-smelling column of smoke that ascended into heaven. . . . Later Joseph got what he did not understand and never had the courage to hope or ask for. These are truly lofty and wonderful examples which we ourselves should learn and also set before others, in order that we may recognize the divine wisdom, goodness, mercy, and power which are most certainly near us.

Pharaoh said to Joseph,
"See, I have set you over all the land of Egypt."
<small>GENESIS 41:41</small>

Wait for the Lord

ut how shall I be steadfast when there is such a mass of trouble?" you will say. Cling to the Word, and conclude as follows: "I have been baptized; I believe in Christ, the Son of God. Come devil and death, it does not matter." There will be no danger from plague, death, or hell; for the Lord sustains you with His hand as long as you have His Word. In this way you will "learn what the acceptable and perfect will of God is" (Romans 12:2). But without renewal you will not attain this knowledge. For this is what precedes: "Be transformed by the renewal of your mind." Then at last you will recognize the goodness of God. And how are we renewed? By rejecting and abolishing the old man, who certainly grieves the flesh violently. Yet there is a renewal from day to day. Thus exceedingly harsh mortification in prison and fetters preceded the liberation of Joseph. Therefore from his example, which is full of virtues of every kind, we should learn to understand the wisdom and goodness of God and the manner of guidance with which God deals with us, that one must wait for the Lord without ceasing, and that no time of tribulation and distress can be so great and so long that it must break us or drive out the Word of faith, which is the strength and power of God for salvation to every believer (Romans 1:16). Therefore one should hold fast.

November 20

Then Pharaoh took his signet ring from his hand and put it on
Joseph's hand, and clothed him in garments of fine linen and
put a gold chain about his neck.

GENESIS 41:42

Civil Authority

hose masks of judges, magistrates, teachers, doctors, and lawyers are necessary; but one must merely use them, not enjoy them. For you are not a man to be adored by the rest, but it is God's will that this life be governed and preserved, in order that the works of the devil may be abolished and peace and discipline may be retained. This must be the goal of all government. For God does not pay consideration to any "person" position when He confers salvation. Why, then, does He create and set up these ranks and grades of human society? He does so in order that He may humble you under this burden and lead you to the recognition of your weakness and wretchedness. This plan of God you abuse and turn into the opposite, that is, toward pride and arrogance, although it is God's will that under these masks you should serve His ordinance and man's need. In this way God wanted to come to the aid of man's need, and for this reason He has commanded that honor be bestowed on the government, as is written: "Respect to whom respect is due, honor to whom honor is due" (Romans 13:7). Without these masks peace and discipline could not be preserved. Therefore use these gifts to the glory of God and for the common good.

Joseph called the name of the firstborn Manasseh. "For," he said, "God has made me forget all my hardship and all my father's house." The name of the second he called Ephraim, "For God has made me fruitful in the land of my affliction."

GENESIS 41:51–52

Unparalleled Works of God

oseph retains the memory of his wretchedness and troubles, and he wants to say: "Behold, I was an exile and poor. Nevertheless, God, who has regard for the humble, the afflicted, the lost, and the condemned, has also had pity on me and has given me a son, Manasseh, in order that I may forget all my misfortunes. Then He has added a second son, in order that I may grow and multiply in the land of my suffering and grief." . . . And this was outstanding praise and glorification of God, whereby Joseph praised the wonderful works of God, namely, that He makes all things out of nothing. We should also acknowledge these works and exercise ourselves in them. For we must be humiliated and mortified, and the grain of wheat that has been thrown into the ground must die and rise again with manifold fruits (John 12:24). For He is the God of . . . fruits, but in the land of . . . mortifications. And it is a perpetual and unparalleled rule of the works of God to make all things out of nothing.

When Jacob learned that there was grain for sale in Egypt,
he said to his sons, . . . "Go down and buy grain for us there,
that we may live and not die."

Trust but Do Not Tempt

t the end of the preceding chapter Moses said that the famine prevailed all over the earth and that for this reason people gathered from all regions to buy food in Egypt (Genesis 41:57). In the meantime, however, Jacob, together with his people, also began to be hungry. Therefore he addresses his sons in this manner and urges them to go to buy grain. . . . We are ordered to believe, and to trust in the goodness of God, but not to tempt God. For we cannot live our life according to the rule which He Himself has, but we must live as opportunities and the times decide. Yet faith and hope must be preserved. Therefore Jacob does not say: "Remain. Wait. The Lord has the power to send bread from heaven. Perhaps He will cause grain to rain in this land and nourish us." This is not what the promise means. Although there is no doubt that God is able and willing to nourish and defend you, you must not avoid the opportunities offered for help and protection. You can avail yourself of these without sin. Otherwise you will be tempting God.

Joseph saw his brothers and recognized them, but he treated them like strangers and spoke roughly to them.

GENESIS 42:7

Harsh Words in Order to Save

oseph deals rather harshly with his brothers. It is his purpose to urge them on to repentance and the acknowledgment of their sinfulness, to slay their smugness and drive them to despair by threatening death and punishments of every kind. . . . He wants to arouse grief and contrition and to induce them to seek health and cleansing for themselves. Thus God afflicts us with various disasters, not to punish us, although this really is a punishment. But He takes no pleasure in it. What, then, does He mean by sending so many troubles, vexations, sicknesses, etc.? He does this in order that you may be led to a knowledge of your sin. He knows that you cannot make satisfaction, and He does not return evil in accordance with our merits; for we deserve nothing else than death and hell. But the sin that clings to our nature is hidden from our eyes, and He brings it to light. . . . Indeed, we must even fall most horribly, in order that we may recognize our wretchedness and weakness. Thus David fell in a horrible manner on account of his smugness and pride, in order that he might learn what sin is and be able to say from the heart: "Against Thee, Thee only, have I sinned" (cf. Psalm 51:4).

"Let one of your brothers remain confined where you are in custody, and let the rest go and carry grain for the famine of your households, and bring your youngest brother to me."

GENESIS 42:19–20

The Law Is a Custodian

 oseph loves his brothers most tenderly. He wishes them no evil. Nevertheless, he treats them most cruelly and allows them to run the risk of death. They themselves behaved in a far crueler manner toward Joseph; for they were planning to kill him. . . . Here, however, Joseph thinks only of their life and welfare, although he lets something else be seen. . . . Thus God gave the Law to reveal sin and to work wrath (Romans 4:15). Therefore it is a discipline and a rod, or, as Paul says, "our custodian" (Galatians 3:24), without whom the flesh does not understand sin. Thus a pupil whom his teacher spares will never make progress but will remain a stump and a log, for without the discipline or chastisement of the teacher he has no knowledge or understanding of his stupidity and his evil plight. Therefore knowledge of sin is necessary, although it alone is not sufficient. . . . This is the measure and goal of all punishments and vexations, just as parents chastise their children in order that they may be corrected and return to the way. . . . In this manner the example of Joseph should be applied to the kingdom of Christ, who punishes, not to cast off or disinherit but to preserve the inheritance which He has acquired for us with His blood.

November 25

"Let one of your brothers remain confined . . . and let the rest go and carry grain for the famine of your households, and bring your youngest brother to me."

True Repentance

Joseph practices the true, proper, and perfect use of the Law on his brothers. For this means leading them down to hell, mortifying and confounding them, not with a view to their destruction but rather for their life and salvation. For the Law was not given to the end that it should kill, although it really does kill when it works wrath and reveals sin. But it does not kill in such a way that one must remain and perish in death, as Judas and Saul perished, but only that it may perform its function. To this the promise must be added, lest despair follow, just as these brothers will finally come almost to the point of despair. Had they not heard the statement (Genesis 45:4) "I am Joseph," it would have been a trial unto death. But Christ does not seek this. No, He seeks humiliation, contrition, and condemnation unto life. Accordingly, true repentance is not contrition alone; it is also faith, which takes hold of the promise, lest the penitent perish. But these brothers have not yet arrived at perfect knowledge of sin. Therefore Joseph will continue to plague them. They must be put through the mill even more.

*"My money has been put back; here it is in the mouth
of my sack!" At this their hearts failed them, and [the brothers]
turned trembling to one another, saying,
"What is this that God has done to us?"*

GENESIS 42:28

An Evil Conscience

hus the sons of Jacob have an evil conscience. . . .
These brothers of Joseph are not only troubled about
the sin of which they were conscious—although they
took pains to cover and conceal it—but they were also afraid
of all their words and deeds, and they imagined that there
was new guilt in every action or thought. Yet in such great
disquiet and confusion they are dumb and do not confess
their sin. This was true of Adam in Paradise, when he was
almost dead from fear of the voice and wrath of God. Nevertheless, he does not open his mouth and is not able to say:
"I have sinned." But the same folly and perversity accompa-
nies sin in all the sons of Adam—as was detected at the very
beginning in our first parent—until the spiritual use is added,
when Christ says: "Ephphatha" (Mark 7:34). In the meantime
the bond of the tongue remains—the bond with which the
devil has stopped the mouth, so that although it is terrified,
it nevertheless does not seek a remedy. For the devil does not
allow the sinner to say from his heart: "I have sinned against
Thee, Lord God; pardon me; I repent of my sin."

When they came to Jacob . . . they told him all that had
happened to them, saying, . . . "But we said to him,
'We are honest men; we have never been spies.
We are twelve brothers, sons of our father. One is no more.'"

GENESIS 42:29–31

Sin Does Not Want to Be Revealed

gnorance of sin necessarily brings with it ignorance of God, Christ, and the Holy Spirit and all things. . . . And if you want to engage successfully in theology and the study of Holy Scripture and do not want to run into a Scripture that is closed or sealed, you should learn above all to understand sin correctly, and the Epistle to the Romans should be your door and key to Scripture. Otherwise you will never penetrate to an understanding and knowledge of it. But when you have done this, you will understand what a great evil sin is. It is on account of sin that God sent His Son, in order that it might be purged away by the blood of the Son of God and that ineffable sacrifice. Therefore the evil itself must be indescribably great. But just as these brothers proceed obstinately to cover their sin, so that horrible plague and misery is raging throughout the world, because sin does not want to be laid bare and to be what it is. For it wants to be pure and clean, contrary to its nature. It wants to be beautiful.

But [Jacob] said, "My son shall not go down with you, for his brother is dead, and he is the only one left. If harm should happen to him on the journey that you are to make, you would bring down my gray hairs with sorrow to Sheol."

GENESIS 42:38

The Weakness of the Flesh

hy does Jacob, who also has the promises and yet forgets them, still mourn? He is wholly carnal; sin not only fights in his members (Romans 7:23) but makes war on him and takes him captive. Or is it not unbecoming for us to be plagued and weakened in this way by our flesh? On top of this, the devil approaches, takes the opportunity offered by the flesh, and increases disbelief, mistrust, and forgetfulness of God. This, then, has been written for our consolation, that Jacob sinned so grievously against the promise he had. He should have said: "What do I care, whether my son dies or lives? It costs only a son. I have God, who promises, consoles, and defends; who is kind and gives bountifully; who can heap many more and even greater blessings upon me. Why, then, do I mourn? Why am I sad?" . . . Accordingly, this doctrine of the Holy Spirit is set forth in this example . . . namely, that the natural affections, which produce this grief and sorrow, remain in the saints, and that God is the author not of the destruction of nature but of its healing. . . . Although this weakness of Jacob is a sin, nevertheless it is beneficial to him for humility, for fear, faith, and prayer, as well as for greater joy of heart.

November 29

Then their father Israel said to them, "If it must be so . . . take also your brother, and arise, go again to the man."

GENESIS 43:11, 13

Entrusted to God

t last faith conquers and triumphs, and Jacob hands his son over to Judah. He neither despairs nor blasphemes but determines thus in his heart: "Hitherto I have resisted you and have wanted to try everything rather than send my dearly beloved son to Egypt. I did not want to tempt God, and for this reason I sought various means to avoid bringing him into danger. Now at length, since we are driven by extreme necessity, I shall entrust him to God's predestination and goodness." This is an illustrious example, and we should follow it in all our actions and in our whole life. For when we have done all that was possible in our tribulation and distress—just as Jacob here opposed the plans and wishes of his sons with great zeal—and there has been no help in those means, then indeed we should say: "Well and good! I have done what I could. I have not tempted God. As for the rest, I must rely on the promise He has given and entrust everything to His will and good pleasure." Then you will have the most rightful excuse of necessity, and God will liberate you in a wonderful manner or will certainly give you something better than you could foresee. Only do not lose heart.

"As for me, if I am bereaved of my children, I am bereaved."

A Son Is Offered

At the end of all his misfortunes Jacob is hurled into such grief that he cries and sobs: "I am bereaved! I am bereaved!" He must offer his son. Just as Abraham sacrificed Isaac, so Jacob offers Joseph and Benjamin, to whom, as he knew, all hope and faith in the promise were attached. It was indeed a very heavy cross. Therefore he is also exalted. These examples have been set before us in order that we may learn to imitate and follow them. Although the suffering of Christ should be before our eyes continually above all, yet the weaker examples of the fathers affect us more than that sublime example of the Son of God. In Christ there was a greater humiliation than in all the fathers. But it does not enter our heart, for the fact that we know that Christ is God stands in the way. The patriarchs, however, move us more strongly. They were men like ourselves in all things when they were involved in extreme difficulties. Christ's example is more wonderful in the Sacrament and in the gift by which He became our Redemption and Salvation.

December 1

And the men were afraid
because they were brought to Joseph's house.

GENESIS 43:18

The Remedy for Affliction

hy do they not take hold of the Word, which can buoy them up and strengthen them, so that they can be without fear of death and dangers? So great is their bewilderment that they are unable to recall the promises and the sermons of their father which they had long since neglected. Because they despise the Word, let them have the lie, be afraid of themselves, and imagine tyranny and punishments of every kind for themselves. For these are the well-known Furies, the tortures of a disturbed conscience because of the sin which has been committed—the tortures with which it burdens and afflicts them in vain and without any cause. . . . [When the Law comes,] it accuses and terrifies, I am killed; and I persecute, attack, and torture myself with vain thoughts that amount to nothing. Thus over and above the fact that we sin gravely against God, we also afflict ourselves; we take a stand against ourselves and fight until a brother comes up to console and buoy us up with the Word and say: "Why are you insane? Why are you imagining things in your dreams? You are mistaken. God is not angry with you; He has taken away your sin, etc." For a heart that tortures itself needs such a remedy and the comfort of a brother.

It Is Well

oseph wishes them peace. This is the way the Hebrew reads. It means that he greets them in a friendly manner. Psalm 122:6 says: "Pray for the peace of Jerusalem!" This means: "Pray that prosperity and health may come upon it." In our salutations we wish others well by saying: "God grant you grace!" "God give you a good morning, a good evening!" "God bless you, and be your Benefactor!" "God be gracious to you, and grant you success and salvation!" For this is what peace means to the Hebrews. Thus Joseph continues to show kindness and special love toward his brothers. As a result they are firmly persuaded that he is kind, mild, and favorable. And yet he conducts himself in a manner that befits a magistrate who must keep discipline—a magistrate of whom mercy and kindness are the chief adornment. Then he inquires about the health of his father. "Does your father, this old man, have peace?" he asks. They reply: "There is peace." And from this reply one can gather the force of this word, just as above, in Genesis 37:14, Jacob sends his son Joseph to see whether his brothers, the sheep, and the cattle have peace, that is, whether it is well with them.

And he lifted up his eyes and saw his brother Benjamin. . . .
"God be gracious to you, my son!"

GENESIS 43:29

A Beloved Brother

[oseph] sees [Benjamin] in his house. . . . Here his natural affections assert themselves, and he weeps at the sight of his brother and at the mention of his father. "God be gracious to you," he says, "and show you favor, my son!" These words stirred his heart very deeply, for he is affected not only by the sight of his brother but also by the recollection of his mother and his father and of everything that had happened at home. He recalled that his very sweet mother had died in childbirth on account of this son Benjamin in the year before he was sold. At the same time he thought of the many great troubles his parents and he himself had to endure throughout their life, especially during the two years before his mother died, and that he had been sold to the Ishmaelites at the end of the year in which Benjamin was born. There is no doubt that he saw all this in his mind's eye when he caught sight of his brother. And his heart burned with the most tender affection toward Benjamin and his parents. Therefore he says: "God be gracious to you, my son." It is as though he were saying: "With what great pain our mother bore you! With what great difficulties and cares my father and I were tormented until it was granted me to enjoy the sight of you and your company!" Now his heart melts in tears.

December 4

Joseph said to his steward, "Up, follow after the men,
and when you overtake them, say to them,
'Why have you repaid evil for good?'"

GENESIS 44:4

Self-Confidence Abolished

he brothers, who had been treated in such a kindly manner and had been filled with joy, flattered themselves with wonderful rhetoric and congratulated themselves on the success of their plans. . . . They undoubtedly intended to relate at home that they had been affectionately invited by the ruler of the land and had been treated very sumptuously, not at an inn but at the court of the ruler, but that Benjamin above all had been treated with the greatest honor, since his portion was increased fivefold in comparison with the share of the others. . . . But this glorying in their righteousness and wisdom disappears in a brief moment. Therefore whether the days are good or evil, we should learn to fear God in a spirit of such steadfastness and equability that we sing psalms to the Lord in our hearts not only in peaceful and pleasant times but also in times of misery. If fortune is favorable, enjoy it, and be grateful; but if it is adverse, call upon God to remove or mitigate your troubles, yes, to be your one and highest Refuge. For this confidence and glory in the merits of wisdom and righteousness—the confidence with which these brothers boasted of having reached such great honor on the strength of their own virtues—must be mortified and abolished.

December 5

Who, Me?

he brothers] rely on their righteousness and merits to remove the crime with which they have been charged, and they want to be completely exonerated. For this confidence in man's righteousness and freedom from danger is so great that it thinks God is a fool and a weakling who is not able to hold such saintly men responsible for any crime. But they will have to learn the prayer of David (Psalm 19:12): "Who can discern his errors? Clear Thou me from hidden faults." . . . We are corrupted by original sin, so that we can be accused and found guilty before God in a thousand ways when to ourselves we seem to be completely righteous. And if we ever are proud and do not remain in the fear of God and faith, He sets a huge mass of sins before us—sins of which we were ignorant, as Moses says in Psalm 90:8. . . . But these brothers are not only smug in regard to secret sins; they also claim innocence in the very worst cause. "There is no need to be worried; we know that we are innocent!" Indeed, they even bring the hardest sentence against themselves by saying, "Let him with whom you find the cup die." This is indeed the fruit of self-righteousness, which makes men smug and stubborn. . . . Therefore they are hurled down to the depths of hell by God's thunderbolt.

December 6

[Joseph's steward] said, "Let it be as you say:
he who is found with it shall be my servant,
and the rest of you shall be innocent."

GENESIS 44:10

Mortification Will Be Turned to Joy

 od is not planning evil against [the brothers] and is not aiming at their destruction. No, it is His purpose to humble and mortify them, in order that the subsequent glory, freedom, and joy may be greater and sweeter. Accordingly, the master of Joseph's house does not cease examining the sacks of each one after finding the money but goes on searching for the cup. He discovers it in the sack of Benjamin, who was the most innocent one of all. Now all pride, smugness, exultation, and triumphing perish wretchedly in one moment, since they were at the highest point of smugness and could not be in doubt about Benjamin's sanctity, and all the rest were guiltless. Here they are suddenly cast down in spirit, and all the confidence they had gained is taken away. Now all joy is over and completely gone, so that it could not have been removed more ignominiously. This is what our Lord God does.

December 7

[Judah said,] "How can we clear ourselves?
God has found out the guilt of your servants."

GENESIS 44:16

The Moment of Confession

 e can offer nothing for our justification," they say; "we are guilty and at fault; we confess our sin." This is the epitasis [the main action] in the comedy. Joseph has now brought them to the final outburst of emotion, so that they say: "We are thieves and scoundrels. How can we purge or excuse ourselves with at least some pretext? If we say that a theft has been committed in your house, we shall be accusing either you yourself or your domestics." Yet they are innocent, and they know that an injustice is being done them. But they dare not and cannot support their innocence. Nor can they offer anything else as an excuse except to say: "We have sinned. God has found out our iniquity." Thus they do not have the courage to accuse either God or Joseph. This is at last the confession of sin which Joseph has wrung from them. For now they are delivering themselves into slavery, and they will confess more than they have committed, in order that with this humility they may somewhat soften the heart of him whose kindness they had previously experienced.

[Judah said], "Let not your anger burn against your servant."

The Pattern of Prayer

his is a perfect pattern of prayer, yes, of the feeling which should be in a prayer. Judah is bold and confident and thinks neither of the might and power of Joseph nor of his own insignificance. His prayer and need make him bold. Consequently, he approaches Joseph without any trepidation. If we were able to pray so perfectly, especially in the name of Christ, our Savior and Mediator, it would be impossible for such a prayer not to be heard. . . . Now it is necessary above all to know for certain that we have the Word. For this is the foundation and basis of our assurance that we are hearers and that God is speaking with us. Concerning this no one should be in doubt; for he who does not know it, or doubts, will surely mumble prayers with the vain repetition customary among hypocrites. . . . But where this foundation, which is the Word of God, has been laid, there prayer is the ultimate help. No, it is not help; it is our power and victory in every trial. Thus God's Word declares: "Call upon Me in the day of trouble; I will deliver you" (Psalm 50:15). And in Isaiah 65:24: "Before they call, I will answer; while they are yet speaking, I will hear." And Gabriel says to Daniel: "At the beginning of your supplications a Word went forth" (Daniel 9:23). For when the heart prays seriously and ardently, it is impossible for those prayers not to be heard by God as soon as one begins to pray.

December 9

"I am Joseph."

GENESIS 45:3

How God Deals with Us

his is a very beautiful example of how God deals with us. For when He afflicts the godly and conceals the fact that He is our God and Father and rather conducts Himself as a tyrant and judge who wants to torture and destroy us, He says at last in His own time and at a suitable hour: "I am the Lord your God. Hitherto I have treated you just as if I wanted to cast you off and hurl you into hell. But this is a game I am wont to play with My saints; for if I had not wished you well from My heart, I would never have played with you in this manner." These matters are depicted in this way in the government of the saints for our consolation, in order that we may learn to endure the hand of God when He instructs and vexes us to cause us to know and humble ourselves and to mortify that horrible evil which is called original sin. For this is not done in order that we may be condemned and cast off—although our cross and affliction is similar to perdition and death—but the sin clinging to our nature must be cleaned out, in order that we may learn the meaning of what the Lord says concerning Himself in 1 Samuel 2:6–7: "I kill and bring to life; I bring down to Sheol and raise up; I make poor and make rich."

"I am your brother, Joseph, whom you sold into Egypt."

GENESIS 45:4

Triumph in Christ

his should be repeated and urged more often, because it is the special wisdom and teaching of Christians, who should be so stouthearted that no evil can happen to them to prevent them from glorying and triumphing. For they have the Word, absolution, Baptism, the remission of sins, and the promise of eternal life. And whatever adversity must be borne either in death or in hell— no evil is excepted, whether it is an evil inwardly or outwardly—they should say: "I triumph and am proud, because I am lord over death, sin, hell, the world, and all evils, so that for a Christian there is no difference between life and death, wealth and poverty, disgrace and fame. Consequently, he becomes a lord powerful in battle and has been placed above the horror of death, hell, and all adversaries. To be sure, this is not our own doing, because nature cannot accomplish this. But it comes to pass because our Savior, our Lord and Conqueror, the Son of God, sits at the right hand of the Father. He frees, defends, and governs us. Therefore let death terrify us, and let Satan drag us off to hell! What then? My Lord and my Redeemer lives!"

This knowledge surpasses all reason and human wisdom, and the saints as well as David and Paul were unable to attain to it perfectly. Although Paul was an exceedingly great apostle, he nevertheless confesses in regard to himself in

2 Corinthians 12:7–9: "A thorn was given to me in the flesh, a messenger of Satan, to harass me. On this account I besought the Lord three times that it should leave me; but He—namely, the Lord at the right hand of God—said to me: 'My grace is sufficient for you.'" Paul would have been glad to be rid of this thorn. "What do you think of My love for you?" says the Lord. "My strength cannot reign except in your weakness. You must be weak. You must suffer, sigh, groan, and be weak and wretched for your own good, in order that by enduring and fighting you may conquer and become a great apostle. If you are not weak, My strength will have nothing to do. If I am to be your Christ and you My apostle, you will unite your weakness with My strength, your folly with My wisdom, My life with your death." This is the doctrine of Christians.

December 11

*"Do not be distressed or angry with yourselves
because you sold me here."*

GENESIS 45:5

Remedy for Grief

oseph deals here in a most kindly and friendly manner with his brothers to give them more courage. For he was a wise man. He had an understanding of the struggles of conscience. Therefore he applies remedies which soothe the grief. He applies them at the right time. "Let there be no anger in your eyes. Do not think that I am angry. All has been pardoned, forgiven, and consigned to oblivion. I love you heartily and like a brother." This indeed is what it means to forgive a brother his fault from the whole heart (cf. Matthew 18:35), especially when he is distressed and grieving. . . . We see with what great long-suffering and kindness Christ deals with His disciples after the resurrection, how gently He addresses them, shows them His hands and His side, and offers Himself to be felt, heard, and seen, eats with them, and has very pleasant conversations with them. Yet they cannot compose themselves at once. And when the angel orders the resurrection of Christ to be announced to the disciples, he wants it to be made known to Peter in particular, because he was in the greatest distress. . . . For it is much more difficult to console an afflicted conscience than to wake the dead.

December 12

God Sent Me

Behold the wonderful doctor and illustrious theologian and interpreter of the words and deeds of God! "You have betrayed and sold me," [Joseph] says. "This is altogether certain. But listen now, and learn God's plan, what you have done and what you have not done. You have destroyed and killed me. This cannot be denied. But this destruction and killing of yours, what has it been in the eyes of God? For in the same work God's plan is one thing, and your plan is something else. God has used your plan and your exceedingly evil intention for life, not only mine, which would be a matter small enough, but universally. The Lord has sent me to bring to life, for life. You have not sent me, but the Lord has sent me through you." . . . Therefore this passage should be especially noted with regard to the counsel of God, which is also proclaimed in Isaiah 55:8–9: "For My thoughts are not your thoughts, neither are your ways My ways, says the Lord. For as the heavens are higher than the earth, so are My ways higher than your ways and My thoughts than your thoughts." . . . Therefore let us learn not to follow our own thoughts or to measure and understand by our own counsels our misfortunes or works and experiences. . . . Before the world Christ is killed, condemned, and descends into hell. But before God this is the salvation of the whole world from the beginning all the way to the end.

December 13

"God sent me before you to preserve life."

GENESIS 45:5

Solace in Times of Trouble

 t is our only solace in the greatest troubles to cast all care on the Lord, entrusting ourselves to His judgment and will, whether He disciplines us publicly or privately. Let matters take their course. Thank God that you have the Word and the promise. Strive with high courage for the ability to sustain and overcome every assault of Satan, of death, and of tyrants. Peter strongly commends that zeal for and faith in the Word when he says: "And we have the prophetic Word made more sure. You will do well to pay attention to this as to a lamp shining in a dark place, until the day dawns and the morning star rises in your hearts" (2 Peter 1:19). He bids us fix our eyes and keenness of mind on the Word alone, on Baptism, on the Lord's Supper, and on absolution, and to regard everything else as darkness. I do not understand, or care about, what is done in this world by the sons of this age; for they crucify me. I cannot escape or draw away that horrible mask which hides the face of God, but I must stay in darkness and in exceedingly dark mist until a new light shines forth. . . . For it is admirably stated by Paul that "God is faithful, and He will not let you be tempted beyond your strength, but with the temptation will also provide the way of escape, that you may be able to endure it" (1 Corinthians 10:13), that one may rejoice.

December 14

He kissed all his brothers and wept upon them.

Healing the Wounds of Sin

he example of Joseph is a true and clear picture of the resurrection of Christ. And such things happen daily in the Church. For it is the peculiar duty of bishops and pastors to teach, buoy up, and comfort, not hardened and foolish persons who cannot be set right with words and should rather be left to the executioner and hangman, but to apply the balsam of Holy Scripture to the afflicted and the distressed. "Do not fear! Have confidence, my son! Your sins are forgiven you!" (Cf. Matthew 9:2.) But how difficult this application is both my own experience and that of others testifies. I have read the Bible with the greatest zeal and diligence for about 30 years, but I have not yet been cured in such a way that I could with full confidence find rest in the remedies shown by God. I would desire to be stouter and stronger in faith and prouder in Christ, but I cannot be. Therefore the wound is healed in the inn after oil and wine have been poured on it (cf. Luke 10:30–35). For the churches are nothing else than lodging places of this kind in which the people who feel sin, death, and the terrors and vexations of an afflicted and wounded conscience are healed. There, to be sure, faithful and diligent care must be exercised by the ministers by pouring on oil and wine. For sin is a very cruel disease, and conscience is a very delicate thing.

December 15

To each and all of them he gave festal garments.

GENESIS 45:22 (according to Luther's translation)

Festive Robes

e have translated *vestes mutatoriae*, "changes of cloth-ing," with "festal garments," not the everyday gar-ments we wear when doing household chores but festal apparel suitable on days of rest and on the Sabbath as neater clothing for the body. In Psalm 102:25–26 it is stated: "Of old Thou didst lay the foundation of the earth, and the heavens are the work of Thy hands. They will perish, but Thou dost endure; they will all wear out like a garment." Heaven and earth are gradually changing, growing old, and directing their course toward corruption. But later they will put on a new garment. For God will make not only the earth but also heaven itself far more beautiful when it has been stripped of its old garment. These are only workday clothes; afterward they will put on an Easter coat and a Pentecost garment. . . . In the same manner God also cleanses us from sins and frees us from death. This is the work of the six days of this world. But when these are past, when we have entered into His rest, then our torn and filthy garment will be changed into the garment of the eternal Sabbath (cf. Hebrews 4:3–9).

"I am God, the God of your father.
Do not be afraid to go down to Egypt."

GENESIS 46:3

Do Not Be Afraid

od appears in a vision and says: "Do not be afraid or despair, as though you were sinning against My promise. But I order you to proceed, and I endorse your descent." . . . From this one can conclude that although God does not deceive in His promises, He nevertheless reserves their execution for Himself and carries out His promises in such a way that everything seems contradictory and far different from the Word. . . . With this He tries us. This is God's wonderful government in regard to which Paul exclaims (Romans 11:33–34): "O the depth of the riches and wisdom and knowledge of God! How unsearchable are His judgments and how inscrutable His ways! For who has known the mind of the Lord, or who has been His counselor?" . . . My pastor consoles me and says: "You have been adopted by God as His son. You shall be a child of life. You shall be an heir of eternal life." But despite this God hurls me into a trial and makes me doubtful, perplexed, and despairing by confronting me with things that conflict with the promise. . . . Satan likewise attacks us with darts (Ephesians 6:16) and stratagems of every kind, and here I feel and see that God is punishing me and exposing me to the gravest evils and dangers. Nevertheless, He has mercy on me; for I have His promise.

December 17

"I Myself will go down with you to Egypt,
and I will also bring you up again."

GENESIS 46:4

I Myself Will Go with You

 e are taught by this example that nothing should be undertaken and attempted contrary to or without the Word of God. Therefore we should arrange our life in such a way that we are sure of walking according to the rule of the Word, whether we are awake or asleep. Finally, we should know that everything we do is of God, who commands, calls, and blesses. For human life is most wretched and is subject to the devil, death, and countless trials, full of the most burdensome troubles and hardships. Therefore it is necessary for the godly to be fortified by the Word of God against Satan, sins, and dangers. . . . Therefore it is a great gift of God to live in the light of the Word and the divine calling. For this is the golden and round crown that shines around the heads of the saints, as they are commonly depicted, namely, the Word, which directs the course of life day and night. Thus David says in Psalm 119:105: "Thy Word is a lamp to my feet," and 2 Peter 1:19 says: "You do well to pay attention to the Word as to a lamp shining in a dark place, until the day dawns, etc." Reason is in darkness. Therefore it has need of the light of the Word as a leader and guide.

December 18

Jacob said to Pharaoh,
"The days of the years of my sojourning are 130 years."
GENESIS 47:9

Years of Sojourning

hese are words of the spirit and of faith that thinks about another life. For [Jacob] does not want to deem this most wretched life, which is full to overflowing of endless crosses and troubles, worthy of being called a life; but he calls it only a wandering, a most miserable way of living to which one must nevertheless render service because of God's command and will. . . . Thus the Epistle to the Hebrews, in chapter 11:8–10, explains this and other, similar passages very beautifully when it says: "By faith Abraham obeyed when he was called to go out to a place which he was to receive as an inheritance; and he went out, not knowing where he was to go. By faith he sojourned in the Land of Promise, as in a foreign land, living in tents with Isaac and Jacob, heirs with him of the same promise. For he looked forward to the city which has foundations, whose Builder and Maker is God." . . . For to those who believe and have God's promise, this life is a wandering in which they are sustained by the hope of a future and better life. . . . Accordingly, before God we are all citizens in hope; but before the world we are sojourners in fact.

December 19

"The Angel who has redeemed me from all evil,
bless the boys."

GENESIS 48:16

The Angel of Blessing

 acob calls God an Angel in the same way in which he said above after the struggle: "I have seen the Lord face to face" (Genesis 32:30). For this Angel is that Lord or Son of God whom Jacob saw and who was to be sent by God into the world to announce to us deliverance from death, the forgiveness of sins, and the kingdom of heaven. And this Angel is our ["Redeemer"] or Liberator. He sets us free with perfect justice and liberates us from the power of the devil, who is subject to the Law because he killed the Son of God. And now the Law, death, and Satan are compelled to be silent and to stretch forth their conquered hands to the victorious and triumphant Christ. Therefore one must note carefully that Jacob is speaking about Christ, the Son, who alone is the Angel or Ambassador, born a man in time from the Virgin Mary—not the Father, not the Holy Spirit. For he makes a clear distinction among the three persons. Yet he adds: "May He bless these lads." That act of blessing he clearly ascribes to God alone.

Then Israel said to Joseph,
"Behold, I am about to die, but God will be with you
and will bring you again to the land of your fathers."

GENESIS 48:21

God Will Be with You

ook, I ask you, at Jacob's faith and at his extraordinary comfort. For when he says: "God will be with you," he has no doubt whatever that God will take care of them, just as we in the New Testament are certain that Christ will be with us until the end of the age (cf. Matthew 28:20). . . . Therefore we encourage fearful hearts in this manner: "Believe that you have been baptized into Christ. I absolve you from your sins in the name of Christ, who died for you and rose again, and said: 'Because I live, you will live also'" (John 14:19). This is solid and firm consolation. In it alone the godly can find rest. . . . This is the voice of a believer and of one who awaits the future life and resurrection from the dead with completely certain faith and hope. "My death will harm neither me nor you," [Jacob] says, "because God will be with you and with me. Yes, I will be with Him." So certain he is that God will console them and bring them back into the land of their fathers, as though they were all going up together now and the fact itself had been placed before their eyes. So great is the power of faith. It makes us live after we have died. And indeed in the very hour in which we begin to believe and to take hold of the Word we also begin to live in eternal life; for the Word of the Lord remains forever (1 Peter 1:25), and God, who speaks with us, is eternal and will be with us forever.

December 21

"Behold, I am about to die."

GENESIS 48:21

No Need to Fear Death

We are in death. We see that we die and breathe out our life, that the body decays and is consumed by worms. . . . But he who believes, as Jacob, full of confidence, here promises himself life, he regards death as nothing, because faith represents life as being very close and concludes as follows: "Although I die, yet I have been baptized, and I believe. Therefore I am alive and saved." . . . And we who believe have this beginning, that even when we feel death, we nevertheless do not fear it as others, who are tormented by an evil conscience and grow pale even when the word "death" is mentioned, feel it. But the godly and saintly martyrs despise death and laugh at it. . . . Therefore let us listen to the patriarch Jacob as he speaks of death as if he were speaking of sleep. For if you should ask him: "Why are you not terrified at the sight of death, Jacob?" he replies: "To be sure, I shall die and be buried in the tomb; but God lives. He has promised the land into which He will bring you back, but He will transfer me into another, far better land; for He has given His promise."

December 22

"Assemble and listen, O sons of Jacob,
listen to Israel your father."

<small>GENESIS 49:2</small>

Threat and Promise

he main teaching and argument of this chapter is why and to what end God threatens and promises. He does so to keep faith in the Word at work. He who wants to deal with God must learn this, so that he does not live by bread alone but by every Word which proceeds from the mouth of God (cf. Deuteronomy 8:3). If bread is lacking, a strange god should not be called upon on this account. No, then the heart should be strengthened by faith in the Word. God has promised that He will be my God and Lord. If He wants to slay me with hunger, let Him do so by all means. I will hope in Him despite this (cf. Job 13:15). Faith and fear should exist in the hearts of men, because a promise and faith, like a threat and fear, are correlative. There is no promise if faith is not present; and, on the other hand, there is no faith without a promise, just as there is no fear where a threat is lacking. But God defers both in order to test us. And since the world is not willing to endure this trial, it despises both and neither fears Him who threatens nor believes Him who promises.

December 23

The Kingdom of Christ

his golden text should be specially noted. It says that the kingdom of Christ will not be like the kingdom of David, which, of course, endured up to the time of Christ. . . . Therefore the kingdom which was governed by arms, the sword, and violence has now ceased, and the kingdom of ["Shiloh"], which followed, is not violent or bloody but consists in hearing and obeying or believing the Word by which it is administered. . . . Thus Christ says: "Go into all the world and preach the Gospel to the whole creation" (Mark 16:15). For that Word is most powerful. It is able to save from the hands of death and the devil as well as from the power of hell, and to translate into the kingdom of God. To this king, then, the nations shall listen; that is, they will be ruled by the Word. The work will be done through preaching. This will be the mark distinguishing the kingdom of Christ from the empires of the world, which are ruled by the sword and physical might. "The weapons of our warfare," says Paul, "are not worldly but have divine power to destroy strongholds" (2 Corinthians 10:4). "I absolve you; I baptize you; I declare you to be a child of the kingdom; I announce to you the remission of sins; I promise and offer you victory over the devil. Believe, and you will be saved."

December 24

*"He has washed his garments in wine
and his vesture in the blood of grapes."*

GENESIS 49:11

What Christ's Blood Brings

We should give thanks to God for having been baptized and absolved unto the promise of the forgiveness of sins. But if sins are still left, they are not charged against us. We have also been called to the certainty of the hope of life and of the kingdom which we are awaiting, and to contempt for death and the devil. Only let us become inebriated more fully with the consolation and joy of grace and of the blessings of Christ. . . . Yet one must state and diligently maintain that we are all baptized into the death and blood of Christ by which we are washed, as is stated in 1 Corinthians 6:11: "And such were some of you. But you were washed, you were sanctified, you were justified in the name of the Lord Jesus Christ and in the Spirit of our God." . . . And the Gospel which we have heard, that very obedience to Shiloh, is the very blood of Christ, as Peter calls it when he says: "For obedience and sprinkling, etc." (1 Peter 1:2). Those who hear the Word of the Gospel concerning Christ are sprinkled with the blood of the Son of God. It is all the beautiful red blood of Christ, so that everything we have through the Holy Spirit in the Word, Baptism, the Lord's Supper, absolution, consolation, and whatever pertains to the remission of sins and eternal life is understood as having been gained through the power of the blood of Christ. All this is the blessed blood of the Son of God.

December 25

From Cleansing to Cleansing

e are not only made drunk by the Spirit and know what "the Spirit of wisdom and understanding, the Spirit of counsel and might" spoken of in Isaiah 11:2 is, but we are also washed every day. For sin still clings to our flesh, and spirit and flesh are opposed to each other. But the promise of the Holy Spirit is operative in us and washes its garment, namely, us, during the whole time of our life. For it is always purging away the sin that is left; and we are washed and purified, not with water but with wine and the blood of grapes, with red wine, that is, with the most abundant gifts of the Holy Spirit. For sin is not destroyed, as the sophists dream, by our acts of contrition, preparation, and satisfaction. . . . We are not in a state of perfection. No, we are in a state of becoming and transition, or in a state of movement from virtue to virtue from day to day, from cleansing to cleansing. After being sanctified we are still being sanctified.

December 26

"I wait for your salvation, O Lᴏʀᴅ."

GENESIS 49:18

I Will Wait

understand this statement to mean that the great man and patriarch Jacob foresaw that the most grievous calamities and dangers were threatening this nation from which Christ was to be born, that for this reason it had to be ruled and preserved by God, and that this could not be done without the greatest struggles and difficulties among the heathen and their enemies, who, as he knew, would gather all their strength for the purpose of destroying and extirpating these new guests in the land of Canaan. . . . Thus this statement is correctly added to stir up faith, which is necessary even in physical matters, just as Isaac had to be conceived by faith before he was begotten physically by Abraham. For if Abraham had not believed that Isaac would certainly be born from him, that is, that God is true in His promises, he would never have begotten Isaac. In this manner faith even in physical things that are not yet apparent is identical with faith in justification and in the forgiveness of sins, because of which we conclude that God is propitious and favorable toward us and is carrying out what He promises. Therefore on behalf of the children of Israel and his descendants Jacob expresses this wish: "I will wait for Thy victories, O Lord." Where? "In my seed, and in this land, which has been promised to him, until Shiloh comes."

This is what their father said to them as he blessed them,
blessing each with the blessing suitable to him.

GENESIS 49:28

Suitable Blessings

I f [these prophecies] are compared with the New Testament, we have a prophecy that is far clearer. For the fulfillment is far greater and clearer, except that we do not pay attention to or trouble ourselves about that ineffable majesty and infinite abundance of the Holy Spirit who has been given to us, "which," as Paul says in Titus 3:6, "He poured out upon us richly." For this reason the prophets and the whole Bible should be read with the greatest diligence; and I indeed, whenever I make a comparison of these things, am angry with myself and am ashamed of my life and full of regrets, because after Christ has been revealed, we have such a cold attitude toward our gifts and believe the Word so weakly, whereas the fathers believed with such great steadfastness and lived in faith in the promises. In this way they overcame great dangers and difficulties. . . . Therefore Peter says: "We have the prophetic Word made more sure. You will do well to pay attention to this" (2 Peter 1:19). . . . We have Baptism, liberation from death and from sin; for the Son of God says: "God so loved the world that He gave His only Son, that whoever believes in Him should not perish but have eternal life" (John 3:16). In this manner we should compare our glory and wealth with the revelations made to the fathers, so that we, aroused by the greatness of this light, may embrace and retain the Gospel with exceedingly joyful hearts.

December 28

Falling Asleep in Faith

his is a form of speech which belongs entirely to the saints and the godly . . . for it testifies that ever since the beginning of the world the saints fell asleep in faith and in the hope of the resurrection. . . . But just as in the Church we are said to be gathered to our people through Baptism, through the Gospel and the Sacraments, and we know that we are among our people, so when we die in the promise of Christ made to Abraham, we are transferred by the angels into the bosom of Abraham, or to our people. . . . Therefore let us give glory to God, and let us bestow this honor on Him, that we conclude that His wisdom is boundless and that He has many more wonderful ways to preserve us than we are able to comprehend with our senses. He preserves us in one way in our mother's womb, in another way in the cradle, in another way in sleep, and in another way in sickness. It is sufficient for us to know that the saints in the Old Testament who died in faith in the Christ who was to come and that the godly in the New Testament who died in faith in the Christ who has been revealed are gathered to their people. . . . Therefore the death of the saints is honorable and, as is stated in Psalm 116:15, "precious in the sight of the Lord."

Joseph said to them, "Do not fear, for am I in the place of God?
As for you, you meant evil against me,
but God meant it for good."
GENESIS 50:19–20

Meant for Good

ow, because [Joseph] hears that his brothers have doubts about his pardon—although they have obtained the forgiveness and pardon of God and their father Jacob—he says: "If God has forgiven you, why would I not forgive all offenses?" And he adds an exceedingly serious statement: "It is indeed true that you meant evil against me, but God is wonderful in His counsels and has turned your worst thoughts to our advantage and the greatest good." Accordingly, he does not want them to deny or forget their sin and their plans to murder him. "But," he says, "behold the wonderful work of God, who has turned everything to the greatest service, in order that I might be of help to many nations which would have died of hunger and would not have learned to know God or heard His Word if I had not been sold by you into Egypt. Thus God has wrought the greatest good from such a great evil. Therefore I readily pardon you, since I see that through your very evil plan God has been of the greatest help to me and countless others." And this is what Paul says in Romans 8:28: "We know that all things work together for good to them that love God, to them who are the called according to His purpose."

December 30

Joseph said to his brothers, "I am about to die, but God will visit you and bring you up out of this land to the land that he swore to Abraham, to Isaac, and to Jacob." Then Joseph made the sons of Israel swear, saying, "God will surely visit you, and you shall carry up my bones from here."

GENESIS 50:24–25

God Will Surely Visit You

 ere Joseph declares his faith when he desires to be among those who were to be raised with Christ. And I believe that he returned to life along with the other saints of whom mention is made in Matthew 27:52–53. Indeed, he wants to rest in the land of Canaan, even though the place and the burial are of little importance. For he could have been buried in Egypt, and it would not have been difficult for Christ to raise the fathers from Egypt or from anywhere else. But in order to bear witness to his faith in Christ he gives orders that his bones be borne down to the land of Canaan. For he also knew that the people of Israel were to be multiplied in the land promised to their fathers. Therefore he wants that tomb to be before the eyes of all his descendants, in order that his children and grandchildren may remember their father and their ancestors and, in accordance with their example, may persevere in the same faith and promise in which he had fallen asleep with his fathers.